BETWEEN NATIONS

Between Nations

SHAKESPEARE, SPENSER, MARVELL,

AND THE QUESTION OF BRITAIN

David J. Baker

STANFORD UNIVERSITY PRESS
Stanford, California

Stanford University Press
Stanford, California

© 1997 by the Board of Trustees of the
Leland Stanford Junior University

Printed in the United States of America

CIP data are at the end of the book

For Mary

Acknowledgments

In writing this book, I have incurred debts in many places. A seed money grant from the University of Hawai'i at Manoa enabled a stay at the Huntington Library in San Marino, and I would like to thank its staff for their helpfulness. This book was begun in Baltimore, where its first readers were Stanley Fish and Jonathan Crewe. Their personal and intellectual generosity was sustaining over many years. For the care and attention that they brought to their reading of chapters, or pieces of chapters, or précis of chapters, and for accepting promises of future chapters, my thanks also go to Marcie Frank, John Guillory, Laura Lunger-Knoppers, Laura Lyons, Rick Rambuss, and Valerie Wayne. Julia Reinhard Lupton's reading of the manuscript for Stanford University Press was incisive and useful. I want to acknowledge three scholars especially. The citations here do not do justice to the pervading influence of Homi Bhabha, though my title is a gesture toward his exacting analytic of "the *in-between* spaces through which the meanings of cultural and political authority are negotiated." This book may be considered an attempt to put his powerfully suggestive thinking to work in a perhaps unanticipated context. John Pocock's influence on *Between Nations* will be patent. My book simply could not have been written without his British historiography, which is at once magisterial and innovative. The usual caveat is, of course, doubly in force here: he should bear no responsibility for the uses to which I have put his ideas. Jonathan Goldberg, though, will have to take more than a little credit for *Between Nations*, since

viii *Acknowledgments*

he has done so much to make it possible. I have borrowed his clarity of mind and singleness of purpose so often that any strengths this book now has are in some great measure his.

Finally, for their *aloha* and for teaching me much about "the condition of living on an island," I would like to say *mahalo* to the people I have come to know on the archipelago of Hawai'i, where *Between Nations* was finished, and to Helen Tartar, an exemplary editor, for suggesting that I do so.

Passages from Chapter 1 appeared in *English Literary Renaissance* 22 (1992), and from Chapter 2 in *Spenser Studies* and *Representing Ireland: Literature and the Origins of Conflict, 1534-1660*, ed. Brendan Bradshaw, Andrew Hadfield, and Willy Maley. I am grateful for permission to reprint them here.

D. J. B.

Contents

Your excellēt wysdome (as you [Henry VIII] haue an eye
to euery parte and membre of your Dominion) hath
causde to be enactede and stablyshede . . . that there shal
herafter be no differēce in lawes and language bytwyxte
youre subiectes of youre principalytye of Wales and your
other subiectes of youre Royalme of Englande mooste
prudently consyderynge what great hatred debate &
scryffe hathe rysen emongeste men by reason of
dyuersitie of language and what a bonde and knotte of
loue and frendshyppe the cōmunion of one tonge is.

—William Salesbury, *A Dictionary in Englyshe and Welshe*
(1547)

For the rest, such as in habits, English manners of
attendance, &c., [the Irish] do much abhor them, as they
count all those that use them *Boddagh Gall*, that is,
foreign boor or churl; and in their rhymes and daily jests
they hold nothing more ridiculous and reproachfull. . . .
So much for marks of difference.

—*A Discourse for the Reformation of Ulster* (1598)

There is no difference betwixt London and Edinburgh;
yea, not so much as betwixt Inverness or Aberdeen and
Edinburgh, for all our marches be dry, and there are
ferries between them.

—James VI and I (1603); quoted in G. W. T. Omond,
The Early History of the Scottish Union Question

We may conceive an hope that the next [Irish]
generation will in tongue and heart, and every way else,
become English, so as there will be no difference or
distinction but the Irish Sea betwixt us.

—Sir John Davies, *A Discovery of the True Causes Why
Ireland Was Never Entirely Subdued [And] Brought Under
Obedience of the Crown of England Until the Beginning of His
Majesty's Happy Reign* (1612)

Introduction

Several years ago, I found myself reading an essay by J. G. A. Pocock, "British History: A Plea for a New Subject." The projected "British history" of the title would be devoted to the entity known for some centuries now as "Britain." So much seemed obvious. "But when one considers what 'Britain' means," Pocock pointed out, "that it is the name of a realm inhabited by two, and more than two nations, whose history has been expansive to the extent of planting settlements and founding derivative cultures beyond the Four Seas . . . it is evident that the history of this complex expression has never been seriously attempted."[1] A great sweep of history was implied in this sentence, but what intrigued me most was the slippage in a certain phrase—"two, and more than two nations." One of the "two nations" in question, of course, was England, and the other Scotland. Ireland and Wales were the remaining members of the geopolitical conglomerate that since 1801 has been called "Great Britain,"[2] and they would need to be included in any comprehensive history of what Pocock called, with a bracing literalness, that "island group lying off the northwestern coasts of geographic Europe."[3] But that this inclusion might have implications for the "nationhood" of *all* of these members had not occurred to me till then. If England and Scotland were nations, I began now to ask, just what was it that made them nations? And if Ireland and Wales might (or might not) also be nations, what sense of the term "nation" was Pocock applying to them? By what process did two of the members of "Great Britain" become distinct nations, while these other two were relegated to a more ambiguous status—"more than two"? And specifically when was it that these diverse entities became or did not become nations, in whatever sense of the word Pocock was using? I asked these questions with some urgency because I was beginning to suspect that they might help to open up a debate (if that was what it was, since the principals rarely addressed one another directly) that had, for me, come to seem more and more stalled and impacted.

When Pocock first issued his call for a history of Britain in 1974, the chronology of nation formation in this area of the world was a matter of distinct disagreement, and it still is. Individual treatments of this development can be nuanced, but the overall argument tends to organize itself around one of the British entities—England—and then to drift to either of two poles. It is often said, usually by established historians, that England not only was a nation by the early modern period, but that it emerged then as the paradigmatic nation, the one from which others would eventually derive. G. R. Elton, a scholar with definite views on the subject, declared in 1953 that "we are familiar with the notion that the sixteenth century saw the creation of the modern sovereign state [in England]: the duality of state and church was destroyed by the victory of the state, the crown triumphed over its rivals, parliamentary statute triumphed over the abstract law of Christendom, and a self-contained national unit came to be, not the tacitly accepted necessity it had been for some time, but the consciously desired goal."[4] And Liah Greenfeld, in a related argument, has more recently asserted that "at a certain point in history—to be precise, in early sixteenth-century England—the word 'nation' in its conciliar meaning of 'an elite' was applied to the population of the country and made synonymous with the word 'people.' *This semantic transformation signaled the emergence of the first nation in the world, in the sense in which the word is understood today, and launched the era of nationalism.*"[5] In the by now considerable literature on the development of the nation, however, including most of the classic discussions, early modern England is quite specifically *not* one of the entities so called. The nation "in the sense in which the word is understood today" comes later: "most current political theory limits national identity to a post-nineteenth-century location, a product of the presumed social homogeneity produced by industrialism."[6] John Breuilly, to name one such theorist, resolutely places early modern England in a precursor stage. Its "nationalism," he says, does not conform to a more stringent definition of the term; intrinsic to a properly identified "nationalism" must be the sense that the "interests and values of [a] nation take priority over all other interests and values."[7] Breuilly notes that Shakespeare's *Henry V* (a frequently cited example and one that will be discussed in this book) "provides ample proof of . . . 'national' consciousness" in his time, but "generally . . . the 'national' [in the play] refers to the customs and manners of the common people; it does not shape the values and actions of those who hold power."[8] Against E. D. Marcu,[9] Breuilly emphasizes that "certain sorts of national consciousness in sixteenth-century Europe . . . should not be confused with nationalism"[10] as such. The dispute over the nationhood of early modern England, it had seemed to me, divided itself between those who saw this polity as an achieved nation, indeed, as the seed bed for all future nations, and those who saw it as an uncertain construction, perhaps more medieval than modern,[11] whose value was chiefly as a defining example of what the real nation was not. What did it mean, I now wondered, to introduce into this unresolved argument the presumably still more complex problems of British nationalism? If Pocock intended to contribute to the discussion, he had picked, I thought, an equivocal way of doing so.

It was soon clear to me, though, that Pocock was not so much "contributing" to the discussion as he was supplementing it, and, moreover, that it was just this both/and stance toward nationalism, or what he in one place called a "twofold consciousness,"[12] that gave his British historiography its flexibility and analytical strength. "The nation-state model produces some unexpected results when applied to 'Britain,'" as he noted in a later essay on the same topic.[13] In fact, he concluded there that, after some analysis, "the concept of nation-state is failing us at all points."[14] This was decidedly not because none of the British entities had become nations at some point in their histories. On the contrary, one of those entities, England, had certainly done so, and the "history of how it has done so . . . constitutes one of the great historiographical enterprises of the world."[15] And Pocock was insistent—as he has remained insistent—that the study of British history was not meant to supplant this enterprise.[16] Nonetheless, he argued, the concept of the nation-state must fail us when we try to write a British history for reasons that go to the creation and definition of that field itself. First, because if we concentrate solely on the history of England, the one definite nation-state on the British Isles for many centuries, we will be led to ignore the histories of the many other entities that existed on the two islands. These either never were or only later on became nations. To a degree, of course, this exclusion might be remedied by doing other sorts of history as well. For example, "the obvious first step, pedagogically speaking, in passing from 'English' to 'British' history would be to make sure the student read as much of Irish as he did of English historiography."[17] But that alone, Pocock implied, would not make an English history British.

What if the material out of which, say, an Irish historiography could be made was not extant? What if it had been "deleted," not all at once, of course, and not totally by any means, but excised nonetheless, and more or less deliberately, over many centuries? And, most important for our purposes, what if those who did this acted not only out of national self-interest but also in order that they might become a nation in the first place? "It is not enough to succeed," it has been said; "others must fail." The success of English nation building came about in part, this historian noted, because others failed to build nations of their own or were prevented from doing so. But what makes for good nation formation may also make for bad history. The nation-state model now fails us in turn because it itself is invested in interested denials and exclusions of history—or rather, of histories, the chronicles that others in Britain might have left had they been possessed of the great textual apparatus that helped to build an English nation. By the time of the Stuarts, said Pocock, the "English monarchy, largest, wealthiest, and most expansive of the British political cultures, had for centuries been depositing official records. . . . The guardianship of one's past is power; the court of record is the kernel of English government; and from the political culture which has not enough self-determined and self-preserved history shall be taken even that which it hath." [18]

Inevitably then, I realized, in writing the history of England as a nation-state today what we are writing is the textual history of the English rulers writing their own textual history, and doing so, quite often, by "unwriting"—suppressing, assimilating, ignoring—the textual histories of the other not yet or never-to-be nations that also existed (or might have existed) among the British Isles. As Michel-Rolph Trouillot more recently put it in his subtle investigation of this historiographic problem:

> Inequalities experienced by the [historical] actors lead to uneven historical power in the inscription of traces. Sources built upon these traces in turn privilege some events over others. . . . That some peoples and things are absent of history, lost, as it were, to the possible world of knowledge, is much less relevant to the historical practice than the fact that some peoples and things are absent in history, and that this absence itself is constitutive of the process of historical production. [19]

Pocock's response to such a predicament, it seemed to me, was at once tough minded and original. On the one hand, he offered little hope of an exit from this historical/textual nexus or of an escape from its professional consequences. England became a nation, he said, because the "English ruling structure" was able to "organize a geographically defined culture into

a nation and in some sort of state." "The history of how it has done so is
not free from blind spots," he noted,[20] somewhat dryly it seemed to me,
especially since he was describing a national history that was *constituted* by
blind spots, one that owed its *topoi*, its overarching narratives, and its sense
of what did and did not matter to centuries of active exclusion and passive
indifference. Nonetheless, there was little more than this history to be written. "The history of an English domination is remarkably difficult to write
in other than English terms," Pocock observed.

> The conqueror, after all, sets the rules of the game; he determines, in propor-
> tion to the extent to which his domination becomes effective, what people
> shall do, how they shall think, and what they shall remember. And the con-
> quering culture may be—and was in the case we are considering—the culture
> which maintains rules, speaks a language and preserves a history so powerfully
> effective that it obliges others to act in the same way and submit to, if they do
> not acquire, its consciousness.[21]

In Britain, the conquerors who left behind the texts by which our sense of
the period has been shaped were English. And it occurred to me, as by now
it will have occurred to the reader, that one of the prime repositories of
this triumphal "consciousness" was the archive that we call the literature of
the English Renaissance.

On the other hand, Pocock insisted, "the fact of a hegemony does not
alter the fact of a plurality."[22] He might believe that, historically speaking,
the English "consciousness" had come to be ubiquitous across most of the
British Isles, but he did not hold that the possibility of a British historiography was thereby extinguished. Instead, he called for a "plural history
of a group of cultures situated along an Anglo-Celtic frontier and marked
by an increasing English political and cultural domination."[23] How exactly
this history was to be written, given the methodological problem that he
himself had defined, Pocock did not discuss. But, after all, in 1974 "British
History" was meant as a "plea" for a new historiography that did not yet
exist. It set out the propositions from which such a historiography might
be derived. And these "premises must be," Pocock asserted, "that the various
peoples and nations, ethnic cultures, social structures, and locally defined
communities, which have from time to time existed in the area known as
'Great Britain and Ireland' have not only acted so as to create the conditions of their several existences but have also interacted so as to modify
the conditions of one another's existence."[24] (With these premises in mind,
let me say that, from this point on in my Introduction and in this book,
the term "nation" should be understood equally, but depending on con-

text, *both* as a distinct geopolitical entity *and*, variously, as one among the "peoples," "ethnic cultures," and/or "locally defined communities" that such an entity may have displaced, subsumed, or integrated in the early modern period. In every case, each sense of "nation" will imply the possibility of the others; I hold that no one of these "nations" can exist except in defining relation to the others. I offer this omnibus definition not to blur the distinctions among types of "nation," which are real, but because it is important to keep a congeries of "nations" before us when we consider "nationalism" and "nationhood" in this period. As it happens, Renaissance English itself was fully adequate to these complexities. All of the groupings Pocock mentions could be called "nations" in this period.[25])

As late as 1982, Pocock could say that "we have little or no 'British history' . . . most of what passes by that name is English history and makes little pretense of being anything else."[26] Earlier, he had noted that one of the few figures to attempt a British history before him had been Francis Bacon, who, upon the ascension of a Scottish king, James VI and I, to the English throne in 1603, "proposed . . . a history which would make that of England and that of Scotland as simultaneously visible as had been the histories of Israel and Judah in the books of *Kings* and *Chronicles*." But, said Pocock, "one has only to walk through the relevant section of any library and glance at the shelves to see that [Bacon's] advice has not been taken."[27] As it turned out, though, a good many others besides myself had been reading Pocock's essays, and, in 1997, if we were to take a walk through that same library and glance at those same shelves, we would find that scholars have since been taking Bacon's (and Pocock's) advice quite seriously. As Pocock puts it, "the tide has abruptly turned . . . [and] we can now claim 'British history' as a field of study well enough established to have both its paradigms and its critics."[28] Distinguished work is being done by historians on both sides of the Atlantic that traces at least some of its genesis to Pocock's "seminal article," which, as Steven Ellis says, "provided a powerful theoretical framework for 'a pluralist and multi-cultural perception of British history.'"[29] It has now become more than possible, and even necessary, to consider the formation of the English nation as a contingent process that is imbricated at every point with the histories of the other nations—as defined above—that coexisted with it on the British Isles.

Between Nations, as will be quickly apparent, is not a work of British history. This is in part because, as Ellis points out, the dictates behind British history "may be intellectually sound, but translating [them] into practice is another matter, if only because research on the subject frequently requires detailed knowledge of Celtic languages and cultures."[30] *Between Nations* is a book that is, unavoidably, the work of a critic trained in English—and English literature at that. In its choice of evidentiary texts and in the reading it applies to them, *Between Nations* is a work of literary criticism. Here, I attempt to read—or, often, to reread—certain instances of early modern English literature in light of the premises and imperatives of the developing British historiography. The texts with which I am most concerned are William Shakespeare's *Henry V* (1599), Edmund Spenser's *A View of the Present State of Ireland* (1598), and Andrew Marvell's "An Horatian Ode upon Cromwell's Return from Ireland" (1650), as well as his "The Loyal Scot" (circa 1670). Inevitably, *Between Nations* owes a good deal to my first reading of Pocock's "British History" and to the historiography that has been written after it. Each of this book's chapters is tacitly organized around a question, and I have been able to ask this question because it has first been made available to me *as* a question by Pocock. When, for example, I consider how Marvell's "An Horatian Ode upon Cromwell's Return from Ireland" might answer to the specific exigencies of British history in 1650, I am appealing to the claim made originally by J. C. Beckett that the "English Civil War" could more properly be called the "War of the Three Kingdoms."[31] This reassessment was first brought to my attention by Pocock in "British History"[32]; its overall premises have been applied to the events leading up to that convulsion by Conrad Russell in *The Fall of the British Monarchies 1637–1642*.[33] In this at times indirect fashion, some of the larger claims that Pocock made in 1974, and the elaborations that followed, find their way into the argument of *Between Nations*.

If this book is Pocockian in its inspiration, though, it is not always so in its application. The key difference between Pocock and myself has to do with the degree to which we are willing to attribute an independent, self-confirming existence to the early modern British nation. "Whether 'Britain' is to be a nation," wrote Pocock, "possessing a locus in which a self is to be invented and self-invented, or an association of such nations and a conversation between such selves, is a problem at the outset of the seventeenth century and looks likely to be a problem at the outset of the twenty-first; though in stating that there is a question, one must be careful to avoid suggesting that one already knows the answer."[34] In this book, however, I have taken up neither of these ways of thinking of Britain; both of them, I suspect, come down to much the same definition (Britain is either self-invented as a nation or emerges as a nation in the engagement between "such [self-invented?] selves"). Instead, I regard early modern Britain itself *as a question*. I am so far from thinking that I know the answer to this ongoing question that I have made the historical fact of it into my very argument. The Britain that I consider here is not an achieved nation, nor even such a unified polity *in potentia*, but an unresolved political and cultural problem: what is Britain? This question preoccupied many among the British of the early modern period, English and otherwise. How to construct Britain as a nation, a distinct geopolitical entity, they can be observed to wonder, when its constituents—England, Scotland, Wales, Ireland—remain stubbornly discrete and, by a seeming paradox, also resist exact definition? How to limn the whole when the parts will neither cohere nor stabilize? Jenny Wormald points out, for example, that when, in 1603, James I attempted to establish a "Great Britain" across his divided realm, what prevented him was not only that his encompassing vision of a "perfect union" was tacitly rejected by most of his subjects. It was also that "what was wholly lacking . . . was any less radical model which might provide a viable alternative." On the one hand, a unified Britain made scant sense to the (alleged) British of the time. On the other, the conjuncture that was proposed to them "was not simply the bringing together of two kingdoms, although that was how it was described, but the addition of another kingdom to the multiple kingdoms of England and Ireland, with the dependency of Wales thrown in."[35] Nations that were not at all nations in the contemporary sense were asked to subsume themselves within a union that we might recognize as a nation, but that bore little resemblance to any polity that the diverse British peoples were prepared to think of as their own. Where James wanted unity, he got divisiveness, and not just that, but a discord among "multiple kingdoms" and kingdoms within kingdoms that refused to add up to an organized federation, much less to a singularity. Britain was, and continued to be throughout the early modern period, a powerful but unrealized trope.

The Britain that I want to chart in *Between Nations*, therefore, is less a fixed and distinct domain than an ontological predicament, a knot of conundrums entangling the several peoples who in the early modern period were compelled to share that "island group lying off the northwestern coasts of geographic Europe." Pocock argues, quite rightly, that early modern England as a nation can attribute much of its political and cultural existence to the differential relations it established with the other entities—some, perhaps, nations in the strong sense, but some certainly not—on the British Isles. As the sixteenth century turned, there existed a "discourse concerned with a nation and kingdom to be known as 'Scotland',," and another "concerned with the union of this entity with another [nation and kingdom], described and self-described as 'England',," and the possibility of "a third entity to be known as 'Britain'."[36] But there, it often seems,

Pocock wants to stop. That England or Scotland (or Wales or Ireland?) finally had a national "self"—self-invented or mutually invented or both—and that discrete "discourses" adhered to each are foundational premises. I want to propose, however, that we will get much further toward understanding why Britain was so radically unstable both as a polity and a trope if we do not rest our thinking at any point on the a priori assumption that Britain as a whole or any of its constituent parts was or could be a national "self" in the sense Pocock appears to mean. Is there a residual commitment to "nation-as-essence" circulating through Pocock's arguments? If so, it is just this that his own historiography brings so powerfully into question. Here, I will instead be entertaining the somewhat counterintuitive notion that early modern Britain was not a "locus" of (self)subsistent nations, but a nexus, rather, of relations of alterity among "England" and "Scotland" and "Wales" and "Ireland," among, that is, the self-displacing sites that took on those names and among the "discourses" that adumbrated them. By saying this, I do not mean to "deconstruct" Britain or any of its member nations, nor to deny the actuality of the differences among them. I mean, rather, to account for those differences. Other critics have pointed out that it was in the early modern period that "the borders between both conceptual and national territories were redrawn as solid rather than dotted lines."[37] I agree; to an extent, these lines were drawn within Britain too. But I differ from these critics on what the "solidity" of these lines connotes. For me, it is not only separation, but also mutual implication. In these pages, I have wanted to "establish the cultural boundaries of the nation so that they may be acknowledged as 'containing' thresholds of meaning that must be crossed, erased, and translated."[38] If it is true that "crossing lines is not . . . the same as denying their existence,"[39] it is equally true that a border that cannot be crossed is not a border. It is a multinational "*process* of cultural production"[40] that is at work in formation of any given nation, and this, I say, is what should be analyzed, without denying the actuality of the nation thus produced. Intra-British boundaries seemed to be—and were—no less real for the British themselves because they were sometimes illegible or multiple. Britain as a nexus of wavering lines was no less consequential because it was thus (dis)organized. Britain was a zone where nations were written between the lines and across them.

There has been a persistent ambivalence in Pocock's dealings with the question of British nationhood. In 1982, he stressed that a British historiography has an "ideological consequence: it reveals the ideological falseness of the claim of any state, nation, or other politically created entity to natural or historical unity." His historiography, he said, was not only "multinational", it was "antinational."[41] But more recently, Pocock has been warning against the "premise that national sovereignty and history never existed, never should have existed, or are at the point of disappearing forever (and a good thing too)." "The history of the United Kingdom," he says, was not "an illusion, a mistake, a crime, or an episode closed off by its ending."[42] Well, as the epigraphs to this book show, the history of Britain as a vision of trans-island hegemony has certainly not been an illusion. Britons of many sorts have longed for a "Dominion" that will obliterate "differēce." Understandably, "consyderynge what great hatred debate & scryffe hathe rysen emongeste men by reason of dyuersitie." If this vision was a mistake, still, as I will be saying later, for many it was what a theorist has called a "grounding mistake . . . [one] that enable[s] us to make sense of our lives."[43] And this vision, it may be, was not a crime, though many appalling things were done—and are now being done—in its name. Certainly, the history of this imagining is not over; the episode of Britain is not closed. Which is why it is all the more important "at the outset of the twenty-first" century, I think, to understand why and how it was that Britain did and did not emerge as a precursor nation "at the outset of the seventeenth." As Wormald has said, the resistances that prevented a union in 1603 are still with us. There is an "ingrained reluctance to ask, let alone answer, fundamental questions about the nature of Britain." This "has been, and remains, constant."[44] To an extent, Pocock participates in this reluctance. His ambivalence over early modern England and its coeval polities on the "Atlantic archipelago"—are they nations, are they not?—repeats an ambivalence that is still writ at Britain's shifting center. I would argue, though, that if this ambivalence were to be recognized for what it is—the constitutive principle of Britain "itself," the question that defines it—then that, for reasons both political and analytical, might well be a good thing indeed.

In *Between Nations* I have in some places argued for this ambivalence by turning to early modern British "selves" who were "national" (or diversely nationalized) in a more personal sense. What of those English, Irish, Scots, and Welsh, I have wanted to know, who arrived at some sense of who they were by means of and in the midst of the charged question of Britain? This often brutal and radically unequal contest for geopolitical existence among superseding nations was rarely anything so benign as a "conversation." Pocock begins to touch on their problems in "British History" when he speaks, for example, of the "characteristic ambivalences of empire: the conquerors' uncertainty whether to impose their consciousness of the world upon the conquered or exclude them from it altogether; the uncertainty of the conquered whether to accept the dominant consciousness unequivocally, to accept it in order to modify it, or to reject it altogether and construct a new ordering of historical consciousness out of their awareness of the dilemma in which they are involved."[45] But this hardly does justice to the "ambivalences" of early modern identity within Britain. What of the English conqueror who came to realize that in imposing his "consciousness" on the conquered Irish, he himself had come to participate in their alien thinking, and that he was now "more Irish than the Irish themselves," as the saying went?[46] Or, conversely, the Irishman who found that he could not simply "reject" English consciousness "altogether" because centuries of English invasion, settlement, and then mutual assimilation had left him ineradicably both English and Irish in his "consciousness" and affiliations? Or, more convoluted still, what of the "Irishman" who learned that his identity changed with the place he occupied, that he was an Englishman in Ireland and an Irishman in England, as Christopher St. Lawrence, one of those who figures in this book, will complain? For such an "Irishman," "Irishness" was a quality that could hardly emerge without the constant implication of "Englishness" (and vice versa), but neither of these, of course, could be entirely adequate to his sense of himself. Throughout most of British history, as Pocock observed, playing the "game" of identity politics meant playing by English "rules" so far-reaching that they often shaped "consciousness" itself, and this was so, no doubt, on both sides of every national divide. But this "game," I suspect, was more uncertain, less one-sided, and even more dangerous than Pocock was willing to consider.

This both/and quality of many early modern British national "selves" has a consequence for Renaissance studies as well: it opens up within that discipline what Pocock called "the single greatest methodological difficulty in the construction of British history."[47] A both/and model requires, at the very least, two elements. But often, in the literary scholarship of this period what we have is one such element, England, and nothing but. This predicament is not ours alone. "The [British] history which [the investigator] is invited to reassess," said Pocock in his inaugural article, "is not only history as seen by the dominant culture; it is actually the history of the dominant culture itself, somewhat to the exclusion of others, since the data, the traditions of scholarship, and the currently operative paradigms he is to criticize are all preponderantly the product of that culture—which is one important reason why it is dominant."[48] The triumphal culture, Pocock told his colleagues, would not only monopolize most of the textual resources it came across. Often, it would also dictate the way in which those texts were to be viewed and block from view the artifacts of those it had ostracized. This same national obscurantism will be a problem for those who read Renaissance literature if what we want is to recover the traces of England's missing "other(s)," and this "for reasons," as Pocock put it, "relative to the maintenance of a number of historically based identities." [49] Of course, we do want this. Just as crucial, though, what we also want, and must want, is to understand the texts of the dominant culture itself—"English literature." But if the import of early modern *English* works can be discerned only insofar as it emerges from within the cross-hatching of those other British influences that situate it, and if those other influences inhere in and proceed from cultures that are now partially lost to us, how can our grasp of even English works be more than partial? And then there is this further difficulty. If we cannot dispel this inherited ignorance, neither can we claim that we do not, willy nilly, perpetuate it. "What is [hard] to face," says Pocock, "since guilt comes easily to us . . . is that we live at the outcomes" of the violent invention of nations "and have to decide what to do with the many legacies they have left us." [50] Being English in the time of Shakespeare, Spenser, and Marvell meant taking part in nation-creating traditions of exclusion and denial. How could it mean anything but this? These are our traditions still. How could they not be? The "dominant culture" that England created (and that created England) is not something that we, most of us, can claim to stand entirely apart from. It is very much *our* culture, and certainly this is so for those who profess a belated discipline called "English."

Anglo-American literary critics have dealt with this problem, mostly, by ignoring it, and often for the very good reason that this has been the response that Renaissance literature itself demanded. Pocock noted that historians had to "acknowledge that there [were] extremely powerful and valid professional and historical reasons pressing us toward the continuation of the Anglocentric perspective." [51] In literary studies, a simple fidelity to the claims that our texts make for themselves has left anything but Anglocentrism looking decidedly skewed. For instance, most of the works of literature that I will be considering here are resolutely committed to the advancement of something they call "England" and are thoroughly enmeshed in the apparatus that produced it. They work to promote this entity by explicitly denigrating or tacitly ignoring the peoples of the other nations on the British Isles. This distinguishes them from the rest of the literature of the period in almost no way. As Andrew Hadfield reminds us, most English writers in this time "tend to elide the distinction between Britain and England as geographical, political, and literary communities."

> There is an obvious nationalist motive at work here for English writers who
> wish to appropriate a wider heritage for their own ends. . . . English writers

rigorously excluded other peoples and nationalities from [their] privileged domain . . . denying other forms of cultural identity the right to exist within the boundaries of the [English] state. Such writers may not have had more than a vague conception of what audience their texts would have reached, but in constructing an implied reader they did not intend to speak to Scots, Irish, or Welsh.[52]

Instead, they intended to speak to the English and expected their acknowledgment to be reciprocated by readers who understood that it was as English—and English only—that they were being addressed. Many of the readers who have taken up these texts later have allowed themselves to be constructed by the same powerful demands. Consequently, these works now come accompanied by a legacy of Anglo-American exegesis that accepts them as exemplary expressions of an English Renaissance "nationalism." Even when it is not assumed that England is an achieved nation-state, it is almost always taken for granted that this nation is the *only* nation in the period that needs to be considered. *Henry V*, as is well known, has frequently been read as a paean to its English prince, Hal, and as a manifesto of English patriotism (while the *patriae* of other British characters such as MacMorris and even Fluellen have been mostly ignored). The *View of the Present State of Ireland* has often been understood as, quite simply, the anti-Gaelic screed of an Englishman displaced in Ireland (while the complexities of Spenser's tacit antagonisms to homebound Englishmen and his oblique affiliations with the Irish among whom he lived have also been discounted). And it has long been possible to read Marvell's "An Horatian Ode upon Cromwell's Return from Ireland" without giving much thought to the implications, in 1650, of his sojourn across the Irish Sea. Such works have been touchstones for a tradition of Anglocentric reading, and this tradition is quite directly linked to the tradition of Anglocentric historiography that the new emphasis on a British past is presently disrupting.

If, however, a history of the British Isles "cannot be written as the memory of a single state or nation" and will perforce be "plural" and "multicontextual,"[53] equally, a literary criticism that hopes to do justice to the literature(s) of this same archipelago must refuse to house itself in a single archive. In *Between Nations*, therefore, I have taken up Pocock's cogent historiography to argue that, even as the interactions of the British peoples, clans, and tribes on the two islands off the European coast were creating an English nation in the early modern period, they were also defining an extraordinarily complex intercultural site. The engagements between the various island peoples within Britain—English/Welsh, "mere" Irish/Old English/New English, Scottish/English, and many more—shape a heterogeneous territory—"Britain"—that exceeds and traverses the boundaries of any one of the nations that make it up.[54] And I go further than Pocock, perhaps, in claiming that, in this zone, identity (national and otherwise) is ceaselessly under negotiation. On the British Isles, the existence of each nation is dependent on the simultaneous existence of other nations, all of which are caught up in a process of mutual self-definition (though often it is precisely this that is denied by the nations in question). In *Between Nations*, I have wanted to show how Shakespeare, Spenser, and Marvell were placed in this "expanding zone of cultural conflict and creation"[55] and to trace the consequences of that placement for their writing. Often, I will say, what Shakespeare, Spenser, and Marvell are meditating on in their works *is* this zone, Britain itself, and on the very processes by which an English nation is being produced *by them* out of that multiple and uncertain domain. Again, the complicated things that these three indubitably English writers have to say owe much of their complexity to the complex British history that situates them. To consider the history of the English nation only is to elide both British history and these authors' responses to it. Whereas, I urge, if we broaden our sense of what early modern England was as a nation, and see that this developing polity was, simultaneously, the site of intersecting nations, and that England *always* implies Wales and Ireland and Scotland, then, at the very least, we will be alert to the operations by which these other nations are being written out of the English national text, more or less conspicuously. "Silences are inherent in history," Trouillot says, "because any single event enters history with some of its constituting parts missing. Something is always left out while something else is recorded."[56] Inevitably, the other British nations enter English literature with some of their "constituting parts missing." But this book is written out of the belief—I plan to show that it is more than a hope—that the other British nations have also left behind in that canon some fragments of what they were. Sometimes, we can begin to reconstruct what is missing from what is not. For me to read English texts with a British history in view is not only to try to recover the Welsh, Irish, or Scottish histories that may be pertinent to them. It is also to locate my reading at the moment and in the places when these histories were being obliterated, and to try to detect, in the text that does the obliterating, traces of what was being obliterated. By analyzing the mechanism of that obliteration, I mean to restore to these texts a historical dimension—a mostly silent but not altogether empty dimension—that disappeared for most readers along with the Welsh, Irish, and Scottish histories these texts "unwrote."

"We are reminded," Pocock has said, "that traditions are invented and communities imagined, and . . . selves invent and imagine others in the act of inventing and imagining themselves; the English . . . could not have invented themselves without imagining the Welsh, the Scots and the Irish . . . in the process, while the Irish . . . had to begin imagining themselves as a people largely in response to the ways in which the English imagined them."[57] This Pocock takes to be the contribution the "new historicism" has made to a British historiography by "applying itself to the study of Elizabethan literature" and discovering there "a process of interaction, highly and even paranoically complex and very often both brutal and tragic."[58] And, indeed, the "new historicism" has done a certain amount to work out the implications of English nationalism in differential terms.[59] Clearly, *Between Nations* owes a great deal to the literary critics, and especially the Renaissance critics, who have come to be called "new historicists,"[60] and it is undeniable that a book like this could not have been written without the presumption of a body of historicist techniques (some of which I use here) and assumptions (one of which is that the history of the early modern period matters crucially to the reading of its literature). I would argue, though, that most "new historicist" work (pace Pocock) has either taken English nationalism as a given or charted its autonomous emergence. The relation of English to British nationalism had hardly been considered.[61] Richard Helgerson's *Forms of Nationhood*, to cite an imposing example, starts with the shrewd observation that there was pervasive "uncertainty concerning [the] name and territory"[62] of early modern England, a nation that in this period was variously conflated with or detached from any or all of the other British nations to form a highly unstable polity. Helgerson's treatment, however, rarely mentions these other nations. Generally, what it concerns itself with is the discourses that went into the almost uniformly English "national cultural formation" that its author claims has "survived the last four centuries on the British Isles."[63] Now, again, in this period England *was* becoming a nation, a polity of a certain sort. But there is a gap between this claim and the acknowledgment that this nation was formed on islands that were British, not merely English, and a good deal of history—for example, Irish history—disappears into that gap. Such a tacit leaning toward one of the early modern British nations proceeds in part, I suspect, from Helgerson's use of historians embedded well within an Anglocentric tradition of historiography. The statement of G. R. Elton's that I quoted earlier, for instance, also appears early in *Forms of Nationhood* and seems to underpin much of Helgerson's approach.[64] To men born in the middle of the sixteenth century, this critic says, "things English came to matter with a special intensity both because England itself mattered more than it had and because other sources of identity and cultural authority mattered less. The large political shape of this change is well known,"[65] he says, rather blandly, and goes on to quote Elton. But how, after all, did it come to be known that in the early modern era "England itself" mattered more and that "other sources of identity" mattered less? The tradition of English historiography "rests upon a sense of identity so secure as to be unreflective and almost unconscious,"[66] said Pocock in 1974. It is not that Helgerson needs to be reminded that "traditions are invented and communities imagined." *Forms of Nationhood* is impressive in its clear-sighted sense of the constructedness of the polity it treats. Like Pocock, Helgerson wants to "unmask the nation's claim to a 'natural' or 'immemorial' origin."[67] "Neither the nation nor the state has always been there," he argues. "Both were constituted and have been continually reconstituted in an ongoing exchange between individual needs, communal interests, and discursive forms."[68] But when Helgerson comes to address the "different discursive forms and communities in which and by which the nation-state was written," it turns out that the nation-state in question is England and that what these diverse communities "provided" was "competing and even contradictory ways of being English."[69] As no doubt they did. What I argue in *Between Nations*, though, is that the communities that were caught up in the uneven and often bloody writing of the nation of England were not all of them English, and that in those communities there were many for whom "being English" was not always possible or desirable, or was so only ambiguously. These people wrote the English nation too, even, sometimes, as they were being written out of it. This exclusion has consequences: it is no more possible to construct a thoroughgoing British literary criticism out of the archive of English literature than it is to construct a thoroughgoing British historiography out of the archive of the English political culture (in fact, they are often much the same archive). But it is possible, I have claimed, to scrutinize the specific textual means by which these archives were assembled and to get a sense of what was left in and what was left out and of the oscillating relation between them. The *thesis* that an early modern English nationalism is inherently relational and invented is not one, it seems to me, that critics of the period will need to rediscover. But the *reading* that follows from that thesis has remained to be worked out. This book is an essay at such a reading. It traces the passages between nations.

Imagining Britain

WILLIAM SHAKESPEARE'S 'HENRY V'

"Divide your happy England"

In act I of William Shakespeare's *Henry V*,[1] the archbishop of Canterbury makes a well-known comparison of England's realm to a beehive. The honey bees, he tells King Henry, are "Creatures that by a rule in nature teach / The act of order to a peopled kingdom" (1.2.188–89), and therefore, he concludes, just as these insects are in "continual motion" (1.2.185) for one purpose, "many things, having full reference / To one consent, may work contrariously" (1.2.205–6). Like many later commentators, Canterbury insists that English national power in this drama has an exalted integrity that contradictions only apparently violate. But we should notice that the splendid wholeness of this "England" depends for its very definition on a threatening otherness that is almost, but not quite, elided. Canterbury's evocation of the beehive English state is a response to his king's fear of "coursing snatchers" (1.2.143) on the borders, and especially "the Scot," who may, if England is left undefended, come

> pouring like the tide into a breach
> With ample and brim fullness of his force
> Galling the gleanèd land with hot assays.
> (1.2.149–51)

"Power is voicing" in this scene, as Jonathan Goldberg has noted.[2] Henry articulates with a "full mouth" (1.2.230) a declaration of royal prerogative that extends out across the territory he means to conquer and forward into the history—"From this day to the ending of the world" (4.3.58)—he intends to command. His sovereign voice announces its unwillingness to tolerate any rival. His "history" (1.2.230), he asserts, will "[s]peak freely" (1.2.231) wherever he establishes an English dominion, without the encumbrance of other voices. These will have disappeared from his "large and ample empery" (1.2.226). But the "ampleness" of the "empery" Henry imagines for himself is inevitably positioned against another, equally "ample," also British domain, also "full" (to the "brim") of "force," that of the marauding Scots. To his English listeners, Henry represents Scotland as a counter-hegemony, as a dangerous simulacrum of their own power. The violation it threatens will turn back on English might a version of itself, transforming England's "pith and puissance" (3.0.21), at the point of entrance, into an emptiness to be filled with "hot assays." This intra-British rape (for that is what it is) can be defended against—"Once more unto the breach, dear friends, once more" (3.1.1)—but its possibility cannot be forgotten.

What makes Henry's anxiety over the marauding Scots especially charged, of course, it that within five years of the first performances of *Henry V* in 1599 (as some in the audience may well have been able to anticipate), Scots *would* "pour . . . like a tide" into England, but at the heels of the newly crowned James I, late of Edinburgh. The king was liberal in his patronage to those of his own nation, so much so that one Englishman complained that he "suffered [the Scots] like locusts to devour this Kingdom; from whence they became rich and insolent, as nothing with any moderation could either be given or denied them."[3] To James, the appearance of these Scotsmen in England proved not that the integrity of the English body politic had been violated, but rather that a larger coherence, that of "Great Brittaine," had been restored. "I am the Head," he announced in his first address to the English Parliament, "and it"—"the whole Isle"— "is my Body."

> I hope therefore no man will be so vnreasonable as to thinke that . . . I being the Head, should haue a diuided and monstrous Body. . . . I pray you was not both the Kingdomes [of Scotland and England] Monarchies from the beginning, and consequently could euer the Body bee counted without the Head, which was euer vnseparably ioyned thereunto? So that as Honour and Priuiledges of any of the Kingdomes could not be diuided from their Soueraigne; So are they now confounded & ioyned in my Person, who am equall and alike kindly Head to you both.

James, who had been hailed as "*England, Scotland, France* and *Ireland*"[4] by the messenger bringing him news of the death of Elizabeth I, offered the peoples of the British Isles in turn a corporeal unity under his sovereignty; "I am assured, that no honest Subiect of whatsoeuer degree within my whole dominions, is lesse glad of this ioyfull Vuion then I am."[5] In 1604 he announced that "wee have thought good to discontinue the divided names of England and Scotland out of our Regall Stile, and doe intend and re- solve to take and assume unto Us in maner and forme hereafter expressed, The Name and Stile of KING OF GREAT BRITTAINE, including therein ac- cording to the trueth, the whole Island."[6] But, as James had already dis- covered by then, many of his subjects felt differently than he about joining with one another, and the British "Body" would remain "diuided." Despite the "Union of Crowns" that James effected, the moment when a "per- fect" union might have been achieved passed early in his reign, stymied by suspicion in his home country of Scotland and by "subtle, intense, and con- stant opposition"[7] in both houses of the English Parliament. For a number of reasons — legal conflicts, economic impediments, sheer xenophobia — neither nation could tolerate a juncture with the other. While James had hoped, as he said in a letter, that a British union could be "left to the matu- rity of time, which must piece by piece take away distinction of nations," time seemed rather to exacerbate the many conflicts among his subjects. The very animosities that *Henry V* enunciates, the English feeling that the Scots are those who, given the chance, "will make raid upon us / With all advantages" (1.2.138–39) kept the realm split and "monstrous." And these animosities persisted. Nearly twenty years into his reign, James was told by a pamphleteer that "they make a mock of your word 'Great Britain.' "[8]

In this scene, then, *Henry V* prefigures the disharmony that would frus- trate the plans of James I and delay a union of Scotland and England until the middle of the next century.[9] As he makes his plans, the politics of Shake- speare's Henry V are British, but uneasily so. He recognizes that dominance within Britain is not necessarily moored to the southern and eastern sec- tor of England. It can shift northward, toward Scotland, which "hath been still a giddy neighbor to us" (1.2.145). Or, attacks from there can impinge on his own domain, as they did in the time of his great-grandfather, till "England, being empty of defence, / Hath shook and trembled at the bruit thereof" (1.2.153–54). His English borders, he knows, are nebulous and per- meable. Canterbury assures him that "They of . . . [the] marches," the lands at the edge of and overlapping the kingdom's boundary, "Shall be a wall sufficient to defend / Our inland from the pilfering borderers" (1.2.140–42). But Henry seems to realize that the march is a "zone of war," as one histo- rian has called it, where "the king . . . can make [his] presence effective only in arms," and where there are "power structures beyond [his] immediate reach."[10] The rhetoric of this English king, quite unlike that of the hopeful James I, is shot through with reminders that the domain he rules is an unstable amalgam of disparate parts, and that the body politic he heads is a site of violent and violating contestation.

Despite these suggestions of British rivalry, however, until recently *Henry V* was read, almost invariably, as an unequivocal testament to Anglopatriotism, "a celebration of English prowess against the overdressed French,"[11] as Harold Bloom put it. One of the great critical "facts" about *Henry V* is that it evokes, and was meant to evoke, English national pride[12] —"the nearest approach on the part of the author to a national epic," wrote H. A. Evans in 1917.[13] Little, apparently, has happened to change this judgment: "a powerful Elizabethan fantasy . . . [that] represented a single source of power in the [English] state," wrote Jonathan Dollimore and Alan Sinfield in 1985, some seventy years later. (They repeated this opinion in 1992, when their essay was reprinted.)[14] An "attempt to stage the ideal of a unified English Nation State," declared David Cairns and Shaun Richards in 1988.[15] Of course, since Hazlitt, readers have disagreed passionately over just this aspect of *Henry V*, professing to admire or loathe its fervid jingoism and its glorification of English war.[16] But "more than almost any other play of Shakespeare's, and certainly more than any other 'history,' " as Annabel Patterson has observed, "*Henry V* has generated accounts of itself that agree, broadly speaking, on the play's thematics—popular monarchy, national unity, militarist expansionism—but fall simply, even crudely, on either side of the line that divides belief from scepticism, idealism from cynicism."[17] That *Henry V* was meant to inspire English bellicosity in the face of an odious French arrogance seems clear. "Men and women decide who they are by reference to who and what they are not,"[18] as Linda Colley has noted succinctly, and, in England, as she has shown, Francophobia has long proved useful in arousing domestic Anglophilia. In this chapter, though, I want to look at the equally complicated matter of the international relations that pertained *within* the British Isles and that were registered within *Henry V*. If, I ask, an English audience could be brought together in xenophobic solidarity by such dramatic exhortations as *Henry V*, could this same concord be achieved when they confronted the sometimes tacit, sometimes violently overt divisions within Britain—English against Irish, Welsh against English, Welsh against Irish, and so on—on Shakespeare's stage?

Most critics assume so. The "opposed" readings of *Henry V* that Patterson mentions almost all rest on the premise, not at first implausible, that in 1599 Shakespeare had dedicated his theater to a specific, royally mandated project: the creation of a Britain out of the overlapping ethno-cultural groupings within the realm of Elizabeth I. They read the play, in fact, as a piece of Jacobean propaganda for union *avant la lettre*. Loyally, this playwright dreamed of a common British realm to be dominated by the Crown of England and offered up his dramaturgy and his playhouse to its establishment. By its conclusion, say Dollimore and Sinfield, *Henry V* is "a representation of the . . . hoped-for unity of Britain."[19] Of course, as I noted in my Introduction, a polity made up of the four kingdoms of England, Ireland, Wales, and Scotland *was* emerging, albeit haltingly, in the early modern period. And Shakespeare's *Henry V*, quite obviously, *does* participate in the attempt to consolidate this union. The play, as has often been observed, assembles a diverse cast of British types—MacMorris the Irishman, Fluellen the Welshman, and Jamy the Scotsman, "the co-captains of the all–British Isles team which King Henry fields at Agincourt," as David Quint jocularly calls them[20]—and unites them under the command of an exemplary English king. "The Irish, Welsh, and Scottish soldiers manifest not their countries' centrifugal relationship to England," argue Dollimore and Sinfield, "but an ideal subservience of margin to centre." These British subjects, it seems to these readers, succumb to an "effortless incorporation" into their conquerors' nationhood.[21] Claire McEachern concurs: "Perhaps the most evident personification of the coincidence of hegemony and collectivity is that of 'Britain' constructed in the four [ethnic characters]. The four parts of Britain have unified in a fight against the greater evil of France; individual wills and Britain's traditional regional feuding are subsumed to greater purpose within a fantasy of national (male) bondedness."[22]

But the unanimity of this critical verdict, and the regularity with which we hear it pronounced, should make us pause. What is the status of "Britain" here, both as a political and a literary trope, and can it be as stable as these readings seem to imply? The historical formation of a Britain on the two islands off the coast of the European continent was complex and protracted, and was far from complete as *Henry V* was being staged. "Britain" as a unifying term came into force in the early modern period by an ongoing effort of both suppression and invention, and Shakespeare wrote as identities on the two islands were still being reconfigured and subsumed under the name "British." "In Britain," as Perry Anderson has said, "the organizing definition of the national was inescapably imperial—the 'British' people, strictly speaking, emerging as an artefact of an empire-state, from the various island nationalities. The ostensible nation . . . was overwhelmingly the creation of its rulers."[23] When critics locate *Henry V* at a moment in the emergence of Britain, therefore, and when they insist on regarding the "incorporation" of its Irish, Welsh, and Scottish characters into British identity

as entirely successful, even "effortless," they are implicitly endorsing a particular version of the history of the British Isles, one whose inevitable telos
is England's long-term domination of, and even elimination of, the other
"island nationalities" that Shakespeare represented in this play. Such critics read with a privileged sense of the final necessity of English cultural
and political hegemony, retrospectively granting the play the subordinating
power to which they think it must aspire. Cairns and Richards, for instance,
explain that "the Welsh, Scots and Irish must . . . be seen to speak English as
evidence of their incorporation within the greater might of England, but
they must speak it with enough deviations from the standard form to make
their subordinate status in the union manifestly obvious. What cannot be
acknowledged is their possession of an alternative language and culture, for
to do so would be to stage the presence of the very contradictions the play
denies." For *Henry V* to be a British play, apparently, it must be without
the "contradictions" that, I will argue, are just what it seems to imply. That
other "cultures" actually persisted within Britain in this period (and long
after) is acknowledged, but any sign of these "cultures," except as the effect
of a self-confirming Englishness, is evacuated from the play by a "devastating act of cultural elision"[24] that is then attributed to Shakespeare.

Perhaps the best known and critically consequential of these readings
is found in Stephen Greenblatt's "Invisible Bullets." "By yoking together
diverse peoples . . . represented in the play by the Welshman Fluellen,
the Irishman Macmorris, and the Scotsman Jamy, who fight at Agincourt
alongside the loyal Englishmen," he says, "Hal symbolically tames the last
wild areas in the British Isles, areas that in the sixteenth century represented . . . the doomed outposts of a vanishing tribalism."[25] Greenblatt,
by now notoriously, reads *Henry V* as "an effort to intensify the power of
the king and his war."[26] The play, as he understands it, is pervasively, perhaps totally organized by the appeal to royal sovereignty it makes, and it is
in the name of this imperative that "subversion," to use his terms, is "contained." Note, however, the linkage between this recuperative reading of
Henry V and the ambitions toward a British (really English) nationalism that
Greenblatt thinks he sees in it. Henry, a "charismatic leader who purges the
commonwealth of its incorrigibles and forges the marital national state,"
appears, he says, in a "celebration, a collective panegyric to 'This star of England.'"[27] Although Greenblatt's *Henry V* calls up the most subversive of
"paradoxes, ambiguities, and tensions of authority," he collapses these, eventually, into the audience's "imaginary identification with the conqueror,"
and affirms that, "in Maynard Mack's words, [Henry is] 'an ideal image of
the potentialities of the English character.'"[28] Greenblatt likens the other

British characters in *Henry V* to "humorous grotesques"; they are dramatic stereotypes catering merely to English prejudices. "Even a spectator"—an English spectator, presumably—"gaping passively at the play's sights and manipulated by its rhetoric is freer than these puppets jerked on the strings of their own absurd accents."[29] Although Greenblatt allows that there are "moments in which we hear voices that seem to dwell outside the realms ruled by the potentates of the land"[30] (a zone he does not specify), finally, he seems unable to imagine such voices speaking where Britishness is announced. In such works as *Henry V*, the "momentary sense of instability or plenitude—the existence of other voices—is produced by the *monological* power that ultimately denies the possibility of plenitude."[31] The British nation arrives on Shakespeare's stage: the British peoples disappear into it.

But as the conflicted and often bloody history of the British Isles reminds us, these peoples did not disappear into an indiscriminate Britishness, nor did their "contradictions." And at the turn of the sixteenth century, "the potentialities of the English character" as they might have been represented by Shakespeare are not givens, far from it. Instead, I would argue, "English character" and its relation to other newly emerging definitions is just what must be negotiated among the various British groups, even (or especially) in *Henry V*. Just the notion of an "England" itself in this period is problematic. As Richard Helgerson has observed, not only did this kingdom take on a number of names—"Albion," "Britannia," "Poly-Olbion"— but the "national territory designated by these names [was not] any more stable. For many Englishmen, 'England'—or whatever they called it—included Wales. Did it also include Ireland and Scotland? For some it did; for others it didn't."[32] And this holds just for those Helgerson calls "Englishmen." How much more complex would these questions become if we were to ask what kingdom "Welshmen" or "Irishmen" called their own? To say that *Henry V* enunciates a fully developed "English" "nationalism," not to mention a "British" "nationalism," would be to frame the geopolitics of 1599 in terms that could apply, and then only roughly, to the England of a much later era. Here, therefore, I investigate "Britain" as a multivalent trope that, in the early modern period, subsumes a volatile and overdetermined political situation on what J. G. A. Pocock has called the "Atlantic archipelago."[33] And I exploit the complexity of this trope to read Shakespeare's *Henry V* not as a fait accompli of Britishness but as an episode in its ongoing and (still today) unfinished construction. Britain, I argue, is being put together in this play as we watch, and the incoherences that bedeviled this confederation in practice are not always eliminated from its performance. Nor, indeed, could they be. If Britishness in *Henry V* is coming into being by means of the very exclusions, the assertions of difference that are employed here to define it, then Shakespeare can only represent a Britain on stage by reminding his audience of the other nations that this Britain is meant to incorporate, and thereby invoking, however dismissively, their incipient but still powerful nationalisms. His *Henry V* forges what we might call, altering Benedict Anderson, an "imaginary community"[34] of Britishness for an audience whose own multiple allegiances and identifications—as "Englishmen," "Irishmen," "Welshmen," and/or as hybrids of these various designations—are, inevitably, in excess of and perhaps counter to the unified realm he so posits. This is not only to say, as critics often do, that *Henry V* stages a Britain that, given the realities of intra-British conflict, could be achieved only in some authorized fantasy. It is also to say that it cannot be achieved in *this* authorized fantasy. Because of the dynamics of Britain's own constitution, such British self-identity can never be fully represented or completely realized—on stage or off. At the turn of the sixteenth century, as Andrew Gurr points out, for Shakespeare to "unite the different domains of Britain into one army was . . . unhistorical." His source for some of the play, Holinshed, "notes the presence of Welsh as well as Scottish mercenaries fighting not for the English but for the French *against* Henry's army." Nor was the England of 1599 that much closer to a political union of the four British kingdoms, as James I would soon discover when he proposed the merger of Scotland and England to an intractable Parliament. Shakespeare may have composed *Henry V* as a "not particularly subtle piece of political prophecy . . . an Elizabethan rewriting of English history,"[35] as Gurr suggests, but, despite its possible exaltation of some future union, the play seems to imply the near impossibility of bringing a Fluellen together with a MacMorris in the present.

To make this argument, I insist, is not to deny that *Henry V* is a "nationalist" drama. It is, though in a sense whose complexities are specific to the period. *Henry V* projects a "nation-space" that, as Homi Bhabha has put it in a related context, is "in the *process* of the articulation of elements: where the meanings may be partial because they are *in media res*; and history may be half-made because it is in the process of being made; and the image of cultural authority may be ambivalent because it is caught, uncertainly, in the act of 'composing' its powerful image."[36] As such a proto-Britain emerges on Shakespeare's particular sceptered isle in the late sixteenth century, *Henry V* glorifies his own English nation, most especially in the person of Henry V. But, in the other, equivocally English, displaced characters who share the stage with the king—especially MacMorris the Irishman and Fluellen the Welshman[37]—Shakespeare implies the very discordances that this nation is meant to eliminate. The several British nationalisms that find an often ambiguous articulation in *Henry V* trouble any sense of sturdy Englishness the play might promote, and even disrupt, as we have seen, the exultant rhetoric of England's ideal king.

"Irish negligence"

In the summer of 1599, as Joel Altman has shown, London was a tense and rumor-racked city. "All the previous fall, news of Tyrone's rebellion had arrived in London, colored by details of barbarous atrocities committed by the Irish upon the English settlements."[38] Elizabeth's government had raised levies of men to go with the earl of Essex to Ireland and had been confiscating monies from every possible source to support them. Both efforts were widely resented and resisted. Once the campaign got under way, Essex's failure to achieve the quick triumphs he had promised—"By God, I will beat Tyrone in the field"[39]—soon became obvious. "Sometime in June there was an apparent crackdown on public information, for on the thirtieth George Fenner wrote to a Venetian correspondent that 'it is forbidden, on pain of death, to write or speak of Irish affairs; what is brought by post is known only to the Council; but it is very sure that Tyrone's party has prevailed most.'"[40] In September, after negotiating a suspiciously convenient truce with Tyrone at the Yellow Ford, Essex fled his command and bolted to London to importune the queen—and perhaps to consolidate his position in the realm in a more direct fashion. For this effrontery, he was soon arrested and, in June of 1600, tried before a special commission. The story of his abortive revolt in that year, and his execution in the following, is well known.

Here, to suggest the British, that is to say, trans-island politics of Essex's campaign, I want to turn to John Donne's "H. W. in Hibernia Belligeranti,"[41] which provides us with a sensitive register of the desires and fears that, among many of the English, attached themselves to that excursion. It will be helpful in locating the first performances of Shakespeare's *Henry V* in relation to these politics as well. "H. W. in Hibernia Belligeranti" is a verse epistle to Henry Wotton, who was then absent with Essex. "Went you to conquer?" asked Donne of his friend, "and have so much lost / Yourself, that what in you was best and most, / Respective friendship, should so quickly die?" (1–3). Wotton had not been writing home, and Donne sent this poem to remind him of the dangers of service in the Irish kingdom. Among them were not just "shot, and bogs, and skeins" (9). These might take Wotton's life, but far worse might happen, the poet implied: Donne himself might be forgotten. Rather than this, "young death is best" (11).

More troublesome still was that an unsettling change in Wotton might leave
him worse than dead. "Let not your soul," pleaded Donne,

> (at first with graces filled,
> And since, and thorough crooked limbecs, stilled
> In many schools and Courts, which quicken it,)
> Itself unto the Irish negligence submit. (13–16)

What does Donne fear? Is the "Irish negligence," the "lethargies" (9) that
might "prey" on Wotton's "waking mind" (8), simply the indifference of
a traveler to the affairs of his homeland, and so to his epistolary obligations to Donne? Or, more disquietingly, is it a "negligence" that might
have entered into Wotton from Ireland itself, a "negligence" that is of the
Irish, and now corrupts and subdues the very "soul" of his English friend?
Donne's verse epistle is made uneasy by the precariousness of English identity on its Irish frontier. As Andrew Hadfield and Willy Maley have argued,
"Donne perceives in the colonial experience the risk of a loss of identity, an
abandonment of self." The "colonial adventure" that has taken Wotton to
Ireland can be "an opportunity to fashion an identity . . . as the archetypal
English gentleman"; it can also be an "abyss into which [that] identity may
disappear." The poem, thus, is caught in a double articulation of assertion
and anxiety. When Donne begins by asking, "Went you to conquer?" he
reminds Wotton that he is bringing English civility to Ireland and that his
existence as a trueborn Englishman there will be guaranteed, quite properly, by force of arms against the debased Irish traitors. Here, "the determination of an English self depends upon the subjection of an Irish other,"
as Hadfield and Maley say.[42] If the earl of Essex succeeds, Donne seems to
imply, he will have achieved not only the supremacy over court rivals that
he himself so obviously desires but also an enhanced sense of identity and
pride for his followers, and even for his entire conquering nation of England. Essex may yet subdue Tyrone and his rebels, and then Donne will
have no need to fear that his friend has been "lost" in Ireland. (We should
note that this provisional confidence in the triumph of English might over
Irish sedition allows us to date the poem with some specificity: it was written and sent before the autumn of 1599, when Essex returned to England
from his by then botched campaign.)

But when Donne frames that first line as a question, he also intimates
that a counter-conquest may have taken place, and that Wotton does not
write because he no longer can write, not as an Englishman. He is not
the man whose "soul" was once, like Donne's, "quickened" by the alchemy
of the court of Elizabeth I. Now, in Ireland, he is fashioned otherwise. If

"H. W. in Hibernia Belligeranti" is invested, albeit with ambivalence, in the establishment of Wotton's English self by military means, it also expresses the terrors that accompany that project and seems to look forward, presciently, to the disruptions that will follow the Essex debacle. Throughout, Donne works to dissociate himself (and, implicitly, Wotton) from the earl's maneuvers. "In public gain," Donne declares to his correspondent, "my share' is not such that I / Would lose your love for Ireland" (4–5). Essex's operations are a greed-driven land grab, Donne implies, and for Wotton a kind of personal bankruptcy is, perhaps, to follow. In Ireland, the poet hints, wealth and glory may be had only at the expense of self-relinquishment. As if uneasily aware that these suggestions are impolitic, Donne tries to open other channels of communication. He asks for letters that need not "fear / Dishonest carriage; or a seer's art" (18–19), letters, that is to say, that circumvent the competing spy networks of the earl and his enemies—and the censorship that Fenner described—and that establish, somehow, an authentic discourse between friends, not "such as from the brain come, but the heart" (20). In this poignant plea for Wotton to withdraw himself from the earl's Irish adventure, we can measure the consequences of the failure that is to come. If Donne was writing this ominous epistle while Essex was still in the field, what might he have written after that commander had returned so ignominiously baffled and defeated?

While we may ask this question hypothetically of "H. W. in Hibernia Belligeranti," in the case of *Henry V* this question is not hypothetical in the least. There are, as is well known, two existing texts of *Henry V*, the Folio of 1623 and a so-called bad Quarto, printed in 1600 by Thomas Creede.[43] (E. K. Chambers thought of it as a "continual perversion"[44] of the Folio.) Both of these editions are crucially shaped by the events of 1599. It has long been assumed, of course, that a working script of *Henry V* was written before Essex returned to England because, in the Folio, the Chorus compares Henry to him and invokes him as the "General of our gracious Empress / . . . from Ireland coming, / Bringing rebellion broachèd on his sword" (5.0.30–32). Clearly, Essex was not yet in England and not yet in disgrace when this was penned. Like Donne's poem, the early drafts of *Henry V* (later incorporated into, if not entirely reproduced in, the Folio) predate the return of the earl of Essex. And these first drafts may well have included many of the troubling scenes we now tend to remember from contemporary productions: the churchmen scheming to manipulate Henry into war, the king standing before Harfleur threatening mass rape and slaughter, a French peer bemoaning the havoc inflicted on his country. This was probably also the version that London audiences first saw. As Altman notes, the "likely date of performance" for what is now the Folio version "can be determined within a few months."[45] "Sometime before" Essex's defeat became apparent—"between 27 March [when Essex left for Ireland] and 30 June, if George Fenner is to be believed—the Lord Chamberlain's servants must have performed *Henry V* for the first time."[46] Had we seen the play in the months *after* Essex's return, though, drawn, perhaps, by a spectacle which promised, as Thomas Nashe put it, "cunning drifts ouer-guylded with outward holinesse . . . [and] stratagems of warre,"[47] we would have witnessed none of these scenes. Between September 28, 1599, when Essex returned, and the summer of 1600, when (as the Quarto has it) the drama had been put on "sundry times,"[48] all of these scenes, and a good many other passages just as disquieting, were deleted. They do not appear in the Quarto of 1600,[49] and Annabel Patterson has argued that they were probably removed in performance as well: "The Quarto may very well be closer than the Folio to what the London audiences actually saw on the stage at the absolute turn of the century."[50]

In his Oxford edition of *Henry V* Gary Taylor has argued that Shakespeare and his company made these cuts to accommodate the sensitivities of a public aroused by Essex's failed campaign. The pattern of the elisions, he says, shows a deliberate effort to meet the demands of spectators who wanted *Henry V* to exalt their own nationalist fervor and who would have been put off by the irksome complexities of the original. The changes "remove almost every difficulty in the way of an unambiguously patriotic interpretation of Henry and his war—that is, every departure from the kind of play which theatrical convention and the national mood would have led audiences of 1599 to expect."[51] The "crackdown on public information" that put Fenner in danger of his life for "writ[ing] or speak[ing] of Irish affairs" extended, no doubt, to this play as well. Here, I want to take this line of argument further and to suggest that these changes were pervasively implicated in what I have thus far called the question of Britain. In the London of 1599, as I will show, national identity—English, Irish, Welsh, and otherwise—was a matter of emphatic argument, and this ongoing contention could only have been heightened by the recent failure of a campaign to establish the prerogatives of Englishness on the Irish frontier. For many among the English, what was at issue in Essex's expedition, as Donne's "H. W. in Hibernia Belligeranti" implies, was whether or not their nation would be consolidated in the face of the barbaric Gaels. If Essex succeeded, Ireland would become the "locus of a re-generation of a newly developing Englishness." If not, it would be the "site of the 'degeneration' of Englishness."[52] The *Henry V* that resulted from Shakespeare's handling of these tensions over the months of 1599 is not a unitary text. Indeed, it seems to have included (at least) two plays (now called the Folio and the Quarto) and was in performance probably made up of some combination of earlier drafts and redacted scripts. This is the *Henry V* that we do not have and for which we can only conjecture a reading. But we can say that this missing play was much less coherent, and, in one of its contributing versions, less obviously nationalist and dutiful than the one we now often construct. It attempts to mediate these contradictions, but, at times, it signally fails to do so. Parts of this *Henry V* could survive the scrutiny of the theater-going public in the anxious days after Essex's return; parts of it obviously could not. In the parts that could not, the play does *not* suggest that Englishness is a stable quality, or that national identity can be unproblematic for anyone on the British Isles. On the contrary, as I will show, in these passages the play implies that such identity is difficult and treacherous for all concerned.

Ireland/Wales

Wales and Ireland each represented a different challenge to the claims of an encompassing English polity. This was, in part, because the two kingdoms had been integrated into the English realm differently and according to a different schedule of encroachment. Under Henry VIII, as J. G. A. Pocock has noted, "the Statute of Wales was enacted, assimilating that principality to the English nexus of county jurisdictions," while well into the sixteenth century, Ireland remained a hodgepodge of overlapping jurisdictions and culturally autonomous zones. It not only "follows," as Pocock says, "that [as they develop historically] a Welsh political nationalism must be different in character from an Irish,"[53] but that these nationalisms must have had a different valence in early modern England. Ireland, certainly, was the more troubled and troubling locale for English hegemony, and, as we will see, the character of MacMorris, who has been assigned the signifying burden of Irishness in Shakespeare's play, presents a case study in the obliterating effects of English anxiety over the conundrums raised by his inassimilable nation. Eventually, much of what he can(not) say about Ireland in 1599 is pushed out of the play altogether, disappearing from the Quarto. In Fluellen, Welsh nationality works to another effect. While Mac-Morris puts in a brief appearance, delivers his lines in an often overwrought dialect, is finally reduced to outraged and stammering questions, and then disappears, the talkative Fluellen can be heard throughout *Henry V*, holding forth in his amiably accented English on matters of military policy, discipline, and tactics in both of its textual versions. He is truly, as he says of another soldier, "literatured in the wars" (4.7.143). Fluellen appears in the guise of the well-spoken Welshman, conversant in the powerful (and, for him, empowering) language of the English, and this is perhaps because the nation that he represents had been brought, more or less successfully, within the realm of England. Unlike the Irish (and, thus, unlike MacMorris), the Welsh (and, thus, Fluellen) could be regarded by the English as somewhat close approximations of themselves, the outlanders who did the inlanders the honor of imitation. "Our . . . Welshmen," said Thomas Wright in 1601, "when they come to London, are very simple and unwary, but afterward by conversing a while and by the experience of other men's behaviors, they become wonderful wise and judicious."[54] I do think, in fact, that Fluellen is entrusted with so much more of the text of *Henry V* than MacMorris because his language is less urgently reminiscent of the contradictions vexing the English nation in 1599.

To say this is *not* to say, however, that either MacMorris's Irishness or Fluellen's Welshness was unproblematic in *Henry V*. Dollimore and Sinfield, for instance, assert that the "issue of the English domination of Wales, Scotland and Ireland" seems "more containable" in the play than English "lower class disaffection." Wales, Fluellen's country, "must have seemed the most tractable . . . for it had been annexed in 1536 and the English church and legal system had been imposed; Henry V and the Tudors could indeed claim to be Welsh." Jokes about Fluellen's accented English were "an adequate way of handling the repression of the Welsh language and culture."[55] As for Ireland: *Henry V* celebrates a victory over the French, and thus offers, by way of displacement, an "imaginary resolution of one of the [English] state's most intractable problems."[56] But, as these critics themselves argue, "*Henry V* can be read to reveal not only the strategies of power but also the anxieties informing both them and their ideological representation."[57] And if, as I will claim, the "representation" (and elision) of MacMorris and Fluellen in *Henry V* pervasively "reveal" the "anxieties" their respective nations summoned up for the English, then it is hard to see how the "issues" they each imply could have been "contained." Moreover, "containment" in a specific case—here, that of *Henry V*—can scarcely be determined by invoking large-scale historical truisms: "Wales must have seemed the most tractable issue," "Ireland was the great problem,"[58] and so on. What is in question is the extent to which "Wales" and "Ireland" were, or could be, "contained" in a textually hybrid play, performed under specific, volatile circumstances in the months from late 1599 through 1600. As I am going to argue, it was during these months that Essex's return gave *both* Irishness and Welshness a politically charged significance that seemed, albeit briefly, to disrupt the coherence of English supremacy on the British Isles. In the character of Fluellen, Shakespeare registers a threat to the unity of the English nation that was as potent in its way as the Irish insurgency that is intimated in MacMorris. It may be the Irishman who famously asks, "What ish my nation?" and then is no longer heard, but a similar question is implicitly posed by the voluble Welshman. Fluellen, as we will see, is not without a danger of his own. In the following pages, I am going to consider each of these characters at some length, first MacMorris, then Fluellen, and ask: what could these British characters, put on an English stage, both of them, by an Englishman, be permitted to say and imply of their respective nations? And what not?

"He was an 'Irish' man"

The famous question—"What ish my nation?"—is asked in the third scene of the third act of *Henry V*. When Fluellen, who has been pestering his Irish colleague for "a few disputations" (3.3.38), observes, "Captain Mac-Morris, I think, look you, under your correction, there is not many of your nation—," his sentence disintegrates under the force of the Irishman's enraged questions:

> Of my nation? What ish my nation? Ish a villain and a bastard and a knave and a rascal? What ish my nation? Who talks of my nation? (3.3.61–65)

That is to say, MacMorris makes this protest in the Folio. In the Quarto, however, not only do most of the conspicuous references to Ireland disappear, but these lines in particular, along with *all* of the other speeches given to MacMorris in the Folio, are absent. This soldier could demand to know "What ish my nation?" in the spring of 1599. By the summer of 1600, as Taylor notes, the comic "Irishman may have seemed rather less funny."[59] The particular menace of this Irishman in the aftermath of Essex's return will emerge, I propose, if we juxtapose his lines against an incident precipitated by one of Essex's disgruntled followers, Christopher St. Lawrence. This soldier was in London while *Henry V* was in performance. St. Lawrence's contretemps, as Philip Edwards has claimed, is "more important . . . for the understanding of Macmorris's outburst, and the topical placing of *Henry V*, than [has been] realized."[60] It seems probable that the anxieties elicited by St. Lawrence are imbricated with the discomfort that an Elizabethan audience evidently felt in the presence of the uncut version of *Henry V*, and particularly in the presence of MacMorris, the belligerent Irishman.

Essex's revolt was obnoxious to the Crown not only because of his outrageous lèse-majesté but also because this revolt was seen to have disturbed the already fragile equipoise of intra-British politics, especially in London. Rowland Whyte reported that Essex's "soddain Retorn out of *Ireland*, bringes all Sortes of Knights, Captens, Officers, and Soldiers away, from thence; that this Town is full of them, to the great Discontentment of her Majestie, that they are suffered to leaue theire Charge."[61] Essex's negotiations with Tyrone at the ford of Bellaclynthe hinted at unconscionable alliances, and although his campaign against the Irish rebels had gone badly, he had a following in Ireland itself.[62] And, on England's southern border, the earl had also disrupted the marches of Wales. Several Anglo-Welshmen traveled with him in his entourage, including his notorious steward, Gilly Merrick. (This was the man, who, just before Essex's rebellion, would arrange for a performance of "the play . . . of Kyng Harry the iiijth," "an old out-worne play of the tragical deposing of King Richard the second."[63]) Through him, Essex had strong support among some of the Welsh gentry. After the earl's arrest, a conspiracy was alleged which would have rallied these Welsh allies to him. "Did you say," the queen's officers demanded of one witness at an interrogation at Llanthony in March 1601, that " 'Before the corrupt Secretary [Cecil] so should have his will (as to ruin Essex) it would cost 1000 mens lives,' " and that the " 'Tower of London should be broken'?"[64] The government's actions after the downfall of Essex suggest that it was moving decisively to curtail expressions of discontent which had begun with the return of the earl from Ireland and which had seemed to originate in several distant corners of the realm at once. As Patterson says, the "evidence . . . indicates that from February 1599 to February 1601 England witnessed a struggle not only for the popular imagination but also, obviously, for the control of the media"—the theater and Shakespeare's *Henry V* included—"by which that imagination was stimulated."[65] The insurrection of an overmighty subject had threatened to disrupt the accord among the British peoples (such as it was) and even to redirect their mutual antagonisms against the Crown.

Thus, when on October 12, 1599, Christopher St. Lawrence, lately returned from Ireland, lifted his cup in a London tavern and offered a toast to his commander, he was making an exceedingly impolitic gesture. Addressing the company, he "drancke to the Health of my lord of *Essex*, and to the Confusion of his Ennemies."[66] For this, St. Lawrence was officially rebuked and later summoned to the Privy Council to be interrogated by Robert Cecil. Essex's great opposite "told hym" before the Privy Council "that he had vsed vndecent Speaches of hym, and tooke hym to be his professed Ennemy," a charge St. Lawrence was discreet enough to deny, assuring Cecil that "he knew both how to govern hymself, and his Speach toward hym."[67]

Certainly, it was hazardous to invoke the name of Essex at the moment, just two weeks after that commander had returned unbidden from his catastrophic Irish campaign. In fact, Essex was in custody then, and the rout of Welsh, Anglo-Irish, and English supporters he had brought with him from Ireland was still milling about London, to the disquiet of the authorities. But perhaps the risk in St. Lawrence's declaration lay not only in *what* he said but also in *who* it was that said it. St. Lawrence had devoted his youth to prosecuting the queen's wars against Irish rebels, acquiring a "reputation as an active but somewhat quarrelsome officer."[68] And his own commander was certainly no friend of Ireland. Before he left Essex had boasted that he would "shake and sway the branches"[69] of the kingdom and extirpate that "tree which hath been the treasonable stock from which so many poisoned plants and grafts have been derived."[70] But Christopher St. Lawrence, who toasted Essex, was himself an Irishman.

Or at least St. Lawrence could be named an Irishman, but when he raised his cup in that London tavern, his status as a member of any nation on the British Isles, as he discovered, was a matter of anxious complexity. He later claimed before his questioners that he had made his "vndecent" toast because someone had said that he "was an *Irish* Man." And "I am sorry," he went on to declare, "that when I am in *England*, I shuld be esteemed an *Irish* Man, and in *Ireland*, an *English* Man; I haue spent my Blood, engaged and endangered my Liffe, often to doe her Majestie Service, and doe beseach to haue yt soe regarded."[71] In truth, neither the terms "English" nor "Irish" was adequate to define St. Lawrence. A long, angry history of naming and counter-naming had made St. Lawrence who he "was." In Ireland St. Lawrence was what would come to be called "Old English." Born in that country, the eldest son of the ninth baron Howth, St. Lawrence could trace his lineage back to the twelfth century, and to the lords who, under Henry II, invaded Ireland to establish suzerainty there. Even among this influx, however, distinctions had begun to blur. The invasion's commanders, says R. R. Davies, could be termed "Anglo-Norman." Their troops and the settlers that followed them were mostly English; some were Welsh and Flemish. The Gaels of the time called them all *Engleis*.[72] St. Lawrence would have traced a tangled genealogy. By the sixteenth century, he and the conquerors' other scions made up a class in Ireland whose "titles were English but whose style of rule tended towards the Gaelic and whose religion remained resolutely Catholic."[73] Depending on where they lived and the stance they took toward royal governance, they could be known variously as the "degenerate English," the "king's English rebels," the "mixed Irish," or the "king's loyal subjects."[74] Such names were given them by the "New English," the Englishmen who arrived to administer and settle Ireland for the queen and, often, these newcomers regarded their predecessors in exile with revulsion. In 1571, Edmund Campion complained that "the very English of birth, conversant with the brutish sort of that [Irish] people, become degenerate in short space and are quite altered into the worst sort of Irish rogues . . . living near them . . . [they are] transformed into them."[75] And, as we will see in the next chapter, Edmund Spenser, English poet and colonial officer, took it upon himself in his *View of the Present State of Ireland* (1598) to condemn the Old English for their cultural treachery: "the most part of them are degenerated and grown almost mere [pure] Irish," he told his readers, "yea and more malicious to the English than the very Irish themselves." How "is it possible," he asked about St. Lawrence's forebears, "that an Englishman brought up naturally in such sweet civility as England affords could find such liking in that barbarous rudeness that he should forget his own nature and forgo his own nation?"[76] Here, Spenser seems certain that he knows just what the English nation is in Ireland and who belongs to it. But this English nation is an artifact of Spenser's own writing, and he is bringing it into being by the very discriminations that he employs. Spenser *invented* the term "Old English." It occurs for the first time in his *View* and passed from him "into common currency in Ireland, particularly during the seventeenth century."[77] This poet's nation requires the constant denunciation of those who long ago fell away from its newly forged purity. And his irate question — "is it possible?" — tells us that Spenser did not easily impose this typology on those he chose to call "Old English." To him, these English/Irish are an ontological scandal, confounding his lexicon. They fuse opposed categories — "civility"/"rudeness," "English"/"Irish" — making "liking" where he wants proper distinction. What exasperates Spenser about Ireland, it seems, is that it includes too many people who, in the confusions of their very nature, challenge the terms he wants to employ — too many people, that is, like Christopher St. Lawrence.

With this convoluted lineage, then, and with this history of intra-British animosity, what *was* St. Lawrence's nation? Was St. Lawrence's enemy the Gaelic rebel against whom he had been ordered to fight, the same rebel with whom, it could be said, he shared a traitorous patrimony? Or was it rather his own sovereign, the English queen who, in that same year, had declared that she so distrusted the Irish in her army that she would henceforth deny them both commissions and companies. "We command you," she wrote one officer, "not onely to raise no more, [but] when these shall be decaid . . . to keepe them unsupplied that are already, and as they waste to Casse [strip] their bands."[78] And the year before she had directed her council in Ireland to "use all convenient meanes to clear our army of the Irish,"[79] including, presumably, Captain Christopher St. Lawrence.

When St. Lawrence insists that, although he was taken for Irish, he is just as plausibly English, he slides between the various definitions that "British" was attempting to subsume and reminds the Privy Council of something that, perhaps, they did not want to accommodate: the Englishness of many alleged Englishmen was provisional and ambiguous at best. St. Lawrence's outcry demonstrates how powerful—and vulnerable— a proto-Britain was in 1599. If even this outlandish Old Englishman can assert, fervently, that there is a single sovereign entity that gathers the diverse regions of Elizabeth's realm within it and that he belongs to it, then clearly this trope has an inclusive potency that is compelling enough to be worth appropriating and defending. St. Lawrence hopes to take his identity from the trans-island nation he hypothesizes, and he is outraged when those around him will neither join him in this reification nor extend the privileges of this nationality to him. But also, if even this outlandish Old Englishman can seize on the still novel trope of inclusiveness to fashion himself, then the identities that this Britishness enables will still be precarious and under negotiation. It may well have been that St. Lawrence elicited this insult and was stirred to anger because he stood there as a register of all of the anxiety-provoking ambiguities that beset the trans-island realm he wished to join. In this period, what will come to be named Britishness can be both vehemently proclaimed and ferociously contested, and St. Lawrence's dilemma is that both of these possibilities are realized in him. A British nationalism provides him, an Old Englishman whose English forebears had come to resemble the very people they had conquered, the Gaels he now disdains, with a sense of who he can and should be as a trueborn subject. But his own lived contradictions—an Englishman in Ireland, an Irishman in England—disrupt any certainty he might have that he simply *is* anyone in particular on the British Isles. He must acknowledge, willy nilly, that his identity is as it is taken, and that it is taken very differently in different places. A loyal soldier stops for a drink and emerges all but transformed into his own Irish foe. His threatening and ungovernable contradictions cannot be reconciled by anyone involved in this incident: not Lawrence's antagonists in the tavern, who (mis)recognize him as a rebel, not his interrogators, who would find themselves questioning a faithful servant of the queen—whoever accused him, said St. Lawrence to Cecil, "was a Villain, and that if he wold Name hym, he wold make him deny yt; I by God, that he wold"[80]—certainly not St. Lawrence himself, who was lodged in both (and/or neither) of the nations that could be assigned to him. His request that he be regarded as an incontrovertibly loyal adherent of the Crown is a plea for exactly that kind of stability of reference a still inchoate supra-English nationalism cannot afford him. What Elizabeth's officers saw as they considered St. Lawrence was an uncertain amalgam of British traits, a man divided from themselves in no very clear way. There in the Privy Council chamber, an Irish rebel regarded them from the face of a blustering, out-raged English captain.

Now, how did such ambivalences come to be played out in Shake-speare's depiction of MacMorris? It is almost always said that MacMorris is an "Irishman." What has not been noticed is that he, like Christopher St. Lawrence, is more likely a displaced Old Englishman, and that Shakespeare probably took his name from an actual Old English family. In *A Discovery of the True Causes Why Ireland Was Never Entirely Subdued* (1612), Sir John Davies listed among those who "did not only forget the English language and scorn the use thereof, but grew to be ashamed of their very English names," and who "took Irish surnames," the family of "MacMorris" in Munster, one "of the great families of the Geraldines planted there." "And this they did," he declared, "in contempt and hatred of the English name and nation, whereof these degenerate families became more mortal enemies than the mere Irish."[81] MacMorris's Old Englishness suggests there were complexities to his portrayal in *Henry V* that so far have gone unrecognized. Critics tend to assume that he can be only "English" *or* "Irish" and, surprisingly, most con-clude that he is probably more "English" than not. But when MacMorris's nation is talked of in *Henry V*, what is the reference? And who speaks—an "Irishman," an "Old Englishman," a "Briton"—when he does? Do we hear in his oddly accented questions asked on an English stage only the "monological" voice of the English (as Greenblatt would have it), speaking through a kind of British ventriloquism? Or do we hear instead the voice of the Irish, those "others" on whom England imposed its power, whisper-ing of their exclusion in a vocabulary not their own? Some readers have in fact heard MacMorris as a representative of the historically brutalized Irish, and to them, his questions speak of the predicament of subjugated Irish identity. In part this is because, as Taylor notes, "the problems of the British in Ireland have continued to lend [him] . . . the thrill of topical interest."[82] What does it mean, MacMorris seems to ask, to be "of" a nation when you have no recognized nation, when those who insist that you are "Irish" also deny the existence of something called "Ireland," except, perhaps, as a colo-nial adjunct, a debased subsidiary to England, the only true nation? But for most readers this scene is a site triumphantly occupied by English power and thus empty of any voice but one. Here, MacMorris the Irishman, along with Fluellen the Welshman and Jamy the Scotsman, those other ethnic "types" whose accents are heard in *Henry V*, are entirely absorbed into the English ethnic typology and reduced to ludicrous caricatures. Greenblatt, as we might expect, thinks of such scenes as instances of "recording"—the incorporation of other "voices" into the discourse of power, the "acknowledgement of the other [that] . . . issue[s] in the complete absorption of the other."[83] In their individuality, these characters are "curiously formal, a collection of mechanistic attributes."[84] Typically, MacMorris and Fluellen both are said to be so assimilated that whatever they say reveals them as loyal subjects of the English Crown. Many readers, for example, hear MacMorris as objecting to the implication that he is somehow *different* from other servants of the king. "Who are you [Fluellen]," one critic imagines him protesting, "a Welshman, to talk of the Irish as though they were a separate nation from you? I belong to this [English] family as much as you do."[85] " 'What ish my nation?' " agree others, "is therefore a rhetorical question to which the answer is supplied by MacMorris's service in the English army."[86]

But if, as I would argue, MacMorris's questions are troubled by much the same cross-national ambiguities as St. Lawrence's protestations, then I do not think we can be so certain that we know who is speaking or what national loyalties his talk may have implied. "Who . . . speaks when I do?" Goldberg has asked. "Do I speak or does something speak in me, something no smaller than the entire culture with all its multiple capacities?"[87] If this is so when one "entire culture" voices itself, how "multiple" will be the "capacities" of discourse when, as in early modern Britain, not one but several nations at odds with one another meet and conflict within a "single" voice? One of the best registers of these disparities, I think, is the very criticism that tries to police this passage and reconstitute MacMorris as an easily identifiable "Irishman." In order to resolve the dispute between Fluellen and MacMorris into something like a civil "communication," critics have resorted to finishing Fluellen's sentence for him,[88] to paraphrasing MacMorris's riposte,[89] and then to reparaphrasing him.[90] "When Fluellen persists in probing MacMorris's doubtful knowledge of warfare," one reader complains, "the Irishman bursts out in a wholly unreasonable *non-sequitur* effectively prohibiting Fluellen from coming to the point."[91] In fact, we could say that MacMorris's Old Englishness (his implication, that is, in the contested and unstable identity that goes under that name) has the effect of preventing any final meaning—any discursive end "point"—from emerging at all. Here, the voicing of an English nationalism gives way to a discursive heterogeneity, interrogates itself, and finds itself unable to sustain the distinctions on which it rests. As Christopher Miller has said in another context, "the gesture of reaching out to . . . [an] unknown part of the world and bringing it back as language"—the appropriation of MacMorris's "Irish" speech—brings England "face to face with nothing but itself, with the problems its own discourse imposes."[92]

This (dis)ordering of English national identity can also be traced in the language of the Welshman's remark and the Irishman's response. Later in this chapter, I will examine Fluellen's own doubled relation to Englishness. Here, though, note how completely he seems to speak for its verities. MacMorris's outburst seems disquieting and incomprehensible to him, as it is to the other royal soldiers on stage. Fluellen can only respond lamely that MacMorris "take[s] the matter otherwise than is meant" (3.3.66–67) and, as the scene ends shortly thereafter, the feuding captains are warned by Gower, their English fellow, "Gentlemen both, you will mistake each other" (3.3.74). The "communication" (3.3.41) Fluellen has forced on MacMorris has been exploded from within. The Welshman's observation ("I think, look you, under your correction, there is not many of your nation—") implies, of course, that English imperialism has been fully extended over its British neighbors. In Fluellen's remark, we catch him in the act of producing MacMorris as a recognizable "Irish" subject. He suggests that MacMorris, as an "Irishman," can be named and categorized, that however few there might be of his kind, together they form a recognizable "nation" that remains within the English order. He assumes that this English word *refers* to the Irish, and thus he assigns MacMorris a distinct (though certainly subordinate) place in the grammar of English power. The Irish, like the Welsh, Fluellen implies, are "under . . . correction," and he expects to be answered in the same terms he employs. His remarks mime the gestures by which the English incorporated (or excluded) others on the two islands. In Ireland itself, for example, the English language served to define officially sanctioned identity. The "Act for the English order, habite and language" (1537), for instance, declared that the "English tongue . . . [must] be from henceforth continually (and without ceasing or returning at any time to Irish . . . language) used by all men that will knowledge themselves according to their duties of allegiance, to be his Highness true and faithfull subjects." Spoken English was to be the mark of "knowledge." Such voices would be located, as the phrase goes, "within the true." While "whosoever shall . . . not . . . use . . . the English tongue," the Act warns, "his Majestie will repute them in his most noble heart as persons that esteeme not his most dread lawes and commandements."[93] They will be divided from true knowledge and from all civility because they do not speak English. As Spenser declared, "It hath been ever the use of the conqueror to despise the language of the

conquered, and to force him by all means to learn his."[94] And sometimes—
as in Fluellen's remark—this strategy seemed to have had the effect of sustaining English hegemony on the British Isles. Henry VIII, for example, was
told by certain of Fluellen's countrymen petitioning for a union with England that "Your highness will have but the more tongues to serve you."[95]

But though the assimilating nomenclature implied in Fluellen's jibe is
reconstructed in MacMorris's response, its coherence is also disrupted there.
As with Christopher St. Lawrence, MacMorris the "Irishman," who is more
than an "Irishman," begins to represent a certain dangerous excess. It is
not only that in this "Irishman's" speech English has been supplanted by a
"mingle mangle, or gallimanfrie of both the languages,"[96] as many English
travelers to Ireland itself complained. It is also that in MacMorris's queries
the assumptions undergirding England's rule in Britain are dismantled, not
because he rebuts them, but because, far more disruptively, he subjects them
to a relentless interrogation which refuses to acknowledge that these premises could explain the subject—MacMorris himself—who asks them. After
all, who "ish" MacMorris? Who is this self-alienated character, an inter-
loper in an English army, and what does "nation" mean when he says it?
Has he borrowed an English term to denote an Irish synonym (which is?),
or is he speaking now as an Englishman, fracturing a language other than
his native dialect? Even royal authority may have found these questions difficult to resolve because, "in Tudor parlance," we are told, "each *Gaelic* clan
was called a 'nation': a clan chief," for example, "when being recognized in
his authority by the English, would be called 'chief of his nation.' "[97] Within
the English language MacMorris tries to speak, there is a split in reference.
Sometimes a "nation" is what the English have; sometimes it is what they
attribute to those Irish whom they subjugate, those to whom they deny
a "nation" while lending them the word. Which was this Old Englishman's usage? And if his language cannot be identified, how can his already
fractured identity be fixed? His inability to utter the copula, to say "is" as
the English would have said it, becomes a sign of the ambiguity which in-
vades assigned identity when MacMorris speaks the English language. In
the ontology of MacMorris's "ish," there is no distinct presence or absence.
When something "ish," it both "is" and it is not. Like MacMorris himself,
it is recognizable but marked with an elusive difference. What he "represents" in this way is clearly *not* an alienated Irish identity, one which speaks
through him and coherently declares itself. But his lines do stage a disintegration of sense and reference within which his own overdetermined
identity is neither completely effaced nor altogether present. And this plurality of reference troubles each line MacMorris speaks. "It is impossible to

say," Philip Edwards has noted, "precisely what MacMorris means by 'Ish a villain and a bastard, and a knave, and a rascal.' The subject of the sentence may be Ireland, MacMorris, or Fluellen."[98] Or, he might have added, England. MacMorris's assertive voice shifts within the multidirectional terms of his speech. His vilification can attach itself to his antagonist, or turn back on himself, or the nation he serves, or even be directed at Ireland, so that the English violence inflicted on his homeland is, so to speak, revisited on it by himself in his own insistent but equivocal rhetoric. When MacMorris speaks in this tongue, he cannot be loyal or traitorous—not to England, not to Ireland, not even to Britain. Each of these is displaced within the nation of his speaking.

At issue, I want to insist again, is not whether MacMorris articulates a well-defined Irish nationalism in the late sixteenth century (he does not), or whether he escapes being an English ethnic stereotype (he cannot), or whether he truly achieves some supranational Britishness (he does not). In MacMorris, Shakespeare fashioned an "Irish" caricature, and by doing so he "helped determine literary representations of the stock . . . Irishman . . . for centuries to come."[99] As the prototypical stage Irishman, MacMorris is "like a court jester." He may "challenge the audience's superiority," a critic reminds us, "their national, English superiority over his Irishness," but he "must . . . ultimately . . . confirm it, [and] be made to acknowledge the hierarchic order of things."[100] Confronted by MacMorris, most Englishmen, I would suppose, left the theater with their sense of superiority intact and the ranking of nations on the British Isles undisturbed. The "order of things," in its larger outline, remained. "I am busied," wrote Essex from Ireland, "in bringing all this chaos into order: in setting down every man's rank and degree, that those under me may not fall by the ears for precedence and place . . . and bounds, and limits."[101] Essex's sentence multiplies restrictions meant to define. But as we saw, his concern for "precedence and place" and the "order of things" he imposed could not make Christopher St. Lawrence, his Old English officer, a trueborn Englishman. He was installed within that "order," but he was also its disordering. Similarly, in MacMorris, Shakespeare creates a character who is, in one sense, the dutifully assimilated "Irishman" most critics want him to be. But he is also, remember, a character who veers wildly between barbarism and civility, and who thus intimates all of the mutability that Spenser decried among the Old English. He looks for "throats to be cut" (3.3.54) and swears to Fluellen, "So Chrish save me, I will cut off your head" (3.3.72–73). He is, at times, not unlike the Irish rebels who horrify Fynes Moryson with their "rude barbarous Cryes," "terrible Executioners" who "never [spare] any that yield to mercy," not "beleeving them to be fully dead till they have cutt of their heads."[102] And, at other times, he is the dutiful soldier who rages because the "work" of prosecuting the English king's war "ish ill done. . . . I would have blowed up the town, so Chrish save me law, in an hour" (3.3.33–35). To imply the excesses of his overdetermined identity, therefore, nothing MacMorris says is (or needs to be) oppositional. There is no simple oppression and resistance here, no Irish "before" in his speech that, as we listen, is transformed into the stuff of English national sovereignty. Rather, his questions are *repetitions* of the terms by which Britain is being constructed; these MacMorris iterates ("nation . . . nation . . . nation") until, paradoxically, we become aware of the almost effaced differences between nations that linger in this rhetoric. The language of his English military masters is attenuated so that its fault lines are exposed. To put this another way, whereas Fluellen's half-sentence implies all the *answers* that make up England's "truth," MacMorris's outburst rephrases these answers as the *questions* they were designed to preclude. His queries are thus definitive for (and defined by) a certain English nationalism. But by disordering the shape of this "truth," by stretching it in his repetition, he unsettles its certainties. Something happens to change the form of the rhetoric from self-evident assertion to drawn-out interrogation. And as that something happens, the possibility of a more than English, or other than English, nation opens within his lines. So, if there is any point in this scene where an "Irish" "subversion" occurs, it is not marked on the page. An unseen place of shift, it lies in the gap—the literal white space—between Fluellen's insult and the enraged iterations that interrupt, rephrase, and question it.

I have offered this scene as a demonstration of the disruptions that cannot be eradicated from even the most powerfully organized celebration of the English nation. The scene has been called a "furious repudiation of difference,"[103] and in a way I think it is. Clearly, what agitates this moment in *Henry V* is the felt presence, just beyond the reach of England's power, of an Irish alien so radically different that it cannot be represented in itself—that "Wildehirisshcman" who appears in a late fourteenth-century text.[104] This barbarian must be absorbed and converted into the tropes of England's nationalism; in this sense, the threatening difference MacMorris represents *is* furiously repudiated. But the differences that divide the British Isles cannot simply be discarded along with the more frightening representatives of its diverse peoples. MacMorris, like St. Lawrence, "ish" "Irish" and he is not. While he seems to insist that the Old English are to be included, however ambiguously, within the emerging nation, he also implies a category of belonging that no term available to Shakespeare and his audience could

quite figure. "What ish my nation?" asks MacMorris. It is a testimony to
the power of this question that we still cannot answer it. "English," "Old
English," "Irish," "British"—no such retort will suffice.

It is because of ambiguities such as these, moreover, that we should
not assume, as critics often do, that the Crown and its agents could have
"won" the struggle for consolidation that is dramatized in *Henry V*, a play in
whose multiple versions that struggle is literally inscribed. Keep in mind the
divisions in the British body politic represented among Shakespeare's audience in 1599. How, for example, might St. Lawrence, MacMorris's offstage
counterpart, have responded to *Henry V*? "What English blood," Thomas
Heywood asked in his *Apology for Actors* (1612),

> seeing the person of any bold English presented and doth not hugge his fame,
> and hunnye at his valor, pursuing him in his enterprise with his best wishes,
> and as being wrapt in contemplation, offers to him in his hart all prosperous
> performance, as if the Personator were the man Personated, so bewitching a
> thing is lively and well spirited action, that it hath power to new mold the
> harts of the spectators and fashion them to the shape of any noble and notable
> attempt. . . . So of *Henry* the fift.[105]

And among the "bold English" Thomas Nashe held up for emulation in his
Pierce Pennilesse (1592) were "braue *Talbot* (the terror of the French)" and
"*Henrie* the fifth represented on the Stage, leading the French King pris-
oner, and forcing both him and the Dolphin to sweare fealty."[106] That there
are passages in Shakespeare's play, even in the Folio, that work to induce an
Englishness by these dramatic means is undeniable. As Nashe explained:

> There is a certaine waste of the people for whome there is no vse, but warre:
> and these men must haue some employment still to cut them off. . . . If they
> haue no service abroad, they will make mutinies at home. Or if the affayres
> of the State be such, as cannot exhale all these corrupt excrements, it is very
> expedient they haue some light toyes to busie their heads withall, cast before
> them as bones to gnaw vpon, which may keepe them from hauing leisure to
> intermeddle with higher matters.

"To this effect," he notes, "the pollicie of Playes is very necessary."[107] And
so, perhaps a disgruntled Irish/English soldier such as St. Lawrence, goaded
and enticed to make himself one with the spectacle before him, might
have been able to repersonate himself for a while. And admittedly, in places
Henry V seems to hold out the possibility that the excesses of an identity
such as St. Lawrence's can be folded into a unitary realm by a simple logic
of replication. "Rightly considered," says Anne Barton, articulating this very
logic, "Henry's soldiers are part of his body politic and thus extensions of

his own identity."[108] Henry V will be the original. The English warrior will be the true copy. Other men will be the mere simulacra. And the play itself will effect and perpetuate this autoreproduction in the name of England. The proto-English onlooker, seeing himself in the royal exemplar before him, is to be remade by *Henry V*'s "lively and well spirited action." But does *all* of the play work toward this effect, and can we assume it *always* did so effectively? In the third act, Henry charges his "noblest English" troops:

> Be copy now to men of grosser blood,
> And teach them how to war. And you, good yeomen,
> Whose limbs were made in England, show us here
> The mettle of your pasture; let us swear
> That you are worth your breeding. (3.1.24–28)

And no doubt there would have been many at the Globe who thrilled to (re)discover themselves as trueborn Englishmen. But St. Lawrence, we can guess, would have received this injunction with the same mixture of truculent pride and baffled resentment that he displayed before the Privy Council. His limbs, after all, had not been "made in England," but in her Irish kingdom. By "breeding," he was the ambiguously fashioned offspring of an English diaspora across the British Isles. Dispersal and the intermingling of English/Irish "blood" went into his nature. So when *Henry V* held up the purebred Englishman as the national ideal and urged all men of "grosser blood" to model themselves on him, would St. Lawrence have thought of himself as the original or the epigone? The norm or the deviation? He could not have avoided these questions. They are, in fact, the very questions urged upon him by his antagonists in the tavern. And the inevitability of such questions—inscribed in the play itself—implies that *Henry V* could not, in 1599, have been received as espousing an unproblematic, ahistorical, monolithic English nationalism. Those who stress the Englishness of *Henry V* have assumed the Englishness of the English themselves, but this, as St. Lawrence's tavern brawl implies, was just what could be brought violently into question. In the England of 1599, as J. G. A. Pocock has said of an earlier time, "There are normanized Irish and hibernicized Normans [like St. Lawrence or *Henry V*'s MacMorris]; there are bi-lingual Anglo-Welsh [like *Henry V*'s Fluellen], as well as monoglot Welsh and English [like, interestingly, almost no one in *Henry V*; even Henry can call upon a little garbled French]."[109] When an Anglocentric reader such as Greenblatt says that the spectators of *Henry V*, "prodded by constant reminders of a gap between real and ideal . . . are induced to make up the difference . . . to be dazzled by their own imaginary identification with the conqueror,"[110] he forgets (as Shakespeare surely could not) that there were many in England like St. Lawrence, who were precluded from straightforwardly identifying with the conquering English because they themselves were still among, or had once been among, the conquered. It is not possible, it has been said, "to reduce even 'nationality' to a single dimension, whether political, cultural or otherwise (unless, of course, obliged to do so by the *force majeure* of states)."[111] In the late sixteenth century such coercions were often at work in England and sometimes spectacularly so in Shakespeare's *Henry V*. But at a time when the polity that the royal government wanted to promote was distributed across a map that included the Irish wastes from which St. Lawrence arrived just as much as the London streets where both he and Shakespeare walked, the Englishness proclaimed by *Henry V*, I argue, could be, at best, contested, and, at worst, almost wholly defensive. This is why MacMorris's demand to be told "What ish my nation?" is not a throwaway query from a minor character representing a subordinate people. It is the question that confronted every English member of Shakespeare's audience and the question that both organized and disturbed *Henry V*—until its powerful interrogations were erased.

"A scornfull imytation"

One incident in a tavern helped me to (dis)locate MacMorris within Britain; let me begin to (un)situate Fluellen with another. It occurred in "an alehouse in the parish of Llanedy in the . . . county of Carmarthen [in Wales] in or about the tenth day of January in the first yeare" of the reign of James I. A certain Maurice Gwyn, "accompanied," the king was informed by the Star Chamber, "with Robert Jones alias Dolbren, Thomas Griffiths and divers other like dissolute and unknowne persons,"

> did in a scornfull imytation of your Ma[tie] in makinge knights, cause the said Robert Dolbren, Thomas Griffiths and divers others that were then present, to kneele downe before him; and thereuppon drawing owt his sword, lay the same on their shoulders and calling every one of them by their severall names of baptisme, using the like woordes as your Ma[tie] doth in the creatinge of this honourable order of knights, commanded every one of his said riotous companyons to arise as knights; and afterwards in common speech called every one of his said dissolute companyons by the name and title of knight, saying and often tymes swearing that they were knights as good as others then made by your Ma[tie].

It was the understanding of the authorities that Gwyn and his crew were motivated by jealousy. "Whereas your Ma[tie] had bestowed on certain gentlemen of very great estate and regard in that countrie the honour of knighthood, the said Maurice Gwyn, not loving those gentlemen but repining at your Ma[ties] favour bestowed on them, did endeavour most contemtously (so much as in him lay) to bringe the honour and degrees of the said knights into scorn, contempt and derision."[112] But there may have been more point to their antics than that. By their parody these roisters were ridiculing not only the credentials of their fellow Welshmen but also the right of the new Scottish king to confer such honors within the realm. The ritual they mocked was one of the means by which James hoped to make a "Great Brittaine" out of his disparate kingdoms. Early in his reign, James began "the process of creating a genuinely British court,"[113] and some of the 838 knights he created in his first year on the throne were, like the Welsh "gentlemen" Gwyn abused, from kingdoms other than England. In 1607, he instructed Parliament to consider that "Irish, Scottish, Welsh, and English, diuers in Nation, [were] yet all walking as Subiects and seruants within my Court, and all liuing vnder the allegiance of your King." Although James marveled "with what comfort"[114] they achieved this mutual accommodation, there was, as I have noted, much animosity among his various British subjects, and few Englishmen welcomed the newcomers. On several occasions during his reign, Scottish and English peers came to blows, and James had to intervene. Thus, the king and his Star Chamber would probably not have been much surprised if this incident had happened in the environs of London. In 1603, the scorn many English felt for the profligacy with which James created knights was evident. But what must have been the predicament of the Star Chamber as they told James I of this ridicule among Welshmen and in Wales? Here was a king who, after all, was no more English than the perpetrators. And here were subjects who felt confident enough of their own belonging within the realm to mock both him and his desire for a polity more inclusive of the "diuerse Nations" within Britain—including their own. These Welshmen seem to care little that the knights created from among their own nation would also have been objectionable to many of their English neighbors. Unlike Christopher St. Lawrence in London, Maurice Gwyn in Llanedy seems to feel no need to declare an unequivocal belonging within any nation, English or otherwise, or even to protest the lack of such belonging. Instead, he and his cohort take on an identity that is not English, but which allows them to assert "in common speech"— in Welsh—that the recognitions they bestow on each other are "as good" as any the new Scottish king might dispense from the English throne. Clearly, they are not entirely the "true" subjects James wished for, but are they notably "false"? They display themselves in the alehouse as parodic subjects

of the king, enacting a "scornfull imytation" of the very ceremony by which
he designates his loyalists, "using the like [English] woordes as your Ma[tie],"
and then sliding into Welsh to repeat such words in an alien register.[115] From
their hijinks emerges an overdetermined category: Gwyn and company are
not English, but English speaking; they are Welsh, but speak a Welsh which
iterates English; they are British, perhaps, but on their own shifting terms.

The report that is brought to James I from Wales suggests that questions of nationhood remained volatile and convoluted in Wales, as, indeed,
they long had been. In Henry V's own day, the "English people in Wales"
had petitioned Parliament to protect them against Welshmen who were
infiltrating their towns. These natives were alleging themselves to be "English by nature and condition, whereas they be in fact true Welshmen at
heart and of lineage," the petition insisted.[116] Ambiguity, however, did not
diminish animosity. On the contrary, "there grew up about that time," a
Tudor antiquary would recall, a "deadly hatred between [the Welsh] and
the English nation, insomuch that the name of a Welshman was odious to
the Englishman, and the name of Englishman woeful to the Welshman."[117]
And, by 1599, as I am going to show, when Shakespeare was to put Henry V
on stage at the Globe, Wales remained a recalcitrant and confusing site for
English rule.[118] As the incident in Llanedy suggests, in this period the problem of Wales was different in kind, but not necessarily in degree, from the
problem of Ireland. As we consider what Wales may have betokened to
Shakespeare and his audience, it is important, I think, to make a distinction between the legal incorporation of that kingdom in 1536 mentioned
by Dollimore and Sinfield, which was relatively easy, and the cultural assimilation of the Welsh themselves, which was far from "effortless."[119] That
Wales was brought within the circuits of English law did not, of course,
mean that the Welsh themselves were easily accepted as English, or that
they always wanted to be. Far from it. Instead, the encounter of the early
modern English and Welsh entailed, for both, the difficulties *that are intrinsic to assimilation itself.* Contrary to Dollimore and Sinfield, the problems
entailed by Wales in *Henry V* are not rendered entirely—or even largely—
"tractable" because that kingdom was annexed to England in the early sixteenth century.

'Bendith û mamme'

As an index of the disruptions of Wales, I want next to take an extended
look at John Penry's *Humble Supplication*.[120] Penry, a Puritan and a Welshman
himself, offered his proposals to Elizabeth I in 1587. This critical, sometimes

despairing tract on the state of true religion in Wales is revealing not only because it testifies to the very real menace that the region could pose for English governance in this period but also because Penry, in representing that menace, becomes a figure of the sort that Shakespeare would later dramatize in the *Henriad*: the ostensibly loyal — or ambiguously disloyal — Anglo-Welshman whose very language hints at the perils he claims to denounce. His country of Wales, Penry informs the queen, swarms with "southsaiers, and enchanters, such as will not stick openly, to professe that they walke, on Tuesdaies, and Thursdaies at nights, with the fairies, of whom they brag themselues to haue their knowledge." These "sonnes of Belial," he claimed, had "stroken" the Welsh with "such an astonishing reuerence of the fairies" that they would not say their names. In Welsh, they were called *bendith û mamme*, but the people would say only *bendith û mamme û dhûn*, "that is, their mothers blessing (which they account the greatest felicity that any creature can be capeable of) light vpon them, as though they were not to be named without reuerence" (46). Such misuse of the Welsh tongue, he concluded, and the absence of a regulating language in which these sprites could be exorcised, imperiled the queen's dominion over Wales. Inevitably, "grosse superstitiõ" (39) in that principality shaded into Catholic heresy. Purgatory was defended and the "Real presence" asserted, "images &c." adored, and "other infinit monsters" (46) propagated. Among these were "Vngodly welsh bookes . . . fraught with . . . Idolatries" (48) and "profaning the name of God in common talk. . . . Affirmations or negations will bring thirty oathes out of a great many." Transgressions against godly speech, he found, had now deformed the character of the Welsh themselves: "reading . . . hath brought to passe . . . many sinnes essential almost vnto our nation" (49).

For this subversion of his nation, Penry proposed a linguistic remedy. But it is not the one we might expect; he does not call for the extirpation of the Welsh language, although there had been many official attempts to accomplish this. Statutes enacted by Parliament in 1401–2, known as the Lancastrian penal code, imposed severe restrictions on the Welsh — they could not own property in English towns, for instance, or bear arms when they assembled — and one author claimed that the obliteration of the Welsh tongue had also been projected by the English in Wales that same year. It was only because God "mercifully ordained the recall of this decree at the prayer and cry of the oppressed" that this did not happen.[121] The Act of Union that brought Wales into Henry VIII's domain in 1536, noting that in that country "divers rights usages laws and customs be far discrepant from the laws and customs of this realm" and that "the people of the same dominion have and do daily use a speech nothing like, nor consonant to the

natural mother tongue used within this realm" had ordered that "henceforth no person or persons that use the Welsh speech or language shall
have or enjoy any manner, office, or fees within this Realm of England,
Wales, or other the King's dominion."[122] But Penry recommends a strategy
other than silencing. He desires that Elizabeth "raise vp preaching euen in
welsh" (52). Although the queen had granted permission in 1563 for "the
whole Bible . . . with the Book of Common Prayer and Administration of
the Sacraments . . . [to] be truly and exactly translated into the British or
Welsh tongue,"[123] Penry alleged that this Scripture was not to be found in
Wales. "The old testament we haue not in our tongue," he pointed out, and
"therefore the I. lesson is read in English vnto our people in many places
that vnderstand not one word of it." "Publicke reading in welsh" (57) could
bring his people to right understanding, and only that.

Now, Penry assured the queen that his plans to "plant the word in
Wales" (43) tended only toward the betterment of her kingdom, and that
his exhortations were offered "to the glory of God, [and] the felicity of
our soueraign" (45). But Elizabeth, we know, did not take them that way.
Two years later, Penry was forced out of England. Fleeing to Scotland,
he was pursued by the queen's warning that he was spreading "subversive
doctrines"[124] and banished again from that country by her royal cousin,
James VI. What was "subversive," though, about Penry's admonitions?
Surely, his radical Protestant leanings had much to do with his exile. This
"Puritan gadfly . . . often likened to a voice crying in the wilderness"[125]
certainly did not speak with the accents of authority. Then, too, there was
the hectoring tone he often adopted. It could not be that the queen would
"take leisure" in effecting his proposals, he averred, "for that were plainly
to say, her Maiesty waied not the honour of Iesus Christ" (43). But I suggest that we can also locate some of the threat that propelled Penry along
an itinerary traversing the borders of several British nations in the *Humble
Supplication* itself, his oddly ambivalent meditation on the Welsh tongue.
Penry claims that his project for the linguistic reformation of Wales will
extend the control that the English government looks for in that kingdom.
But will it? Can another tongue articulate English power within Britain?

In Penry's time, Wales was an often disrupted, multilingual border
zone, where most of the indigenes spoke Welsh, an English settler population spoke mostly English, and English and Welsh were spoken by an
anglicized comprador class. For example, the Act of Union had mandated
that all legal proceedings be conducted in English, but this soon proved un-
workable, and an arrangement was reached by which judges pronounced in
English, while interrogations and court testimony took place in Welsh.[126]

Penry's *Humble Supplication* articulates, I think, the subtle (in the event, perhaps overly subtle) tactics of accommodation demanded of those in Wales who were both "Welsh" and who had become, as Pyrs Morgan puts it, "approximated to western European norms of behaviour."[127] Penry's treatise, which advocates using a suppressed language—his own—to declare the official dogma of what still could be thought of as an occupying government, indicates how involved was the linguistic state of affairs in early modern Wales and the intricacies of positioning that this polyglot domain required of Welshmen who, like Penry himself, desired to speak for and to their countrymen and to address English power as well. The Wales implicated in his writing is not a kingdom where English hegemony can be assured because only English is spoken. Nor is it a wasteland of mere Celtic strangeness where only Welsh is heard. It is rather a zone of ambiguously imbricating tongues. This churchman operated, perforce, as an intercessor in an intersector where one language was privileged, but two (at least) must be used, and he negotiated between and within these tongues, sometimes fluent, sometimes stammering, as the occasion required. "I dare write," he wrote as he was about to inscribe a Welsh profanity, "that which I durst not vtter in words" (49).[128]

What Penry can or cannot utter in words, and in which words he must speak—these become the unspoken dilemmas of the *Humble Supplication*. His voice is distributed between the Welsh he castigates, but still uses, and the English he has adopted to address the queen. When, for example, he reminds Elizabeth that "southsaiers, and enchanters" roam the countryside of Wales, intimidating the people into misnaming the fairies, he not only implies that her subjects have fallen under the influence of those who can conjure power in another language altogether; he himself speaks this language. *He* names the names "they . . . wil neuer vtter": *bendith û mamme*. He thus makes of himself a figure both menacing and loyal. On the one hand, he calls up for the royal government the ancient and occult language of Wales. Under English domination, this had "become the half-secret code of necessarily subversive and marginal freemasonry on the borders and within the bounds of the . . . monarchy of the English lowlands,"[129] and Penry pointedly informs the Crown that their best efforts have not done much to destroy it. Only a true reformation can deny expression to the treasons uttered in this tongue. That it finds expression in Penry's own text indicates, paradoxically but deliberately, how corrupted Wales has become. On the other hand, Penry presents himself as an agent for that true reformation—a double agent whose facility in both languages, and in the writing of both, will allow him to spread the gospel where (but he does not say this) the English cannot make themselves heard. It will be Penry to whom the Welsh will come: "If they meete with any who can write and read, they wil demand of him whether he can teach them euer a good praier" (48). The control over Welsh discourse Penry imagines for himself is full orbed. Now, his people listen to "Idol pastor[s]" (46). The reading of "vngodlie welsh . . . bookes" (48) "hath brought to pass . . . many sinnes" (49). But if Welsh "preaching were in euery Parish, the people would be stirred vp to read the word priuatly in their houses, and so become acquainted with the phrase[s]" (57) in their own words. By invoking the nearly diabolical capacity of the Welsh to reinterpret the Scriptures, Penry shrewdly places himself between the linguistically powerful and the disempowered in Wales, and reminds the queen—and us—that simple polarities of nationality will not account for the forms of negotiated power that are achieved by crossliminal figures such as he.

"Beastly shameless transformation"

Within the *Henriad*, anxieties over Welsh language, sorcery, and assimilation come together most vividly when Owen Glendower appears in the trilogy's opening play, *Henry IV, Part I*.[130] "At my nativity," he informs Hotspur,

> The front of heaven was full of fiery shapes,
> Of burning cressets, and at my birth
> The frame and huge foundation of the earth
> Shaked like a coward. (3.1.12–16)

And there is no man, he says, who "Can trace me in the tedious ways of art"—magic—"And hold me pace in deep experiments" (3.1.46–47). But when Hotspur dismisses Glendower—"there's no man speaks better Welsh" (3.1.48)—and mockingly asks that, the better to be misunderstood, he "speak it in Welsh" (3.1.116), the rebel pointedly reminds him that

> I can speak English, lord, as well as you;
> For I was trained up in the English court,
> Where, being but young, I framèd to the harp
> Many an English ditty lovely well,
> And gave the tongue a helpful ornament—
> A virtue that was never seen in you. (3.1.117–22)[131]

The historical Owain Glyndŵr was indeed accustomed to English ways. As a young man, he had gone to London for a legal education at the Inns of

Court, and later, in Wales, married a wife of English descent. "The careers of Glyndŵr's ancestors, and his own activities before 1400, fit [the] well-established model of adjustment and co-operation [between the Welsh gentry and the English government] embarrassingly neatly."[132] After 1400, though, the year of his revolt, the "assimilated" Glyndŵr emerged suddenly as a genuine threat to English dominion in Wales and beyond.[133] Pocock reminds us that even today "Welsh nationalists . . . like to point out that had the conspiracy of Glendower, Percy, and Douglas against the English king Henry IV succeeded—which does not seem so absurd to them as it did to the English nationalist poet Shakespeare—a belt of marcher principalities, running from Wales through Northumbria to southwestern Scotland, might have fragmented the advance of both centralized kingdoms"[134]—dividing the various kingdoms, that is, that James I would want to call "Great Britain." But does the possibility of this fracture running down Britain's history really seem all that "absurd" to Shakespeare in 1599? I think the Welsh threat is present everywhere in the *Henriad*. Fluellen appears at the end of a sustained meditation on Wales that extends throughout this trilogy and links him uneasily not only to Owen Glendower in *Henry IV, Part I*, but to his daughter in that play, and, more uneasily still, to the other Welsh-women mentioned there. As Christopher Highley points out, the drama opens with Westmorland's report of

> A thousand of [Mortimer's] people butcherèd—
> Upon whose dead corpse there was such misuse,
> Such beastly shameless transformation
> By those Welshwomen done as may not be
> Without much shame retold or spoken of. (1.1.42–46)

Highley argues convincingly that "Shakespeare's Welshwomen evoke the dangers of native, Celtic women generally," and in particular "the women of Wales" who, during Glyndŵr's revolt, "cut off [the] privities" of English soldiers and "put one part thereof into the mouthes of everie dead man," then sodomized them with their own severed noses.[135] The menace of Wales, implied by these violated Englishmen, resides as a powerful residuum in the *Henriad*. But, as Highley also notes, however threatening they may be, the castrating Welshwomen are "twice removed and doubly mediated" in the play. We hear only Westmorland's report of them, which is "based on the prior report made to [him] by a 'post from Wales'"[136] (1.1.37), and then he will not name the "shameless transformation" that has occurred. If the menace of Wales resides in the *Henriad*, it is also well buried. When Shakespeare arrived at Fluellen in *Henry V*, he did not create (and not surprisingly) an "oppositional" Welsh character who could declare, in an obviously alien rhetoric, unpalatable truths about the corruptions of English patriotism and English war. Far more frequently than otherwise, Fluellen's lines glorify the English King Henry and his French campaign. Nor does Fluellen boast of the magical prowess Glendower claimed (and Penry feared). Instead, Shakespeare seems to have been interested in shaping a character who was ambivalently implicated in the problems of Anglo-Welsh assimilation that are also writ so large in Penry's *Humble Supplication*. These are not the problems of decided otherness—the outrage of an "Irish" MacMorris—but of partial inclusion, of Welshness that shades into Englishness without remaining entirely innocent of the barbarity and ferocity hinted at in Westmorland's oblique report.

Fluellen, just by his presence on an English stage in 1599, pressed on matters of nationhood that remained sensitive for both English and Welsh. "The neighborhood of Wales and remoteness from London," Sir Henry Wallop observed in 1605, "giveth more opportunity to disorder in these parts then elsewhere."[137] But, especially after Essex's return, what would have been disturbing to some in Shakespeare's audience was that such a number of Fluellen's counterparts were not "remote" at all but were to be found in London itself. The century that was ending as Shakespeare wrote *Henry V* had seen a wave of emigration from Wales into England. "Since the time of Henry VII and Henry VIII," when Wales was incorporated into the Tudor realm, wrote George Owen, the Welsh had been "emancipated, as it were, and made free to trade and traffic through England."[138] The Welsh, and especially the Welsh gentry, settled all over the island, in Berkshire, Somerset, Shropshire, and Suffolk. But a large contingent lighted in the capital itself, and these "London-Welsh emerge as the surrogate capital of their . . . homeland"[139]—a city of emigrants within Shakespeare's London. Owen's "as it were" marks the gap between the liberty that full acceptance into English society would have conferred and the more ambiguous status these newly arrived Welsh actually achieved. Many Welshman had been able to make their way to London because they had first learned English (and Englishness) in Wales. At such foundations as Abergavenny, Carmarthen, and Bangor, senior pupils were taught in the classical languages, but all Welsh students, perforce, learned English.[140] Some Welsh students traveled to England, matriculating at such schools as Westminster and Winchester. And some, as Humphrey Llwyd declared in 1573, had larger ambitions. "There is no [Welsh] man to poore, but for some space he setteth forth his children to Schole, and such as profitte in studie: sendeth them unto the

Uniuersities" of Oxford and Cambridge. Llwyd traced the itinerary from the Welsh frontier to service in England:

> it commeth to passe, that . . . [the Welsh] are now enritched and do imitate the Englishmen in diet, & apparell . . . boastyng of the Nobilitie of their stocke, applying them selues . . . to the seruice of noble men. . . . So that you shall finde but few noble men in England, but the greater parte of their retinew (wherin Englishmen excede all other nations) are welsh men borne. For . . . beyng nymble, and well set of bodie: are very apt to do any kynde of businesse.[141]

Predictably, the belonging of these expatriates among the English was tested and contested, as their hosts tried to sort out who was, or once had been, Welsh, and as they debated about what marked off such émigrés.[142] (As Penry Williams puts it, "Londoners liked the Welsh but hesitated to marry their daughters" to them.[143]) Historians often comment on the "teasing and banter . . . usually presented in a good-humoured and affectionate way" that the Welsh received from the English. They were especially "twitted and satirized" for their Fluellen-like (mis)use of the English tongue, "the difficulty they had in enunciating consonants like b, d, or g, and the dreadful muddles they got into over the tenses of verbs and the uses of pronouns."[144] Dollimore and Sinfield, we recall, consider that "the jokes [in *Henry V*] about the way Fluellen pronounces the English language are, apparently, for the Elizabethan audience . . . an adequate way of handling the repression of the Welsh language and culture." But, offstage at least, such jokes could be edgy and unstable. One Elizabethan witticism had St. Peter, oppressed by the "krakynge and babelynge"[145] of too many Welshmen in heaven, luring them all out with a cry of "Caws Pôb"—toasted cheese—and then hurriedly closing the pearly gates behind them. (The joke offers several satisfactions: the revelation of the Welshman as a true foreigner, with his own odd tastes as the instrument of that revelation, and then his disappearance.)

And, with jokes like these, it is not surprising that expatriate Welshmen could, in turn, be edgy about their belonging among the English. In 1567, Gruffudd Robert castigated those of his countrymen who "so soon as they see the river Severn, or the steeples of Shrewsbury, and hear the Englishman but once say 'Good Morrow', they shall begin to put their Welsh out of mind. . . . For he is never seen for a kindly, virtuous man that will deny whether it be his father, or his mother, or his country or his tongue."[146] Though, of course, it was just this willingness to eschew, or seem to eschew, their native tongue and to take up another speech and others' customs that allowed many of these Welshmen to move so well in English circles. "Speak no Welsh to any that can speak English," wrote William Wynn to his son at

Oxford, "no, not to your bedfellows, and thereby you may . . . freely speak English tongue perfectly."[147] Some transplanted Welshmen were spectacularly successful. The original family name of the Cecils, for instance, was Siesyllt. But when a Welsh genealogist wrote Robert Cecil with an offer to trace his lineage back to Wales, the reply, penned across the letter, was: "I desire none of these vain toys, nor to hear of such absurdities."[148] Belonging was precarious.

What, then, did it mean in 1599 for Shakespeare to put on his stage a Welshman, *Henry V*'s Fluellen? Some forty years ago, J. O. Bartley described the early modern Welsh as they appeared to their English contemporaries. The relative ease of travel between England and Wales brought many people from both countries together, he said, and "made the English see the Welsh in two co-existing roles—as provincials and as foreigners; the most remote and strange of provincials and the nearest and most intimate of foreigners."[149] This well-turned phrase, or something like it, is often echoed by historians of the Anglo/Welsh encounter. "The Welsh," we read in one place, "were seen [by the English] as people slightly more strange than provincials, slightly more familiar than foreigners,"[150] and, in another, "the closest and most familiar of foreigners . . . the most distant and outlandish of provincials."[151] Bartley's trope nicely captures the ambivalence of the relation between the English and the Welsh at this time. It recognizes both their mutual tolerance and alienation, and holds these suspended in its balanced periods. But if we listen closely as others ring the change upon his phrase, the relation begins to sound less stable. How, for instance, did the English manage to combine the sense that the Welsh were intrinsically "strange," distant cousins from the provinces, with the sense that they were at the same time nearly related and "familiar"? What quantum of likeness to unlikeness produced Welshness? How was it to be distinguished from Englishness? And, in practice, could it always be so distinguished? The meeting of the Welsh and the English within Britain took place through intricate negotiations over identity, a give and take that, I suspect, could only have become more charged in the aftermath of "ill-starred Essex's" return in the company of "boisterous and ambitious henchmen [who] were Welsh."[152] With what uneasiness, at that moment, would an English audience have regarded a character who could seem so like and unlike themselves? (These questions take on more weight when we recall that the model for Fluellen may well have been Sir Roger Williams, an obstreperous, opinionated Welsh soldier who for many years was Essex's devoted confederate and agent.[153]) If Englishness depends for its fixity and definition on "a series of negative images," as Hadfield and Maley maintain with regard to Ireland,[154] then an "other" who is to be regarded as "strange" *and* "familiar" can only complicate that relation and perhaps complicate it more than *Henry V*'s largely English audience could accept.

That there is *something* disquieting about Fluellen's presence in Henry V's army has been noticed by other readers. Greenblatt allows Fluellen, alone among the British characters, some measure of "subversion": "Only Fluellen (much of the time an exuberant, bullying prince-pleaser) seems at one moment to articulate perceptions that lie outside the official line," he says, but, he is quick to add, Fluellen "arrives at these perceptions not through his foreignness but through his relentless pursuit of classical analogies." Fluellen, remember, finds himself caught up in an analogy he has made between "Alexander the Pig" and Henry V: both are valiant commanders, both were "porn" in cities beside rivers, Macedon and Monmouth (Fluellen can't place the Macedonian river, but, he attests, "there is salmons in both" [4.7.28]), both killed their best friends, the one Cleitus, the other "the fat knight with the great-belly doublet" (4.7.43–44)—Falstaff. As Greenblatt remarks, "the moment is potentially devastating."[155] Note, however, that it is Fluellen's use of a certain structure of argument—one which holds up dissimilar things for comparison and then cheerfully obliterates the differences—that leads him to make this dangerous similitude, almost, we sense, despite himself. "I speak but in the figures and comparisons of it" (4.7.40), he alleges, as if his rhetoric has itself made his sentences indiscreet. Now, is this assimilating drive in Fluellen's rhetoric altogether *un*related to his "foreignness"? Or, more pointedly, to his Welshness? Is it unrelated to the issues of imbricated national difference and sameness that, as we have seen, were of necessity entailed by his portrayal as a Welshman in *Henry V* and that were implicit, for that matter, in Welshness itself in Shakespeare's London? On the contrary, I do not think that we can understand why Fluellen's elaborate declarations of loyalty to the English Crown could have any disruptive charge at all unless we consider that they are uttered by a character whose Welshness, in 1599, is itself being defined, on stage and off, according to a developing and ambiguous logic of national alterity. An Elizabethan audience would hardly have been able to forget that Fluellen, whose lines sometimes seem to be on a search-and-destroy mission for difference—"there is salmons in both," as he airily declares—was a figure who summoned up the most perplexing conundrums concerning the differences that did or did not separate him from Englishness. When Fluellen hears himself saying of English power what he claims not to mean, perhaps it is because he himself, as well as the Anglo-Welsh diction that Shakespeare has given him, insinuates a troubling of, even a collapsing of, categories that does not comport with a uniformly English nationalism.

That Fluellen's Welshness might have been a problem in the first performances of *Henry V* can also be inferred from the differences between its Folio and Quarto versions. So far, I have made much of the disappearance of the Irishman, MacMorris, along with the third scene of act 3, but of course Fluellen, his Welsh interlocutor, also disappears with that scene. There, Fluellen displays many of the qualities that would have marked him as a Welsh "type" for an Elizabethan audience: he is given to colorfully accented, grandiloquent talk, much of it on the "disciplines of the war" (3.3.5), in which he presents himself as an expert; he is given to extremes of judgment on his fellow soldiers (Captain MacMorris is "an ass" [3.3.15], Captain Jamy "a marvellous falorous gentleman" [3.3.21]), and he is pugnaciously willing to engage them in dispute. He is touchy, verbose, brave, and a little absurd. In itself, Fluellen's appearance in act 3 seems unlikely to have caused Shakespeare any difficulty, since it resembles so much that was left unaltered elsewhere. But there is another, more significant change, this one in act 5, not of Fluellen's lines themselves but of a commentary on them by an Englishman, Captain Gower. In both the Folio and the Quarto version of this act, Fluellen revenges himself on the upstart Pistol by forcing him to eat a leek, the symbol of Welsh courage since the battle of Crecy when, as he has explained to Henry, "Welshmen did good service in a garden where leeks did grow, wearing leeks in their Monmouth caps" (4.7.93–95). In the Folio, Gower admonishes Pistol after Fluellen has left:

> Go, go, you are a counterfeit cowardly knave. Will you mock at an ancient tradition, begun upon an honourable respect and worn as a memorable trophy of predeceased valour, and dare not avouch in your deeds any of your words? I have seen you gleeking and galling at this gentleman twice or thrice. You thought, because he could not speak English in the native garb, he could not therefore handle an English cudgel. You find it otherwise. And henceforth let a Welsh correction teach you a good English condition. Fare ye well. (5.1.63–72)

But in the Quarto this passage is altogether absent, and this absence has implications for our sense of Fluellen as a Welshman.[156] In both versions of *Henry V*, Fluellen is given many opportunities to demonstrate his martial valor. He humiliates the cowardly Pistol, confronts Williams as a supposed traitor, and beats the king's soldiers into battle: "Godes plud vp to the breaches / You rascals, will you not vp to the breaches?"[157] But nowhere in the Quarto is there the suggestion that these actions might make of Fluellen

something other than a Welsh mercenary—loyal, but now unalterably foreign—within Henry's English army. In the Quarto, that is, Fluellen *does*
appear, as critics so often claim, as a Welsh subordinate whose violence is all
in the service of his English masters. In the Folio, however, Gower's speech
implies that the consequence of Fluellen's gallantry is that Pistol (and with
him, perhaps, some in the audience) must rethink Englishness and Welshness. Pistol believes that he can claim precedence over Fluellen simply because he himself is taken for English. As he is made to realize, however,
not only does this Welshman have time-honored traditions of his own, but
by his courage he participates in virtues that, by a radical reconstruction
of this term, the play insists are *English*. Fluellen may sound alien because
he cannot "speak English in the native garb," Pistol is told, but the Welshman's knowledge of the arts of applied violence, and his willingness to use
them at the behest of his king—to swing "an English cudgel"—makes him
more English than the cowardly Pistol can ever be. And this insistence has
consequences. Allowing Fluellen to personify English valor also allows this
admirable quality to be represented in a character who is, nonetheless, not
English, or not quite. This shifting across the Anglo/Welsh identity divide
can be tracked through Gower's lines: Fluellen, who speaks like a Welshman and fights like an Englishman, administers a "Welsh correction" in the
name of the "ancient traditions" of his homeland. This punishment trans-
lates, in turn, into a changed "English condition" for Pistol, who learns
who he "is" as an Englishman just as this identity is stripped from him at
the hands of an alien, appropriated by the foreigner who beats him. At the
end of this episode, it is now Pistol, the bombastic English soldier, who has
been changed into a wandering mercenary. As he asks in the Quarto:

> Doth Fortune play the huswye with me now?
> Is honour cudgeld from my warlike lines? . . .
> To England will I steale,
> And there Ile steale.
> And patches will I get vnto these skarres,
> And sweare I gat them in the Gallia warres.[158]

Pistol can come home only by claiming, falsely, to have won abroad the
honor that alone would make him truly English.[159] In England, he must play
the part of an Englishman, while Fluellen, on whose Welshness Gower insists, takes his place as an authentic (though not English) subject of Henry V.
Not that Gower denies that Fluellen has a Welshness about him that sets
him apart from the English. Indeed, he emphasizes those traits—the pride
Fluellen takes in his ancient heritage and his ornate mispronunciations—

that serve to make him the recognizable Welshman he is in most English eyes. But Gower also seems to suggest that, while these qualities do make Fluellen different, they do not make him entirely other. They make him . . . British?

In the Folio, then, Shakespeare places Fluellen in just that ambiguous position that Welshmen—the "most intimate of foreigners"—*did* occupy in London as *Henry V* was first performed. He, like others of his British nation, is in, but still not altogether of, this English society. His identity is still very much in the making, and in May of 1599, apparently, Shakespeare could imply that this contingent formation within Britain would have consequences for the definition of Englishness itself. As the audience watches Fluellen win the recognition of Englishmen such as Gower, he becomes, not simply a version of them, but an Anglo-Welsh amalgam whose ethnic pride can legitimately force the abusive Pistol to learn a new "English condition." The conclusion to which a thoughtful spectator may have been led was that the national pride (which, as we are so often told, *Henry V* promotes) was not reserved for Englishmen. This observer might even have noticed that the very idea of an English nation was both troubled and renewed by Fluellen's insistent but equivocal patriotism. And perhaps it was just these conclusions that in 1599 made this passage inopportune. By the summer of the following year, as we know, this passage in *Henry V* would no longer have offered the occasion for such meditations.

"I am Welsh, you know"

Fluellen's hybrid Anglo-Welsh patois also allows him to articulate a "Welshness" that is pervaded by a sense of history, and, perhaps, by a disruptively British history. As Fluellen speaks, "past" and "present" are juxtaposed in politically unstable alignments that can intimate the muted threat posed by the Welsh nation. By portraying Fluellen as preoccupied with the past and his claims on it, Shakespeare was drawing upon a then well-known characteristic of his Anglo-Welsh contemporaries. Gwyn Williams has shown that, even as the early modern Welsh began to be incorporated into the English realm, they presented themselves as the inheritors of "an aboriginally independent and imperial British identity." "British" is the key word here. A Welsh historiography, famously propounded in the twelfth century by Geoffrey of Monmouth in his *History of the Kings of Britain*, and later taken up by such Tudor chroniclers as John Price of Brecon and Humphrey Llwyd of Denbigh, recalled a "mythical history which established Brutus the Trojan as the progenitor of Britain, Joseph of Arimathea as the founder of its independent Christianity and, buried at . . . Glastonbury, Arthur of Britain as its great hero."[160] This history predated, it was claimed, the incursions of the English into Wales and nominated the Welsh themselves as the "oldest, most illustrious, and most authentic inhabitants of Britain, and those still having the best title to rule over the whole island."[161] Although Fluellen himself nowhere refers to this Welsh counterhistory, interestingly enough, the English characters do. Such a historiography is implied in the "ancient tradition" (5.1.64) of which Gower (in the Folio) reminds Pistol after he has been beaten by Fluellen; Pistol has earned that beating by calling Fluellen, among other titles, a "base Trojan" (5.1.17) — a descendent of Brutus of Troy. Fluellen's own historical recollection, though, when it leaves the antique world of Greece and Rome, most often arrives at moments taken from the annals of the English Crown: "Your grandfather of famous memory, an't please your majesty," he says to Henry, "and your great-uncle Edward the Plack Prince of Wales, as I have read in the chronicles, fought a most prave pattle here in France" (4.7.87–90). His invocations of the past are thus bound up in an English and monarchical historiography. But although Fluellen's history may be royalist in its references, it could not have elided altogether certain appeals to Welsh mythic history and the Welshness it inspired because, in a sense, Elizabethan royal history *was* Welsh history. By 1599, Wales's past had often been both appropriated and rejected by the English Crown in its drive for legitimacy. Elizabeth's grandfather, Henry VII, had, of course, been Welsh himself. He descended from the Tudurs of Anglesey. As Williams points out, he "spoke Welsh and spoke English with a Welsh accent."

> When he landed at Milford Haven in 1485, his agents drenched Wales in the old Arthurian traditions in their novel political persona. Henry took pains to consult a celebrated Welsh diviner near Machynlleth; he depended utterly on a Welsh rally to carry him into England. At Bosworth, he unfurled the Red Dragon of Cadwaladr the Blessed. 'A worthy sight it was to see', says the Ballad of the Rose of England, 'how the Welsh rose wholly with him and shogged them to Shrewsbury.' And to his victory Te Deum in London, the Welsh came shogging in herds, for Merlin's prophecy had at last come. Henry VII made sure it would; he called his eldest son Arthur.[162]

However, by the turn of the century the "Tudor state [was] cast[ing] a jaundicedly discouraging eye on those grandiloquent prophecies," and Elizabeth herself "made little boast of [her] British descent."[163] "Wales," then, was the site of competing and contradictory historiographical strategies, some deployed with the collusion of the royal government, some not. In Wales itself, Welsh history could be called upon to articulate an "intense attachment to locality and a deeprooted antipathy to the foreigner,"[164] especially the English foreigner. Simultaneously, the English Crown could be heard insisting on (and then, sometimes, denying) its own Welshness. Among Anglo-Welsh émigrés, the Fluellens of Shakespeare's day, the Arthurian mythology of their homeland served both to establish their Welsh identity among their English hosts, and, paradoxically, to integrate them into the English ruling class. These displaced Welsh, who spoke and were British, "could recover a respectable and central identity" for themselves, as Gwyn Williams observes, while serving (and appropriating) the claims to Welshness of their English monarchs.[165]

Fluellen's historiography operates according to the same both/and logic that was not only intrinsic to the predicament of the Anglo-Welsh generally in Shakespeare's day, as I have said, but was specifically immanent within their own relation to the Welsh past. On the one hand, Fluellen glories in the present, when, among the English, the Welsh have been "emancipated, as it were." As Fluellen talks, his devotion to Henry V's kingdom of England, and his pride that he is included in its army, sounds in every sentence. All of his fellows (who can sustain comparison with some champion of the past) are eminently praiseworthy. "The Duke of Exeter," Fluellen assures Gower,

> is as magnanimous as Agamemnon, and a man that I love and honour with my soul and my heart and my duty and my live and my living and uttermost power. . . . There is an ensign lieutenant there at the pridge, I think in my very conscience he is as valiant a man as Mark Antony, and he is a man of no estimation in the world, but I did see him do as gallant service. (3.6.6–9, 11–15)

But, on the other hand, Fluellen uses historical similitudes that have a way of distributing praise and blame according to some scale that might or might not be at odds with a purely English nationalism. Here, for instance, we cannot quite tell whether Fluellen esteems these Englishmen because they exemplify the classical martial virtues, or whether he invokes these classical virtues because nothing less will suffice to praise their English bravery, or whether he would even make such distinctions. Fluellen, as he declares, speaks in "figures," and when he deploys these "figures" as far-reaching historical metaphors, he is led to collapse the historical "chronicles" (4.7.89) and ancient treatises that he reveres into the strictly English history that seems more immediately present to the other characters on stage. This can leave any one of them, even the king, exposed to unpredictable comparisons—flattering, denigrating, or, as when Henry becomes Alexander, one *and* the other. The speech above in which Fluellen praises Exeter is one more instance of the doubleness of his estimations. The brave ensign at the "pridge" he admires is none other than Pistol, who is not at all the paragon of Roman courage Fluellen's analogy makes him. The Welshman's lines, however, do not expose Pistol as the sham Englishman he will turn out to be. Rather, they (momentarily) ennoble this soldier by displacing a classical excellence on to him. But, of course, to liken Pistol to a well-known conspirator against the Roman Caesar, in a play of royalist history, is not necessarily to praise him. Within the fluctuating confines of his Anglo-Welsh identity, Fluellen is loyal, but insinuating, whether he "intends" to be or not, and whether we judge him right or wrong about his British fellows.

Fluellen's passion for "history," therefore, cannot have been politically innocent. The past that he calls upon is classical. It is conspicuously *not* the past of Welsh heroism that, as he appeared in *Henry V*, was being invoked in some quarters to establish his British race as the true inheritors of the island. But his lines, which hark back to a past that for the other characters seems to be a dead letter, constantly threaten to revive comparisons and analogies that will reinscribe the present as a historical palimpsest and expose the Welshness underwriting Britishness in Elizabeth I's England. As Fluellen speaks, the possibility lingers that he will reclaim, by some appeal to his mythic heritage, the ancient legitimacy now claimed in the name of his supposedly British king. "I am Welsh, you know, good countryman" (4.7.100), Henry assures him. "All the water in the Wye cannot wash your majesty's Welsh plood out of your body, I can tell you that," Fluellen reminds Henry in turn. "God pless it and preserve it. . . . By Jeshu, I am your majesty's countryman. I care not who know it, I will confess it to all the world. I need not to be ashamed of your majesty, praised be God, so long as your majesty is an honest man" (4.7.101–3, 106–9). The Welsh origins of English royal power emerge in *Henry V*, not explicitly, but enough to hold suspended the question of from whence a truly British monarchy would derive.

Thus, when we are told that *Henry V* promotes the gathering together of the British peoples under the English Crown, we should remember that this trope — "British" — was only tenuously under the control of the royal government and did not necessarily imply subservience to it. "The new 'British-ness'," as has been argued, "unavoidably took much of its tone and colour from those Welsh who had been its first celebrants and were still its most direct inheritors."[166] It might be true that Shakespeare, in his fidelity to the purposes of Elizabeth I's rule, wrote a play that offered a vision of pan-British union to a London audience. But the name for such a unity already presupposed a split within the realm. The Britishness of Fluellen initiates a regress into political origins that cannot be easily halted.

"Here and there"

Why, Annabel Patterson asks of Gary Taylor, should the Quarto of *Henry V*, after Essex's return, have deleted the speeches of the Chorus, "whose voice might itself be thought to embody the essence of an idealizing, unquestioning nationalism"?[167] Answering this question will require us to decide, at perhaps an opportune point in this study, what could have been meant by a "nation" and "nationalism" in the early modern period, and so I want to conclude with a look at just these passages. The Chorus's speeches, which powerfully and problematically shape the reception of the play, are interesting, I think, because they do *not* "embody" such an ethos and may have been eliminated for that reason. What the Chorus "embodies" instead is a dislocating projection across places and times that can make it hard for the spectator of *Henry V* to find him- or herself within the drama's plot, much less within the plotted coordinates of an English nation. Here, a distinction of Benedict Anderson's will be helpful. "In the modern conception," he notes, "state sovereignty is fully, flatly, and evenly operative over each square centimetre of a legally demarcated territory. But in the older imagining, where states were defined by centres, borders were porous and indistinct, and sovereignties faded imperceptibly into one another." The premodern principality was dispersed, an agglomeration of royal holdings, and coherence of rule and extent did not typify it. We can say, then, that if the Chorus's passages in *Henry V* are "nationalistic," they are not so, or not only so, in a strictly modern sense. Indeed, *Henry V* seems to appeal to a sense of the nation that was retrograde, in many ways, even in 1599. In this drama, the principle that most effectively secures claims to land and allegiance is dynastic. Henry wants to reconquer parts of France because, as he allows himself to be convinced, they are in his patrimony. He "Look[s] back," as Canterbury urges, "into [his] mighty ancestors" (1.2.102). *They* give justice to his cause, not as yet the imperatives of the modern nation-state. Henry's authority, confirmed by lineage, does not require a bounded terrain on which to operate. The imprecision of premodern borders, and the diffusion of kingly power across them, made it possible, "paradoxically enough," for "empires and kingdoms . . . to sustain their rule over immensely heterogeneous, and often not even contiguous, populations for long periods of time."[168] That the Crown, the "centre" of a fluctuating ensemble of territories, could command the loyalties of diversely placed subjects was enough to insure a fluid control.

But is the nation implied in *Henry V* strictly premodern? Is it not instead, as we so often put it, "early modern"? As Goldberg cogently argues, this play should be located "before . . . modern regimes are in place," yet it anticipates and participates in the construction of those "regimes."[169] *Henry V* is written at a historical place and moment—"London, England, 1599"—configured between the premodern and modern polities that Anderson describes, and its nationalism is being defined by textual negotiations that cut across and interweave the "regimes" of several sorts of sovereignty. It catches a sense of nationalism—that might be called "British"—just as it is coalescing, uneasily and sporadically, around an imagined trans-island locus. The place of *Henry V*, therefore, is *both* a royal demesne, stretched loosely across the British Isles, *and* the spatially distinct and regulated domain that we have now come to think of as a nation.

Even as the play opens, the Chorus outlines a dramatic space in which his rhetoric cannot quite be trusted to distinguish one nation from another. Imagine, the Chorus instructs us, that we have before us "A kingdom for a stage, princes to act, / And monarchs to behold the swelling scene" (Prologue.3–4). But within this scene the Chorus also invites a recognition that the English national difference cannot always be fixed. Even the "warlike Harry" is neither strictly an English warrior nor exactly an English king: he is "warlike" and "like himself" (Prologue.5). (Henry and his fellow peers are, as the French say, "Normans, but bastard Normans, Norman bastards!" [3.5.10]. "There has not been an 'English' dynasty ruling in London since the eleventh century [if then]."[170]) "This wooden O" (Prologue.13)— the Globe in London—represents the place of battle, but, as the Chorus asks, abruptly widening the national territory, "Can this cock-pit hold / The vasty fields of France?" (Prologue.11–12). What the Chorus seems to offer is a theater in which English identity depends on the constant implication of national "others" who are elided but constantly implied. France, for example, the great enemy, is clearly elsewhere, but it comes "within the girdle of these walls," not as itself, but as England's (almost) specular opposite. Here "Are now confined two mighty monarchies" (Prologue.19–20), mirroring each other uneasily across the "narrow ocean" (Prologue.22) of a difference the play insists on but cannot specify. How is one "mighty monarchy" to be distinguished from another? England, we gather, might just as well be France, and France England, except that somehow they are counter. "No king of England," Henry will say, "if not king of France" (2.2.190). (This interchangeability continues throughout the play. When they appear, the French knights seem suspiciously English. As Greenblatt has noted, although they must remain resolutely foreign, they "say remarkably little that is alien or disturbing."[171]) In the domain the Chorus describes, the nation produces its own distorting simulacrum, and we are witness to transformations and unsettling reversals. As our "imaginary forces work" (Prologue.18) along the Chorus's lines, the "great" (Prologue.11) is "cram[med]" (Prologue.12) into the small; one man is divided "Into a thousand parts" (Prologue.24). Our thoughts jump "here and there" (Prologue.29) according to a calculus of identity that will not add up.

This overdetermination of the nation in *Henry V* is why the Chorus's speeches do not (pace Patterson) "embody . . . an idealizing, unquestioning" fealty to England but rather deploy a series of compressed, high-speed excursuses on the displacements that an early modern nationality must entail. The well-known sceneshifts of *Henry V* also shift between the mappings of premodern and modern royal power. The labor urged on the spectators by the Chorus is just that of assembling a sovereign (modern) nation out of the far-flung pieces of Henry's (premodern) dynastic empire. "Work, work your thoughts," the Chorus directs; "eke out our performance with your mind" (3.0.25, 35).

> Thus with imagined wing our swift scene flies
> In motion of no less celerity
> Than that of thought. Suppose that you have seen
> The well-appointed king at Dover pier. . . . (3.0.1–4)

> O do but think
> You stand upon the rivage and behold. . . . (3.0.13–14)

> Now we bear the King
> Toward Calais. Grant him there; there seen,
> Heave him away upon your wingèd thoughts
> Athwart the sea. Behold, the English beach . . . (5.0.6–9)

> Then brook abridgement, and your eyes advance,
> After your thoughts, straight back to France. (5.0.45–46)

There is, of course, nothing especially disruptive about these shifts. Our dizzying migration across the king's disputed territories, the Chorus implies, will "work" to guarantee royal authority. The power of the prince and the power of the play are to be established in one act of loyal imagination, "For 'tis your thoughts that now must deck our kings, / Carry them here and there, jumping o'er times" (Prologue.28–29). In places, the Chorus draws the audience "home" to affirm the sceptered isle: "O England!—model to thy inward greatness, / Like little body with a mighty heart" (2.0.16–17). But, at the same time, the effect of the peregrinations the Chorus has enforced is to put us ambiguously back into the space of Anderson's premodern imagining, where "borders were porous and indistinct, and sovereignties faded imperceptibly into one another." What has not been noticed is that in *Henry V*, which is said to mark off and celebrate the English nation, it is national borders that most conspicuously collapse. This play is set between nations.

CHAPTER 2

Border Crossings

EDMUND SPENSER'S 'A VIEW OF THE PRESENT STATE OF IRELAND'

"Discourse of the overrunning and wasting of the realm"

On April 14, 1598, the Secretary of the Stationers' Company, upon request of the Warden, entered a manuscript copy of Edmund Spenser's *A View of the Present State of Ireland* into the Stationers' Register on behalf of the bookseller "Mathewe Lownes. . . . Uppon condician that hee get further aucthoritie before yt be prynted."[1] Lownes, the author's representative, did not get that authority. Spenser, who had just returned from Ireland after long service there as an administrator, who had fled Irish insurrection and had his home at Kilcolman burned behind him, who had submitted the *View* to the queen's government as a contribution toward its official policy, was denied publication. Elizabeth's Privy Council, apparently, did not want the treatise to be read.[2]

Now, if the *View* was penned as an official document, and meant to be read as such, why, it is often asked, was it banned? Why, as Jonathan Goldberg has put it, "should the government suppress a work that states its case?"[3] One answer to this question would be that Elizabeth's government did not have *a* "case" to make on Ireland; "there was not in the 1590's, as indeed there never had been among the Elizabethans, an agreed way of comprehending or of dealing with Ireland and the Irish."[4] Spenser's text, as we will see, needs to be positioned in a complex ethnopolitical field that set several such "cases" against one another, both in England and Ireland. Though England's absolute right to rule in the kingdom went unquestioned in royal circles, there was ongoing disagreement at court, between the court and the administration in Dublin, and among diverse factions— Old English, New English, "mere" Irish—across the Irish Sea. On both islands, debate was especially pronounced, for example, over the degree of rigor with which England's control should be enforced, just the issue that Spenser's *View* addressed.[5] Goldberg himself, however, has an answer to his own question, and it is one that I want to consider here because, while it is initially plausible, and a tradition of condemnation of the *View* lies behind it, finally, I think, it leads us away from the difficulties of the *View* and its reception. The treatise, we are told, was censored because it revealed the true brutality of English rule in the Irish kingdom. It lays bare "the premises upon which sovereign power operates. . . . Genuine power would not admit its savagery, and although the *View* speaks the official language of law and reformation, it does not fail to reveal that decapitation, destruction, and constant surveillance are the facts upon which the language rests."[6] What Goldberg's phrasing implies, thus, is not a divergence within the official view on Ireland, which did exist, but a far more radical distinction between that view—that "language"—and the very "facts" of the matter. The one, evidently, is an ideologically biased idiom which refers, with more or less accuracy, to a world standing beyond it; the other is the brute residuum left after this "language" has done its mystifying work, the stuff this discourse cannot shape. But "facts," after all, including emotionally charged "facts" like decapitation, are defined by and within the "language" brought to bear, and such a "language" does not recognize facts for which it cannot account or which it cannot justify. Indeed, an "official language" has this as its specific purpose. When, for instance, Spenser relates that "at the execution of a notable traitor at Limerick called Murrogh O'Brien, I saw an old woman which was his foster mother took up his head whilst he was quartered and sucked up all the blood running there out, saying that the earth was not worthy to drink it, and therewith also steeped her face and breast, and tore her hair, crying and shrieking out most terribly" (62), he is not revealing a brute and brutal "fact" which exceeds the capacity of this description to redeem it. This horrific spectacle came to Spenser already constituted, and he presents it already interpreted and justified. (Here he has implicitly claimed that the Irish resemble the blood-drinking Gauls Caesar described and so display their barbarism and suitability for another Roman conquest.) The only savagery which he admits is the savagery of the primitive Irish themselves. The brutishness of the "mere" Irish, the superior civility of the English, these were "facts" for Spenser and his fellow administrators. Their beliefs rested not on irreducible, nonlinguistic reali-

ties—the self-evident horror of a bloody head and a screaming woman—
but on shared presumptions that gave shape and significance to such "realities" but were themselves beyond proof or disproof. In the 1570's, it was the
practice of Sir Humphrey Gilbert to order that

> the heads of all those . . . which were killed in the day should be cut off from
> their bodies and brought to the place where he encamped at night, and should
> there be laid on the ground by each side of the way leading into his own tent,
> so that none should come into his tent for any cause but commonly he must
> pass through a lane of heads, which he used *ad terrorem*, the dead feeling noth-
> ing the more pains thereby. And yet did it bring great terror to the people
> when they saw the heads of their dead fathers, brothers, children, kinsfolk,
> and friends lie on the ground before their faces.[7]

Official terrorism like Gilbert's leads more than one historian to conclude
that "Elizabethan officers in the closing decades of the century 'believed
that in dealing with the native Irish population they were absolved from
all normal ethical restraints.'"[8] But Gilbert, and Spenser equally, *were* restrained (and compelled) by "norms," the normative assumptions, that is,
of English governance in Ireland. Within the premises of Irish savagery
and the absolute rightness of enforced civilization, severed heads were not
incontrovertible evidence of official depravity, but yet another means of
articulating the "official language" of terror. English officers inscribe their
"language" on the Irish; decapitation is one of the ways this is done. Since
such practices do not stand beyond the "official language" but are themselves articulations of it, it seems improbable that the *View* states for English
brutality a case "that cannot be stated."[9] For Spenser it is not a case that
needs to be made. Wretchedly cruel as English policy now seems, to Spenser
it was not repugnant, simply because within the domain where he moved
and had his being, this policy was always already "justified," or, more precisely, needed no justification at all. In arguing this, I echo W. B. Yeats, who
once remarked that "Spenser had learned to look to the State not only as
the rewarder of virtue but as the maker of right and wrong, and had begun
to love and hate as it bid him."[10] If the *View* does not "expose"[11] a distasteful truth underlying and concealed by "official language," this is because the
overall verities of that "language" shaped what Spenser could see as true of
Ireland even as he encountered it. His view never encompassed the brutal
realities of English administration because for him they were neither brutal nor real. "When Spenser wrote of Ireland," as Yeats said, "he wrote as an
official, and out of thoughts and emotions that had been organized by the
State. He was the first of many Englishmen to see nothing but what he was
desired to see."[12] I would add, however, that there was nothing just there

for him to see, at least not from the point of view from which he wrote his *View of the Present State of Ireland*.

This controversy matters because how we regard the *View*, how we divide up and distribute its "truths," has specific consequences for how we construe its politics. The *View*, we should see, is in some ways a remarkably overt document. Its harsh proposals for the subjugation of the Gaels are notorious and have earned Spenser a well-deserved reputation as an "ill-wisher of Ireland."[13] But, in making these proposals, Spenser told the Privy Council little of the kingdom that they did not know or that they could not have explained quite readily themselves. The tract's potential for disruption, I argue, must lie elsewhere. Goldberg says, in effect, that the *View* was suppressed because it revealed the secret of English ruthlessness in Ireland. He thus opens a space between what the text seems to declare and what it "does not fail to reveal"—the reality of official violence. But what if what the *View* "revealed" was "not so much secrets, but *secrecy* itself"?[14]

To explain, I want to turn to work on Spenser and secrecy by Richard Rambuss, from whom I have just quoted. Rambuss holds that during much of Spenser's career, and especially when he served as secretary to Lord Grey and others in Ireland, he was involved in the "*management* of secrets—protecting them, discovering them, even creating them" (2, emphasis Rambuss's). By a "secret," however, Rambuss does not mean, or only mean, something hidden or obscured. His more subtle understanding of the secret is housed succinctly in his observation that "you do not have a secret if no one else knows you have it" (21). Taking a hint from lines of Richard Mulcaster's, Rambuss asks, "Do we first have a secret, a hidden signified that requires, as it enters into writing, a cover to protect it from penetration? Or does the veil itself, the operations of secrecy, come first?"[15] Does the secret, that is to ask, *always* conceal—and thus potentially reveal—some "fact," or is it sometimes that "secreting" itself creates the illusion that there "is" a "fact" "there," beneath the "hollow shell" (3), to be concealed? And, if some "fact" *is* concealed, is it truly hidden, or is it hidden precisely in order to elicit its own uncovering? Rambuss argues persuasively that secrecy in this sense of doubled knowledge, at once withheld and intimated, "circulates through and traverses nearly all of Spenser's texts, and it provides the deep structure of those texts" (3). He demonstrates, in texts ranging from *The Shepheardes Calender* to the concluding books of *The Faerie Queene*, that Spenser is constantly engaged in a "transitive" labor: "on the one hand maintaining the secrecy of a secret, and on the other inviting the secret's penetration by signalling its existence" (19). His analytic, moreover, suggests why it is that we need not see the *View* as simply "revealing" the gruesome "facts" about

English rule in Ireland. Not only were these "facts" not secrets, but, even if they were, Spenser's relation to them as secrets would have been other than as the instrument of their "revelation." But when Rambuss himself comes to treat the *View*, as he does briefly, the implications of his own reading are not developed. The *View*, he says, advances "an insider account of the 'Irish problem,'" and offers "ruthless solutions to it" (27). It is "of a piece with Book 5" of *The Faerie Queene*, in which Spenser vindicates his former employer, Lord Grey, against criticism for "his extreme measures" (including the massacre of prisoners at Smerwick). As in book 5, Spenser is "not at all looking to subvert absolutist power . . . on the contrary, [he] appears to be championing a more vehement expression of it" than Elizabeth I has been permitting in Ireland. And the *View* is brought forward as evidence that in the latter years of his career Spenser had doubts that the glorious prerogative of the "sovereignty [he] celebrates is consistently expressed in the sovereign" (112) he serves. But is this mode of "vehement expression" likely to be any more characteristic of the *View* than the rest of the Spenserian canon? Does *it* have no secrets (not) to tell? In this chapter, I want to extend to the *View* Rambuss's claim that Spenser is always about the business of veiling and unveiling secrets. This, after all, was the last work Spenser wrote, and thus the culminating text in the poet's "secret career."[16] Rambuss considers the treatise—and rightly, I think—as an apologia for royal absolutism and as a brief for its translation into an implacable intolerance for Irish resistance. Such an "excessive" loyalty to principles that the queen embodied but did not always enforce might account, in part, for the book's first suppression. As Rambuss notes, the *View* "wasn't published until 1633, and even then some passages did not make it past the censors" (112). But it does not explain the book's continued suppression under James I after Elizabeth's death, nor its eventual publication, which took place in Dublin, not London, nor the partial elisions that were performed on it there in that year. To account for the reception of the *View*, both in 1598 and later, it seems to me that we need an expanded sense of secrecy that takes into account the influences of the many sites within Britain that Spenser and his text came to occupy. At the end of this chapter, I am going to return to the publication history of the *View*. But, for now, I want to suggest that, if we should see "the unfolding of Spenser's poetics as a constant trafficking in secrets and structures of secrecy" (9), we also should see that for Spenser, displaced in Ireland, the traffic in secrets was not and could not be confined to the domain of England and the demands for "concealment" that it imposed. Rambuss goes a long way toward demonstrating Spenser's ongoing investment in the culture and techniques of official English secrecy.

While his reading of the major texts of the Spenserian canon is convincing, it excludes the *View* from its complexities and restricts itself mostly to the secrecy involved in Spenser's relation to his English patrons and peers, not the other "British" people he lived among for about eighteen years: the Irish. I will argue, therefore, that in the *View* the paths of secrecy lead across several borders within the two British islands. This text too is set between nations, and moves back and forth over divides that split its imperatives and circulate its secrets in unexpected ways.

Spenser's *View* is a work of many secrets, and of course we cannot know just which of them it was that made it an inconvenient text for official purposes. And some of these secrets, as we will see in the first part of this chapter, do indeed have to do with the poet's relation to the Irish people he was sent to the island to govern. With them, I will say, Spenser's relation is more ambiguous and somewhat more tacitly complicitous than is usually considered. But the secret that would have offended the Privy Council most, I suspect, and the one that probably resulted in the *View*'s suppression, had to do with the operations of English law in the Irish kingdom. This, I think, is a secret that was Spenser's (not) to tell precisely because, as is so often mentioned, he had been "exiled" to Ireland.[17] "Elizabethans who were appointed to service in Ireland were . . . confronted with a range of problems that were generally remote from the immediate concerns of their compatriots at home, and those among them who addressed these problems were of necessity forced to advance novel solutions."[18] One such problem for the displaced Englishman was the very fact of his isolation from those who were both distant and indifferent. Essex reminded Elizabeth of "that infamous observacon, noted by manie, that Ireland yeldith none other frutes to her governors, than disgrace at home."[19] Sir John Perrot thought the kingdom "the greatest prison in the world."[20] But, as Rambuss argues, one solution to this problem is to "parlay . . . the condition of exile into one of (relative) empowerment" by seeing "the distance of exile as opening up a space for saying what cannot be said elsewhere, nearer the centers of power" (107). And this I think Spenser did when he came to treat of the common law in Ireland—except, again, he did not simply adopt a more knowing stance toward his official superiors. How could he? What he knew of legal disintegration in Ireland, and what he wanted to convey, was too volatile for that. Instead, he insinuated, from the margins, the truths the center needed to know. In Spenser's works, Rambuss has said, we can see an "endless oscillation between two questions. What must be done in order to maintain the secret as a secret? But also, what must be done in order to disclose it, to make it known insofar that the secret of keeping a secret does not remain a secret? The undisclosed, in other words, must continue to operate on some discursive level" (62). The secret of the inefficacy of the English common law in the Irish kingdom, I argue, is both what the *View* "knows" and what it "does not fail to reveal" (to resituate Goldberg's claim), the "undisclosed" that Spenser wanted to be able to disavow, if need be, and that he also wanted the Privy Council to register in all its radical severity. On the evidence of the *View*, we can say that Spenser at once believed, and denied that he believed, and allowed himself to intimate, that this law had reached a point of almost total collapse, and that it could be delivered only by the most stringent imposition of royal will.

In claiming this, I am also concurring with the arguments of Ciaran Brady. In response to claims made by both Goldberg and myself, this historian has proposed that "a simpler, though perhaps deeper, explanation [of the *View*'s suppression] would seem nearer to the truth." Spenser's text was "unacceptable not simply because it underlined the costly failure of successive English administrations in Ireland, but because it asserted that the great law [of England] itself lay at the source of this failure."[21] But I would add this crucial proviso. Brady goes on to say that what the *View* revealed, shocking its official readers, was that "English law was not an organic entity that developed and expanded through the history of a community, but an artificial construct that could be imposed by power alone."

> It is extremely doubtful whether Spenser intended these implications to be followed, or whether indeed he was fully conscious of their significance himself. But it is nonetheless clear that out of his critique of the failure of English law in Ireland, there arose a series of questions concerning the essential character of the common law which neither Spenser nor his intended readers were prepared to face.[22]

I urge to the contrary that Spenser was fully conscious of the "secret" implications of his own text, and that the questions that arose concerning the essential character of the common law were introduced by design into a treatise that was meant quite deliberately to disrupt the certainties of Elizabeth's policy makers. Spenser implies that nowhere in Ireland is royal power more self-canceling and incoherent than in the most authoritative code the English could impose: the common law. Elizabeth's law in that kingdom is now a pervasively unstable vehicle for imperial rule. Prone to misinterpretation from all sides, suspiciously akin to the native law it claimed to displace, manipulable and fractured, the common law asserts a power that could not be definitively maintained. "It is dangerous," says Irenius, Spenser's spokesman, "to leave the sense of a law unto the reason or will of the judges who are men and may be miscarried by affections and many other means, but the laws ought to be like to stony tables, plain, steadfast, and unmoveable" (33). If these lines are ironic, it is because the text they are set within can be read—and I think was read—as implying that the law in Elizabeth's British realm has become a chaos of legal ambiguity, subversive equivocation, and pervasive uncertainty.

Spenser, I hold, has a distinct argument on the common law to make. But it is not one that he expresses in the clearly ordered prose of the dutiful bureaucrat. On the contrary, the problems he intimates *are* his argument, and his text arrives at its conclusions only after Spenser has fully exploited the evasions, doublings, and (mis)recognitions that a lifelong experience with the "keeping" of secrets provides him. Enmeshed as it is in its own secrecies, the *View* does not, cannot, declare the law's authority unequivocally. Far from being like to stony tables, its meaning plain, its argument steadfast, and its premises unmovable, it itself demonstrates the impossibility of conducting the queen's policy in Ireland according to fixed terms and unquestioned truths. Subtly and often obliquely, Spenser's text insinuates that in Ireland as it is presently administered, royal truth has been allowed to come into fundamental question. In prose that does not straightforwardly declare legal verities, but twists through manifold arguments, often taking into account more than it should and unavoidably displaying the contingency of what it declares, the *View* both exemplifies and castigates the confusion of English law in Ireland. If Spenser had propounded this message more directly, perhaps, the *View* would have been a less threatening book. Proposals for radical reform in Ireland were hardly unfamiliar to the royal government in London. "Almost every English-born author writing of Ireland during the 1580s and 1590s was insistent upon the development of a clearly-defined radical programme of reform which would involve the erection of a completely new commonwealth upon firm foundations."[23] But, instead, Spenser determined to couch his allegations in a rhetoric that not only implicated, but was implicated in, the perplexities of the legal discourse by which the queen's councillors hoped to rule Ireland. Thus, contra Brady, it was not only *what* the *View* (did not) "reveal"—the incoherence of the common law in Ireland—but *how* Spenser chose (not) to "reveal" it that may have elicited censorship. The *View* could not look like the self-consistent statement of English right to rule that the Privy Council would demand. By its "secret" equivocations, it overwhelmed whatever purposes the Council may have had for an official text. That actual royal influence extended only so far beyond the Pale, that the queen's writ ran only here and there, no one could deny, not even in London. But that within the domain of the English and for an official like Spenser the law in the Irish kingdom had become so concussed with uncertainty that its authority—the queen's authority—was effectively destroyed was not, I suspect, something the royal apologists who sat on Elizabeth's Council could accept. That, I propose, is why the government suppressed a work that seems to state its case.

If, however, Spenser's *View* were offered only as a self-canceling secret, it would not be the poignant text that it is. The legal flux that Spenser's own prose exemplifies horrifies him as well. Spenser's loyalty to the transcendent ideals that he served in the person of his "Magnificent Empresse" should not be underestimated. The larger facts of his life make a case of their own. This poet rendered some eighteen years of loyal service in Ireland to Elizabeth I and to her royal administration. He coveted and accepted the queen's rewards of land and position in the kingdom and was concerned to defend them. For much of his career, he thought of himself as a royal servant, not just by employment, but as a self-appointed apologist and theorist. And writing as a legal officer himself, he is acutely aware—because he makes himself aware as he writes—of the ungovernable complexities of making a coherent argument for royal authority when, in Ireland, it is exactly the tenability of that authority that is put into question. And so, as we will see, Spenser's *View* also expresses an intense drive to rise above the very secrecies that it itself elaborates. Without a secure "center" of authority, Spenser concludes, the law cannot establish order. Even within an English court, its meanings are negotiated, altered, and disputed by techniques of evasion that are not unlike his own. In practice, the "reason or will" of men who "may be miscarried by affections or many other means" can never be excluded, though their contention within the law leaves it incoherent and uncertain. In consequence, the truths which must be established and guaranteed by an authoritative, stable legal discourse are not to be had. As Spenser's own prose demonstrates, in Ireland, even servants of the queen like himself must administer a code whose jurisdiction is indefinite and fluctuating in courts where testimony is suspect and judgment unsure. Worst of all, the royal authority on which adjudication must rest is brought into question because it cannot halt the confused struggle over the law within the precincts of its own tribunals. The *View*, therefore, is also meant as a plea to the government to assert Elizabeth's rightful prerogative and prevent her law from devolving into the kind of indeterminacy that Spenser both condemns and exploits. The solution Spenser hopes for is the immediate and definitive establishment of English law on royal authority. This would require an incontrovertible demonstration from the throne of the absolute centrality of the prince's will throughout Britain and the utter dependence of every legal doctrine on its conformity to that will for its validity. To secure itself completely, regal authority must show that invincible power flows from its inherent prerogative, and this is why, as is well known, Spenser pleads for a full-scale military invasion of Ireland and the eradication of those who deny the queen's supremacy. Royal truth in Ireland must not be only the unrivaled truth, but it also must be capable of ordering the world so that its truth cannot be denied—even by a text like the *View*. Yeats once diagnosed these ambivalences in Spenser. "Like an hysterical patient," he said, the poet "drew a complicated web of inhuman logic out of the bowels of an insufficient premise—there was no right, no law, but that of Elizabeth, and all that opposed her opposed themselves to God, to civilization, and to all inherited wisdom and courtesy, and should be put to death."[24] In a text that was itself denied official sponsorship, the very existence of those who can think otherwise than royal officials want them to is threatening. The truths that Spenser himself subverts may not be refused.

"Uncertain of their loyalty"

The Ireland of Spenser's day was a battleground where "Englishness" and "Irishness" were fought over incessantly. "Ireland is but swordland," as the Irish bard Tadhg Dall Ó Huiginn declared. "Let all be defied to show that there is any inheritance in the land of Fál save that of conquest by force of battle."[25] In the 1570's, when Sir Thomas Smith and others attempted an Irish colony—its capital was to be "Elizabetha"—prospective colonists were told that they would be "either wholly in the warre and half in peace," but to go as if they "were all in warre."[26] Unable to tell who their opponents were or what the extent of the hostilities, half at war, half at peace, the newly arrived English struggled to establish their rule against an enemy at once within and without. War in Ireland was confusing. Some English captains took on Irish soldiers to complete their rosters. English soldiers sold their weapons, deserted to the Gaels, or were hired by rebel lords.[27] (No wonder that military commanders were instructed to deliver "secular discourses" to remind their troops of their English superiority to their adversaries.[28]) Even the well-known Pale could not keep the civilized "inside" apart from the barbaric "outside" in any definitive way. Since Henry II, Ireland was said to have acknowledged the lordship the Pope had conferred on the English Crown. Henry VIII had himself declared "King of Ireland" in 1541, and Irishmen were thereafter to be his loyal subjects (though "the bill had to be read and explained in Irish as well as in English"[29]). But though English monarchs inscribed the limits of their prerogative at the outermost edges of the island, the Crown controlled only "a narrow coastal strip, stretching from Dundalk to a few miles south of Dublin, and even this small area could [only] with difficulty be defended against the depredations of the Irish"[30]—the Crown's supposed subjects. Outside that boundary, but still within the confines of the kingdom, the people seemed exotic, and law was alien. Much of the territory just within or just beyond the Pale was controlled by Irish and Old English nobles. There, along that wavering line, English government sometimes did, sometimes did not function. Another law—native (or brehon) law—often prevailed. At its edges, at the boundary of the Pale, the Pale lost its edges. The boundary collapsed, so that, "as one approached the frontiers of the Pale the evidence of English influence faded away, and a considerable border zone seems to have existed where even the landowners were uncertain of their loyalty"[31]—so confused, apparently, they could barely make sense of themselves.

Across the island, the problems of the Pale were writ large. The very map the English officials drew of the kingdom was a constructed and unstable fiction.[32] The legal distinctions it attempted to enforce broke down constantly, and this had the largest implications, since in Ireland ethnic typology was a matter of law. As Sir John Davies (solicitor general of Ireland, 1603–6, attorney general 1606–19, Speaker of the House in the Irish Parliament, 1613) recounted, Edward III had caused the Statutes of Kilkenny to be promulgated because "the English of this realm . . . were at that time become mere Irish in their language, names, apparel, and all their manner of living, and had rejected the English laws . . . to the utter ruin and destruction of the commonwealth." The Englishman who adopted Irish ways, decreed the statute, would be prosecuted till he "conform himself in all points to the English manner of living."[33] But the statute was not systematically enforced, and, as Nicholas Canny notes, "the distinctions drawn in 1366 were exaggerated and are certainly not valid for the sixteenth century."[34] By the time Spenser wrote, the persistence of Irish dress and speech within the Pale had forced the English to realize that these legal distinctions were ceaselessly eroding and willfully violated. The social categories the English insisted on so vehemently—"mere" Irish, Old English, New English—also visibly failed in some instances, eroded by intermarriage between Old English and Gaels.[35] Even the spoken word did not truly differentiate the English from the Irish. The English took their own tongue as the legal sign of a true subject, but, said Richard Stanyhurst, in Ireland "the meaner sort speak neither good English nor good Irish," but "a mingle mangle, or gallimanfrie of both the languages."[36] And it was not just the Irish peasants who spoke Gaelic; so did the "better sort," the Old English.

Another observer claimed that "all the English and the moste parte with de-
lighte, yea even in Dublin, speak yrishe and greatlie are spotted in maners,
habyte and condicions with Yrishe staynes."[37] By yet another paradoxical
turn, the categories by which English and Irish were to be divided into discrete, comprehensible groupings were vehemently insisted upon, not only
by the New English themselves, but by the Old English, those long established transplants who needed to consolidate their position in the face of
the Englishmen arriving from the home territory. The Old English seized
upon these categories to accentuate their distinction from the barbaric
"mere" Irish, but, inevitably, the Old English themselves came to represent,
for the New English, the collapse of these very distinctions. Thus, much of
the discourse that figured Ireland was actually under the control of those it
had been meant to exclude. "A considerable part of 'the English image of
Ireland,'" we are told, "was . . . manufactured in the Pale, and reflected . . .
the calculated snobbery of a struggling élite within Ireland."[38] To the queen,
these Old Englishmen styled themselves "Inglish gentillmen" of the Pale or
"your graces subjects . . . within the Englishe Pale."[39] But, as we saw in the
previous chapter, Spenser recognized and sometimes declared that in their
"deviance" the Old English violate "Inglish" national identity and threaten
its coherence. He says that the Norman ancestors of the Old English nobles
had followed Henry II into Ireland and then "degenerate[d] from their first
natures as to grow wild" (63), adopting "from the Irish . . . their apparel,
their language, their riding, and many other the like" (66). "Lord," he ejacu-
lates, "how quickly doth that country alter men's natures!" (151).

Divided Voice(s)

Canny has pointed out that much of the virulence of New English reactions to the "barbarism" of the Gaels proceeded from a severe case of what
we would now call "culture shock." In the middle of the sixteenth century,
for "the first time since the original Norman conquest . . . large numbers
of Englishmen [came] into direct confrontation with the Gaelic Irish in
their native habitation." Before this, arriving officials had been "screened
through the English Pale," and, in any case, saw little of the inner reaches
of the island. But now many "went directly by ship to the proposed site of
the colony and thus did not experience the gradual assimilation that an approach through the Pale would have effected."[40] This abrupt clash of two
cultures on the British Isles helps to explain why the New English insisted,
as they did throughout the century, that the "mere" Irish were utterly different from themselves and irredeemably debased. They "live like beastes,"

Barnaby Rich would say in 1578, "voide of lawe and all good order"; they are "more uncivill, more uncleanly, more barbarous and more brutish in their customs and demeanures then in any other part of the world that is known."[41] Famously, Spenser's *View* also flays the "inordinate life and manners" (6) of the Gaels, and it is useful to be reminded, as by Canny, that Spenser can most readily be identified with the New English in particular. His *View* was "designed to serve the interests of those engaged upon the conquest and colonization of Ireland at the end of the sixteenth century."[42] Clearly, though, when we consider the Spenser of the 1590's, who had served some eighteen years in Ireland, we are not dealing with a man still reeling from the shock of first contact with unalloyed "barbarism," and thus one prone to making absolute distinctions. Rather, we are dealing with a mind that is well versed in the ambiguities that would beset such certainties after some years in Ireland, however much those ambiguities might, at times, horrify him. Indeed, it is just this shift in awareness, that, again and again, the *View* uneasily calls our attention to—and condemns. "And is it possible," asks Eudoxus, one of the dialogue's interlocutors, "that an Englishman brought up naturally in such sweet civility as England affords could find such liking in that barbarous rudeness [of Ireland] that he should forget his own nature and forgo his own nation?" (48). Can we hear this question and not apply it to its author? Whatever Spenser was at the end of his life, he was no longer (if he ever had been) purely "English." Spenser, rather, was the product of a life lived on—and "between"—two islands, and the inheritor of the complexly imbricated histories of both.

Living as he did at this confused intersection of island cultures, how does Spenser position himself in the *View*? The poet, of course, takes great care to adopt an official tone. He offered his *View*, he told the queen's Council, not as "a perfect plott of myne owne Invension . . . but as I haue learned and vnderstood the same, by the consultacion and actions of verie wise governors, and Counsellors whom I haue sometymes heard treate thereof."[43] And we are told that if in fact the Lord Deputy had called together any number of the most influential colonial officials, "he would have received much the same information as we find in the *View*, and practically identical advice."[44] Like other English officials, Spenser can speak the language of official terror. And he does—copiously, implacably. He too insists on difference and patrols the boundaries. However, I argue that Spenser's *View* also manages to blur, if not erase, those boundaries, and that in his treatise he implies affinities with the very folk he disparages. As Rambuss notes of the later books of *The Faerie Queene*, there are many places in Spenser where "the secret is constituted as a field in which the operations of concealment and disclosure, veiling and revealing, are made to compete and collude in the exercise of knowledge and power" (115). It may be that Spenser seems rigorously to exclude any recognition of Gaelic interests or values, but is this exclusion perhaps designed to "shield" an affinity that Spenser could find no way to articulate directly? The answer to this question is, of course, nowhere in the text of the *View*, at least, not on its "surface." It is rather in the play of claims, counterclaims, and insinuations by which the reader (and remember, the *View* was meant for an official reader) is pulled into its secrets, and made thereby to "collude in the exercise of power and knowledge" in Ireland. Strict separation—by category if not in actuality—may have been decreed for the inhabitants of Ireland, and Spenser certainly does his part to enforce it. But it seems unlikely that the contested mélange of Englishness and Irishness that really did pertain in the kingdom did not produce in Spenser an awareness that far exceeded the simplicities of the official typology. Whatever Spenser may sometimes have felt about the "degeneracy" and "barbarism" around him, he knew that these were unavoidable features of the experience of Ireland in the 1590's. Inevitably, the two had been very much a part of *his* experience. And it may have been this sense that he wanted to convey, tacitly, to the English officials who were so remote from the realities of governance in Ireland, and who so clearly needed a subtly administered education in those realities. In any case, we can say that, in the authorized rhetoric of the *View*, Spenser manages to imply that his statements do not quite encompass all there is to say. There remains something residual in his declarations, not quite articulated, not entirely absent. Because the *View* is a text compounded of divided voices, no voice predominating and no voice entirely consistent with itself, the reader is allowed to sense that in Ireland another tongue is spoken and another truth given voice.

Let me take first the most readily identifiable voices. Spenser cast the *View* as a Ciceronian dialogue taking place between Irenius, a perceptive and conscientious administrator recently back from Ireland, an observer who has explanations for everything, and Eudoxus, his amiable, though somewhat less acute and informed interlocutor, who needs explanations for everything. As Annabel Patterson points out, many of those who read the *View* now assume that the entire text is a single expression of Spenser's "voice," and that his representative within the text is Irenius.[45] But finding "Spenser" here is harder than that. In this interplay of voices, it is Eudoxus who is usually heard making the direct, sententious observation or asking the baffled question that reveals his complete orthodoxy, while Irenius, whose sympathy is with that orthodoxy, nonetheless appears to confound him and demonstrates that orthodoxy will not suffice in Ireland. The dialectic the two establish is between Eudoxus's articulation of the standard, unquestioned premises of the queen's policy, its enabling assumptions, and Irenius's denial (directly or not) of those assumptions' legitimacy or coherence. The variously construed etymology of their names helps define the roles they play in the dialogue. "Irenius," says one critic, "is from the Greek for 'peaceful,' somewhat darkly punning on Eire, Erin, Ireland" [46] — thought of, we know, as a place of incomprehensible, intractable resistance to English civility, a region of violence and anger. (Davies declared that his charge "might properly be called the 'land of ire,' because the irascible power was predominant there for the space of 400 years together" [223].) The same critic glosses Eudoxus (from the Greek, εὐδοξ-έω, "to be in good repute," "to be honored, famous") as "well-taught," [47] while another says the "name means truth," and continues, "English truth, that is." In the *View*, Irenius, who can be seen at times as "the mouthpiece for Ireland," and at others as "the spokesman for its pacification," both declares the meaning of Ireland, the land whose name his name invokes, and argues for the "peace" — the civil peace — he would impose on it. His name uneasily couples anger and a kind of peace — as they are in Ireland itself. Eudoxus is Irenius's pupil whose lesson is the persistent complexities of the Irish question (in which he is not always so very well taught) *and* he is the standard of official English truth Irenius at once accepts and obliquely questions. Eudoxus sets the terms and defines the assumptions Irenius moves within and moves against. One critic claims that, as "the official view, [Irenius] can always persuade his interlocutor, Eudoxius," [48] but this is only partly so. Irenius occupies an official "position" in the treatise, but the one whose preconceptions must always be taken into account is Eudoxus. He can be persuaded, usually, when the argument is tailored to fit his premises, but he seems to miss altogether the subtle ways in which those premises are rendered untenable. Thus, *his* is the official view, apparently untroubled by skepticism; his is the voice of authority. In this dialogue are interwoven the voices of officially sanctioned truth, unaware of its own instability, and unwilling doubt, all too aware of the insufficiency of the received view.

"It's a long way to Tipperary"

There is a further consequence to Spenser's self decentering: not only is the received truth broken up into disparate and conflicting voices, but, within his text, others — Irish others — begin to make their presence felt. In what follows, I am going to consider two instances of this. First, Spenser's response to the ongoing legal challenge of the Counties Palatine. Here, the claims of an Irish lord and sometime enemy of the Crown made themselves heard in this official's prose. Next, Spenser's treatment of the bards. In this case, affinities between his own techniques of concealment and those of these disloyal Gaelic rhymers begin to emerge.

As autonomous jurisdictions, the Counties Palatine had long troubled the Crown. Davies recounts that Henry II established eight of them to reward the English lords who invaded and then settled in Ireland. Since then, he thought, their autonomy had become a matter of Irish pride and resistance. They had been ceded as self-contained legal jurisdictions, and so these "absolute palatines . . . did exercise high justice in all points within their territories, erected courts for criminal and civil causes, and for their own revenues . . . made their own judges, senechals, sheriffs, coroners, and escheators; so as the king's writ did not run in those counties" (148). By 1596, only one remained, the Liberty of Tipperary, the domain of the tenth earl of Ormond, Black Thomas. The County's immunity from English common law could be "turned to the advantage of fugitives from royal justice" (with or without the collusion of its lord was not always clear); this in itself was a disconcerting exception to official hegemony. But, worse, "almost inextricably mingled with the lands of the 'Liberty' were those of the 'Cross' of Tipperary, directly under the Crown's authority."[49] "And so at this day," says Davies in 1612, "the earl of Ormond maketh a sheriff of the liberty, and the king a sheriff of the cross of Tipperary" (148). Within Ormond's borders, as Davies realizes, the status of English authority was at its most uncertain—at once present and excluded, authoritative and unfounded. Here, its efficacy depended not on its inherent prerogative, but on the assent—sometimes proffered, sometimes withheld—of an overmighty subject. Sir Henry Sidney had tried to set up a presidency for "the xecution of the lawes in those countrees"[50]; it would administer justice throughout the province of Munster, including Tipperary, and extinguish the "pretendid palatyne liberties without which yt is never to be lookid for that Mounstir shall be reformed."[51] Like Davies, Sidney believed Black Thomas was more king than subject; in Tipperary, they had "never herd of other prince than Ormond."[52] But Ormond treated directly with Elizabeth, persuaded her to his support, and Tipperary remained a Liberty. Thereafter, the English both resented and depended on Ormond—resented him because he exercised power which should have been theirs, depended on him because short of total conquest they could govern much of Ireland only through him. "Here," we are told, "was an anomaly that irked the officials, the more that Ormond was too powerful, both in Ireland and at Court, for them to attack openly."[53] For Davies, the Crown's problem and its solution are equally straightforward. There is a single, unquestioned locus of authority, the Crown itself. The lords of the Counties Palatine were pretenders who "could not endure that any kings should reign in Ireland but themselves; nay, they could hardly endure that the Crown of England itself should have any jurisdiction or power over them" (147). The Crown's jurisdiction had been secured forever by Henry II's conquest. Anomalies like the earl of Ormond's sovereignty simply needed to be brought into line with the enduring reality of royal prerogative.

Now, by contrast, here is the attempt of Irenius, Spenser's spokesman, to fix this Irish boundary for Eudoxus, his interlocutor. "I would gladly know," Eudoxus says, "what you call a county Palatine and whence it is so called."

Irenius responds:

> It was as I suppose first named Palatine, of a Pale as it were a pale and defense to the inner lands, so as now it is called the English Pale; and thereof also is a Palsgrave named, that is an Earl Palatine, others think of the latin *palare*, that is to forage or outrun, because those marchers and borderers use commonly to do so; so as to have a County Palatine is in effect but to have a privilege to spoil the enemy's borders adjoining; and surely so it is used at this day as a privileged place of spoils and stealths, for the County of Tipperary, which is now the only county Palatine in Ireland, is by abuse of some bad ones made a receptacle to rob the rest of the counties about it, by means of whose privileges none will follow their stealths, so as it being situate in the very lap of all the land, is made now a border, which how inconvenient it is let every man judge. And though that right noble man that is lord of that liberty do pain himself all that he may to yield equal justice unto all, yet can there not but great abuses lurk in so inward and absolute a privileging. (30)

Notice that a boundary which a more doctrinaire official (such as Davies) could think of as rigid and authoritatively fixed Irenius thinks of as fluctuating and linguistically defined. He is so conscious that a jurisdiction such as a County Palatine is nothing but a mapmaker's construct, consisting of nothing other than lines of demarcation holding apart inside and outside, that, searching for the linguistic origins of "Palatine," he can conclude only that this ability to delimit, exclude, and include—to establish a Pale—defines what it means to be such a thing. The word "Palatine" itself, he says, testifies that this County takes its existence only from the arbitrary limits it defines, while its "Palsgrave," who marks these boundaries, has authority only within the lines thus drawn. The English cartographer who sets such boundaries across Ireland, Irenius implies, is writing his schematic fiction of authority onto the land, much like the poet who writes *these* lines.

There is, moreover, an improvised quality to Irenius's etymology that emphasizes its tenuous hold on the land described. His derivation of "Palatine" is patently a lexical fabrication. He calls attention to his own inventiveness by immediately offering another etymology, "the latin *palare*" of which "others think." And it is at this point that Spenser's prose begins to hint at, and in some sense include, what does not fall within the official view. Irenius suggests that "Palatine" might take its meaning not only from the setting of boundaries, but their violation by the foraging and outrunning "marchers and borderers," and thus momentarily implies that even official language embodies just as much the disruption of its own categories as their establishment. By bringing these aliens into the word game, moreover, Irenius renders his own purportedly official etymology partial and unstable. He makes the necessary first gesture toward the imposition of official categories (his definition *seems* to impose boundaries). And his derivation is "in line" with accepted notions of what it means to establish a jurisdiction in colonial Ireland. But it also declares itself a ceaselessly violated invention.

Still more disquieting are the traces left by the interlopers Spenser has allowed in, here, one overmighty subject in particular—the tenth earl of Ormond. Irenius does not give the obvious etymology for "Palatine," but, as Spenser's readers must have surmised, it derives from the Latin *palatinus*, which in turn is a cognate of *palatium*, a palace.[54] "Palatine," that is, irresistibly suggests the place, the habitation of an imperial or royal figure. The Crown, of course, claimed full jurisdiction over all Ireland, including Ormond's County Palatine, but Spenser's lines announce that Elizabeth harbors in her domain a jurisdiction whose very name suggests a rival monarch. There is some apparent praise here for Ormond, but even this is complicated. Tipperary's lord, Irenius insists, is a "right noble man . . . [doing] all that he may to yield equal justice unto all." Seven years earlier, as Spenser's readers might have remembered, when he dedicated *The Faerie Queene* to Ormond among sixteen others, he had noted that

> where they selfe hast thy braue mansione;
> There in deede dwel faire Graces many one.
> And gentle Nymphes, delights of learned wits,
> And in thy person without Paragone
> All goodly bountie and true honour sits.[55]

We might wonder, though, if Ormond's habitation was once the site of justice, arts and learning, and Ormond himself in every way exemplary, how has Tipperary come to be a "receptacle" of abused privilege and exactly who —other than "Black Thomas"—are the "bad ones" making it so? Ormond cannot quite escape responsibility for the effects of the "absolute privileging" he secured for himself at the expense of royal jurisdiction. The felt "presence" of this almost royal figure, who cannot be named, forces the prose into unsettling conjecture. The rest of the "definition" completes the damage. The paragraph began by demonstrating that a "County Palatine" came into being with the setting of limits, however fragile, but as it continues we find that our sense of those limits deteriorates even more. Instead of erecting an enclosing and protecting "defense to the inner lands," Irenius tells us, a Pale licenses the spoiling of "the enemy's borders adjoining." To possess a Pale, now, is to *be* a "borderer," an inveterate violator of one's own and others' boundaries whose frequent transgressions of these limits call them into question as, precisely, limits, and destroy the peace of the realm.

Here, Spenser's prose hints at a very real problem in the kingdom's political topography. The "Innormities in [Ormond's] Countie" could not be confined, as Sir Henry Sidney (Lord Deputy, 1566–71, 1575–78) once explained to Elizabeth, because Tipperary lay alongside "the rest of your Majesties Country . . . unperfectly lincked with it,"[56] and the very contiguity was subversive. The earl was ostensibly loyal. ("I will never stand in Law against my most dere and dread Soveraine Lady," he once told the queen—while justifying having followed Irish custom instead.[57]) But for all of Ormond's announced devotion, Sidney found, he could not be prevented from exploiting the indeterminacies of the boundaries which so ambiguously confined him. He slipped in and out of Tipperary, introducing into other areas the disquiet that agitated his own Liberty. "As it being out of Order," said Sidney, "the rest cannot be kepte in Order."[58] And in fact we know that "because of incessant warfare and turmoil many areas, such as those bordering the [earldom] of Ormond . . . were completely desolate."[59] For Sidney, Tipperary was a "sinke and receptacle of innumerable cattle and goods stolen,"[60] an inaccessible, inexplicable area where English law fails.

For Spenser, the County is a similarly contradictory locale. Tipperary is, somehow, at once the most civilized and most refractory locale in Ireland, curiously double. Characteristically, even its coordinates are hard to plot. The County Palatine, says Irenius, "it being situate in the very lap of all the land, is made now a bcrder." If we take out a map of Ireland, we can see that Tipperary is set somewhere near the center of the island. But the spatial coherence that a map seems to confer on the Irish terrain does not survive the dislocations of Spenser's prose. Has *it*—Tipperary—been made a border or "all the land"? Is what stands at the shifting heart of Ireland nothing but a margin, a decentered space that unsettles everything around it? Or has the entire country been made a margin to the "receptacle" that opens inside it? The syntax allows for either construction. More precisely, it suggests that this distinction cannot be made. Ormond's borders turn the country inside out. The center moves to the edges. The peripheries collapse toward an "inward and absolute . . . privileging"; "which how inconvenient it is let every man judge."

"A likelihood of truth"

"Idleness," said Sir John Davies, "together with fear of imminent mischiefs which did continually hang over their heads, have been the cause that the Irish were ever the most inquisitive people after news, of any nation in the world" (168–69). A sense that the "mere" Irish were hungry after "news" —of political affairs, past and present—but would not accept the official versions of these pervades English commentaries of the period. Instead, the complaint goes, the Gaels turned to an information network of their own. "Nothing . . . hath more led the Irish into error," asserted Barnaby Rich, "then lying Historiographers, their *Chroniclers*, their *Bardes*, their *Rythmers*, and such other their lying Poets; in whose writings they do more relie, then they do in the holy Scriptures, and this rablement do at this day endeuour themselues to nothing else, but to feed & delight them with matter most dishonest and shamefull." To the English, it seemed obvious that the circulation of bards among the Gaelic populace led directly and perniciously to the combustion of revolt. "For in their speaking and writing," Rich explained, these rhymers "do nothing but flatter [the Gaels] in their vngracious humours, still opening the way with lying praises of their progenitors, what Rebellions they haue stirred vp, and how many mischiefes they haue performed; this is such a whetstone to their ambitious desires, and being thus made drunke with these lying reportes of their Auncestors worthinesse, that they thinke themselues to be reproched for euer, if they should not be as apt & ready to run into al manner of mischiefe, as their fathers were before them."[61] "These people be very hurtfull to the comonwhealle," alleged another, "for they chifflie manyntayne the rebells; and further, they do cause them that would be true, to be rebelious theves, extorcioners, murtherers, ravners, yea and worse if it were possible."[62] That Irish bards could promulgate "news" of their own was one reason, English officials were sure, that the final imposition of order in the kingdom was being frustrated.[63] English standards of veracity were ignored; other truths were given voice, and the moment when England would truly rule in the kingdom was postponed. Therefore, as Davies noted, "the Statute of Kilkenny doth punish news-tellers (by the name of *skelaghs*) with fine and ransom" (169). Attempts to regulate and suppress the bardic orders were ongoing in

Spenser's day, and within a few years of the writing of the *View*, the royal
government of James I would largely succeed in destroying not only the traditional bardic orders but much of the Gaelic culture in which for centuries
the bards had lived and moved and had their being. The *View*, then, is set
on a historical cusp; Spenser takes cognizance of the bards just as the official
apparatus of which he is a functioning part is about to obliterate them.[64]

   "It is odd, given Spenser's vocation," Annabel Patterson has observed,
"that so little attention has been paid to the section in the *View* that deals
with the Gaelic poetic tradition."[65] We might not want to say now, as
an antiquarian did say many decades ago, that Spenser's "lofty spirit was
incapable of envy." "There could be little competition . . . between the
illustrious poet who addressed his gorgeous epic . . . to the English court,
and the Irish country rhymers who sung Gaelic verses to a Celtic public."[66]
What we would say, though, is not obvious. If Spenser were entirely to
be identified with the hostility of the New English toward the Gaels, we
might expect that he would also take a dismissive attitude toward "their
Chroniclers," the bards, or, perhaps, that he would roundly and plainly condemn their devious maneuverings outside (and within) the realm of English
truth. Instead, as is well known, Irenius tells Eudoxus that "Yea, truly, I
have caused diverse of [bardic poems] to be translated unto me, that I might
understand them, and surely they savoured of sweet wit and good invention" (75). He even summarizes one such poem at length in his own treatise,
thus, as Patterson says, "recycling it for a larger audience" by "a curious act
of ventriloquism."[67] (This was an audience, I would add, that could have
been *both* courtly and "Celtic.") For Spenser, a distinction between himself,
the poet who had devotedly offered up his *Faerie Queene* to his monarch,
and the bards, "whose profession," as he says, "is to set forth the praises and
dispraises of men, in their poems or rhymes" (72), may have been hard to
maintain absolutely. Perhaps there can be no question of a direct competition or comparison. But it could be that the links between Spenser and
his Gaelic counterparts were less a matter of identity, in which they were
strictly opposed, than of technique, in which they could be seen to have
a good deal in common. Spenser has Eudoxus make a strong case for the
possible virtues and benefits of the bards (in terms an English readership
could accept, of course). He has read, he says, "that in all ages, poets have
been had in great reputation, and that meseems not without great cause,
for besides their sweet inventions and most witty lays, they are always used
to set forth the praises of the good and the virtuous, and to beat down
and disgrace the bad and the vicious, so that many brave young minds have
oftentimes, through the hearing the praises and famous eulogies of worthy

men sung and reported to them, been stirred up to affect like commendations." Eudoxus, that is, seems to offer an aesthetic in which the rhapsodies of the poet as such are always and everywhere edifying. Irenius, echoing Rich and others, assures him to the contrary that the Irish bards instill only sedition. "Whomsoever they find to be most licentious of life most bold and lawless in his doings, most dangerous and desperate in all parts of disobedience and rebellious disposition, him they set up and glorify in their rhymes, him they praise to the people, and to young men make an example to follow" (73). Thus, Spenser makes sure to give the requisite distinction between English and Irish poets proper emphasis. If, with Spenser, though, we must be alert to the "constant transitivity between . . . maintaining the secrecy of the secret and . . . inviting the secret's penetration" (Rambuss 19), then we might ask whether Spenser's is a distinction we can accept without reservation. What the Gaelic bards may have offered this English poet was a suspect but disturbingly familiar model for his own covert practice. As the enraged English denunciations of the bards make us realize, these rhymers managed not just to evade the official truth but also to operate quite effectively—and subversively—in the very presence of officials, by both implying and denying that they had some secret "news" to tell that the English could not know. The rhymes they bring the Irish populace circulate in the same space as the official line and alongside it, disrupting and doubling its certainties. As we will see in the next section of this chapter, Spenser is preoccupied in the *View* with the ability of the Irish generally, like their bards, to operate in two cultural registers at once. They transform a place in which their loyalties to the Crown should be most definitely articulated, such as an English court of law, into a place where their own allegiances prevail, and do so while seeming faithful to both. Is this so different, though, from what Spenser himself is doing in his treatise? The poet who, in the *View*, aches to tell his government the hard truth about Ireland, and who does so by subtly twisting the premises of the received "view" to fit his own, cannot be without some understanding of the opportunities poetry offers to practice upon (against?) the official truth.

Indeed, if we look closely at Spenser's treatment of the bards, we see that the sense of certainty his text should convey to official readers is relentlessly self-disrupted, and in ways that are not unlike those of the rhymers he castigates. Even as the "spokesman" for Spenser, Irenius seems to acknowledge the uncertainty of his own "view," and links this uncertainty to his reliance on, as Rich called them, "lying Historiographers." He describes his method—the method by which the *View* itself is constructed—as he defends himself against a charge that he has "lean[ed] too confidently unto

those Irish chronicles, which are most fabulous and forged," the annals of
a nation "without letters" and the "remembrances of bards, which use to
forge and falsify everything as they list to please or displease any man" (39).
Eudoxus claims, that is, that Irenius has stepped outside the textual confines
within which English truth rehearses and justifies itself, and, by giving cre-
dence to the sophistical pseudo-truth of the Irish, by recognizing those he
should ignore, has brought the validity of his own declarations into doubt.
In response, Irenius both proffers and withdraws the certainty that official
readers would demand. "I do herein rely upon those bards," he admits, as
do "the Irish themselves," who, although ignorant of

> matters of learning, and deep judgement, do most constantly believe and
> avouch them, but unto them besides I add my own reading and out of them
> both together with comparison of times, likeness of manners and customs,
> affinity of words and names, properties of natures and uses, resemblances of
> rites and ceremonies, monuments of churches and tombs, and many other like
> circumstances, I do gather a likelihood of truth; not certainly affirming any-
> thing, but by conferring of times, languages, monuments and suchlike, I do
> hunt out a probability of things which I leave unto your judgement to believe
> or refuse. (39)

Irenius acknowledges the complicity of his account in the fabricated mythic
history of the Irish, even while disparaging the Irish as a people. The self-
confirming forgeries "most constantly believe[d] and avouch[ed]" that Eudoxus hopes to discredit saturate his own "chronicle." Now, that an alien
tradition permeates what is purportedly an official text suggests that official history and Irish "forgery" are not as dissimilar and are more entangled
than English power could comfortably allow. And this is why Eudoxus,
who wants to believe the Irish are "altogether destitute of letters . . . by
which they might leave the verity of things written" (40), has pressed him
to divide English history from Irish myth, to accentuate English difference.
Instead, Irenius assures him that "ye are . . . much deceived, for it is certain that Ireland hath had the use of letters very anciently, and long before
England." The only certainty Irenius will offer Eudoxus is that the free-
standing truth Eudoxus thinks of as an English possession is subsumed in
a proliferating array of texts, both familiar and alien, within which Irenius
seems to see truth both present and absent. "Caesar writeth," he allows, that
Irish bards "deliver no certain truth of anything"; they can, moreover, be
discounted "since all men be liars and may lie when they will." But this is assertion of skepticism so thoroughgoing that it points every which way and
briefly falsifies every text to which it might be applied: Caesar's pronounce-

ment (now turned into a self-reflexive paradox—a liar may write lies about liars), Irish chronicles, even Irenius's own words. There is no "certain hold to be taken of any antiquity which is received by tradition." No congeries of texts will, in aggregate, import truth since any text may have been penned by a liar. And yet . . . Irenius asks for leave to "show that some of [Irish chronicles] might say truth" (40). Their authors are "unlearned." They suffer from "vanity" and "ignorance." Their "forged" histories "they deliver to fools and make them believe for true." Nonetheless, they share an ability which, implicitly, Irenius has ascribed to himself: they "[write] things according to the appearance of the truth which they [conceive], [they] do err in the circumstances, not in the matter" (42). As his self-described methodology has revealed, Irenius would also claim only to transcribe the appearances of things, and only according to his own conception, from within his own "view." He is willing to admit that he gets the circumstances wrong, that, in fact, appearances deceive him. But he still would insist, as he says of the Irish, that his assertions partake of truth. In some fashion, they contrive to go to the "matter" behind appearances. This is the provisional truth he claims for the text of an artificer—for his own especially, but even an Irish bard's. And this is why, in describing his method, he offers Eudoxus not univocal truth, but a multiplying catalogue of related texts, written and enacted: Irish chronicles, inscribed tombs and monuments, names, words, the playing out of ceremonies, rites, and manners. In the midst of this discursive chaos, Irenius situates himself, adding, as it were, "his own reading," noting "affinity," making "comparison," establishing "likeness." He puts stress on "resemblances" (including, presumably, the mirroring "correspondences" between English and Irish "customs," the practices of antipathetic but kindred societies). In the scheme Irenius constructs, things with their ontological natures and "words" seem almost interchangeable, all tumbled together in this catalogue and, as Irenius applies his method, equally significant. Yet, this intricate conglomeration of "circumstances" and "languages," held together only in the "view" of an observer preoccupied with analogies, even analogies he cannot acknowledge—all this is proffered only as "a likelihood of truth" and a tentative inquiry into the "probability of things." Not that Irenius surrenders certainty; within the "official language" in which he writes, truth claims cannot simply be abandoned. But Spenser does not, as so many English officials do, claim absolute veracity for his elaborate reading of Ireland. Truth, he says, depends on the "judgement" of Eudoxus, whose name, again, can mean "truth," but who also suggests an untutored lack. Within the treatise Spenser drafted and submitted to the judgment of the Privy Council, Irenius shifts the onus for determining truth onto the voice of the received view, but contrives to suggest that the "truth," the very "truth" in which he participates, is the "truth" of a fabricator.[68]

Irenius's unwillingness to adopt a more knowing stance has implications throughout the *View*. Indeed, Irenius can be observed maneuvering around overly simple and definitive notions of truth from the moment of his opening commentary on other "plots" devised for Ireland. Some, says Irenius without noticeable enthusiasm, attribute that country's barbarism to a "fatal destiny . . . whether it proceed from the very genius of the soil, or influence of the stars, or that Almighty God hath not yet appointed the time of her reformation" so that "no purposes . . . will prosper or take good effect" (1). Then, as if to forestall objections to his lack of dogmatism, Spenser puts the critique of a theological account of Ireland in the mouth of *Eudoxus*. "Surely I suppose this but a vain conceit of simple men, which judge things by their effects and not by their causes." The actual cause of Ireland's barbarism, he says, lies in the "unsoundness of the . . . plots which . . . have been ofttimes laid for her reformation" (1). In this, even Eudoxus implies that there is no essential truth to the Irish matter, that Ireland will take shape according to the "plot" through which it is fashioned, and that, within Ireland, what will be true will be what those who script that plot believe (or even decide to believe) is so. But Irenius goes further. Although he does not claim that these deterministic explanations are false, he does note that they preclude official action, and he implies that, in Ireland, if truth is to be valid, it will be so only because it is *enforced*. Thus, he wrenches Ireland out of the providential scheme which encompasses the English. Ireland, he allows his readers to see, is so far removed from the places in which God's will can work that theological explanations which assume unmediated truth can only be naive. Ireland is a place where no law is in effect without power, not even divine law. Perhaps this is why, when Irenius comes to declare his program of religious reformation, he is uncharacteristically reticent. "For religion little have I to say myself, being . . . not professed therein, and itself being but one, so as there is but one way therein, for that which is true only is and the rest are not at all." Religion, therefore, must not be "impressed into [the natives] with terror and sharp penalties . . . but rather delivered and intimated with mildness" (161).[69] Irenius cannot criticize, but also can make no use of, explanatory schemes according to which truth "only is and the rest not . . . at all." This kind of truth, he insinuates, with its proclaimed inherent rightness, cannot be (re)produced in Ireland. Those who live in the kingdom know that its circumstances are not that simple or that divorced from the difficult realities of colonial fashioning. This is one of the secrets that the *View* has to tell.

Common-Law Minds

As I have said, however, the secrets which Spenser's *View* put before the Privy Council were not limited to his ambiguous affinity with the Gaels and their bards. Again, Spenser had a specific (though oblique) argument to make: the law that England imposed on Ireland could not establish royal control, first, because it was not thoroughly enforced, but, more disturbingly, because that law had its own ambiguous affinity with Gaelic law, and this left it open to hostile appropriation. In Ireland, the common law was a weapon that did not serve; it could be turned back on the English, and was. Gesturing toward his official readers, Eudoxus declares that the proper "speech" to adopt is "of grave counsellors which ought to think nothing so hard but that through wisdom may be mastered and subdued, since the poet says that the wise man shall rule even over the stars, much more over the earth" (2). The poet to whom he thus refers might be Spenser himself, the poet who writes this treatise and couches it in the "speech" of "grave counsellors," taking up their hard pragmatism in order both to participate in and to dismantle their power. Almost the first question asked in the *View* is, "Why, Irenius, can there be any evil in the laws?" (3), to which he gives an oblique but devastating answer of "yes" — oblique because Spenser's prose is under scrutiny and seems at crucial junctures to entangle itself in indeterminacy, and devastating because those indeterminacies are precisely the "burden" of Spenser's argument. His shifting declarations push the official view to a conclusion so radical that even its own legitimacy is, eventually, put in question.

The opening lines of the *View* present a question which preoccupied colonial officials: how to explain the baffling failure of English government to subdue the Irish and turn them from barbarism. "But if," says Eudoxus in reply to we know not what observation, "that country of Ireland whence you lately came be so goodly and commodious a soil as you report, I wonder that no course is taken for the turning thereof to good uses, and reducing that savage nation to better government and civility" (1). Fourteen years later, this puzzlement is echoed in the opening of Sir John Davies' *Discovery of the True Causes Why Ireland was Never Entirely Subdued* (1612).[70] Davies moves, like Eudoxus, from wondering admiration of Ireland's natural wealth to bewilderment over England's inability to appropriate it. His

observation of Ireland's resources, its "fruitfulness of . . . soil . . . pleasant
and commodious seats for habitation and lastly, the bodies and minds of the
people, endued with extraordinary abilities of nature," has "bred in [him]
some curiosity," he declares, "why this kingdom, whereof our kings of England have borne the title of 'sovereign lords' for the space of four hundred
and odd years . . . was not in all that space of time, thoroughly subdued and
reduced to obedience of the Crown of England, although there hath been
almost a continual war between the English and the Irish? and why the
manners of the mere Irish are so little altered" (69). English officials in Ireland knew that they had been delegated to refashion the "manners" of a hostile people. The success of their project would depend on how much they
understood about the mechanics of reshaping a recalcitrant society. Since
these administrators saw their own society as structured top to bottom by
a customary legal code, they assumed that the alien culture of the Irish was
ordered in a similar way. To alter Irish customs and convert barbarians to
tractable subjects, they would have to transform or displace native law. They
did not regard this task as simply replacing one legal code with another, but
as bringing truth where before there was only falsehood. Their own law,
they held, was indistinguishable from the foundational principles of their
belief. In this, they retained the medieval notion that the "law was synonymous with right and with custom, the moral sense and traditional social
pattern of a community. Law developed and changed imperceptibly; it was
not 'made' by human will to deal with novel situations."[71] As an extension
of "right," law was an assemblage of truths and was as open to doubt as only
the most profoundly held beliefs could be. As an extension of "custom,"
law had entered into the "second nature" of a people.[72] Between differing
peoples, who owed their very being to differing customs, legal validity was
and must be utterly nonnegotiable. Thus, in Ireland, no rival law—no Irish
"truth"—could possibly be acknowledged. The legally minded Englishman
in Ireland was possessed of a coherent but rigid epistemology. He employed
an appeal to authority—not to the authority of anything claimed to stand
outside his own code of beliefs but simply that code of beliefs itself.

To meet the implicit challenge of a rival law, the English insisted on
its *difference*. They declared that "the law called the Brehon Law, nothing
[agrees] with the laws of England."[73] It was "repugnant to the Queens Majesties lawes."[74] Davies asserted that those who "did reject and cast off the
English law and government" and "received the Irish laws and customs" did
so for love of "Irish tyranny (which was tied to no rules of law or honor)"
(155) whatsoever. Brehon law, moreover, was merely arbitrary and arose
from nothing but passion; reason had no place whatsoever in its workings.

Irish judges, said a traveler, "take upon them to judge matters and redress causes . . . although they are ignorant."[75] The English assumed that, by contrast, the principles of rationality itself inhered in the legal dialectic of their common law. An English court in Ireland displayed Truth in the midst of alien falsehood. At Cavan, for instance, there came before Davies "a lawyer of the Pale retained by [Irishmen whose land had been confiscated] . . . to maintain that they had estates of inheritance in their possessions which their chief lords could not forfeit"[76] by accepting common law. Davies answered that "their own Brehon Law . . . is abolished and adjudged no law, but a lewd custom."[77] When by various arguments Davies had justified the spoiling of these natives, he reports they "seemed not unsatisfied in reason, though they remained in their passions discontented, being much grieved to leave their possessions to strangers, which they had so long after their manner enjoyed."[78] For Davies, the realm of reason is exclusively an English domain and its manipulation an instrument of English hegemony. Once the Irish are compelled to follow the rule of reason, they are ineluctably drawn to see the intrinsic justice of their occupiers' law — and the utter emptiness of their own. While English legal custom was inherently reasonable and guaranteed the common law's immemorial validity, Irish custom justified nothing. It cloaked barbaric violence. English colonizers charged, ironically, that native law licensed the strong to victimize the weak. As Davies alleged, "no man could enjoy his life, his wife, his lands or goods in safety if a mightier man than himself had an appetite to take the same from him. Wherein they were little better then cannibals" (163). And while English legal custom was thought to constrain its practitioners' judgments so that judges decreed as the law ordained, Irish custom was supposed to be infinitely malleable. Said Barnaby Rich, "Custom is a metal amongst them that standeth which way soever it be bent. Check them for their uncleanliness and they plead custom."[79]

"The condition of living on an island"

To get a sense of why this adherence to legal custom had such an extraordinary importance for English/Irish relations in the kingdom, I want to turn to the early, seminal work of J. G. A. Pocock. His arguments on English legal "insularity" will help me to convey not only what was at issue in Spenser's tacit critique of the common law, but also, more generally, the consequences for a reading of Spenser of the British historiography that Pocock himself came to advocate. In the Introduction to *Between Nations*, I described Pocock's call for a departure from Anglocentric historiography;

this has been the impetus to much of the British history now being done and to this study as well. Here, I ask: how can Pocock's own early theses be fitted to his later arguments? How do they modify one another?

Some thirty years ago, Pocock argued in *The Ancient Constitution and the Feudal Law*[80] that the English common law mind was distinguished by its "insularity." His claim, as he says in a later defense, was that "Jacobean [and, presumably, Elizabethan] Englishmen . . . lacked the knowledge which would have obliged them to see the common law as co-existing and interacting with other legal systems, undergoing in a historical dynamic changes incompatible with the presumption of immemorial custom and explicable only as the product of contact with other laws."[81] Common law thinking, that is to say, was typically ahistoricist, since it was held that the law's authority lay in its origin in customs which were themselves without remembered origin (i.e., "immemorial"). Such customs had arisen in a, precisely speaking, "pre-historical" community, and they had since proved their fittingness by surviving unchanged (or changed only in accordance with a dynamic internal to that custom). Law rested on custom and custom warranted itself. For the legally minded Englishman, its existence demonstrated that generations of Englishmen who could have taken up some other usage thought it appropriate for their needs. Elsewhere, Pocock provides a tight "purely structural explanation" of the legal equation giving shape to English law: "all English law was common law, common law was custom, custom rested on the presumption of immemoriality; property, social structure, and government existed as defined by the law and were therefore presumed to be immemorial."[82] When Pocock says the common law was "insular," then, he means that its practitioners believed no alien law had ever intruded to disrupt the unbroken succession of custom. English law had established itself and perpetuated itself; it therefore validated itself.

One of Pocock's prime examples is Sir John Davies, who, as we have seen, was attorney general of Ireland under James I. "As one of the principal advocates of English policy," says another historian, "Davies worked to consolidate and perpetuate . . . military conquest by a series of judicial decisions which transformed the legal and administrative structure of the island. In cases brought before the central law courts in Dublin, Davies' arguments compelled the Irish judiciary to eliminate the Gaelic law and to assimilate the autonomous Gaelic lordships, to reduce corporate liberties and franchises, [and] to impose religious conformity."[83] For Davies, Ireland was a ground contested by two systems of law, and legal authority was a simple matter: either common law or Gaelic law prevailed. Vanquished law was completely void. (Some Irish evidently thought so too. When, under

Henry VIII, a certain overmighty Irish lord was offered the king's greetings, he derisively replied, "what king?"[84]) Davies speaks of the opposed legal systems as great "games"—monolithic, coherent, mutually exclusive. When Henry II's nobles, he says, had dispensed with common law, "the estate of things, like a game at Irish, was so turned about as the English, which hoped to make a perfect conquest of the Irish, were by them perfectly and absolutely conquered" (162). But James I had restored English dominion, and "the Irish game turned again" (217). ("The Irish game, a variation of backgammon, was characterized by a rapid sequence of back-and-forth reversals for the players, so that the apparent winner-to-be could easily lose during the final moves."[85]) Davies understands, says Pocock, that each of the laws pertaining in Ireland—common *and* Gaelic, or brehon law—"has the widest consequences in every department of life—so wide that the whole history" of a people, "of their agriculture, speech and habits as well as their political conduct, can be written in terms of their adherence to one or other law."[86] Law is prior to the cultural fashioning it makes possible: first law provides the organizing principles, then "from observance of one or other system of law there [follow] consequences in every department of economic and social life."[87] He "describes men's actions in terms of the social system of which they form part,"[88] demonstrating an acute sense of what we would term "cultural relativity."

Now, we might expect that for Davies this awareness would represent a potential threat to the validity of the common law. While the English in Ireland castigated the Irish for a code which was based on nothing but custom, their own law, as some of its practitioners realized, was itself such a "system," and was itself based on custom, and only that. But this, Pocock claims, was not so. Davies, despite his wide experience of brehon law, was impervious to any sense of the instability of English common law. He was a cultural but certainly not a legal relativist. Davies did not find brehon law in any way a threat to common law, Pocock claims, because, quite patently, it had never entered into its historical formation: "brehon law had come into contact with common law only when the latter was already well developed."[89] Since the common law took on authority within a tradition which assumed the present recapitulated the past, Pocock says, the law's self-confirming insularity *could* be brought into question, but only by arguments that past law came forth from circumstances peculiar to some specific time. If it could be shown that the past was discontinuous with the present, ancient law might not be valid now, since, in principle, well-founded law derived from customs answering to the particular needs of Englishmen, and conditions in the realm had changed. However, it was just this historical awareness that some common lawyers lacked, or perhaps resisted. They denied, for instance, that James I's prerogative could have originated in William of Normandy's conquest in 1066. His prerogative, they held, was established in common law. Its origins must be lost to memory. Eventually, the recognition that Norman legal forms such as "feudal tenures had been imported into England and imposed upon land and law" signaled the nascence of a more historicist turn of mind, without which, says Pocock, "a history of English law could not be written." [90] And so, Pocock concludes that, until that time, *only* some proof that English common law had not been valid "time out of mind" could disrupt its sense of self-authorization.

To this rigorous argument, however, there is an obvious objection, one that, to his great credit, Pocock himself has now enabled: his understanding of English legal "insularity" in the early modern period is strikingly un-"British" in its assumptions and conclusions. In 1982, as we recall, Pocock claimed that the "premises must be that the various peoples and nations, ethnic cultures, social structures, and locally defined communities, which have from time to time existed in the area known as 'Great Britain and Ireland,' have not only acted so as to create the conditions of their several existences but have also interacted so as to modify the conditions of one another's existence." [91] Surely, this must be so of the tradition of the English common law as well. Of course, it may well be that, before legally minded Englishmen came to recognize that other laws had made a contribution to their own, most could not "think" the interactions between their tradition and others, wherever and whenever these had occurred. Pocock could claim that the absence of any awareness of England's legal debts among Spenser's contemporaries is precisely his historical point. In *The Ancient Constitution*, Pocock investigates the period "before" anything like a more-than-insular consciousness became possible for the common law mind. But if Pocock is right about the interactions that make up British history, [92] then what the early modern English usually did believe (or even *could* believe) of their relation to others is only part of what we will need to know. We will also need to know how the various British peoples, including the English, "modif[ied] the conditions of one another's existence" on two islands, whether or not they were all of them disposed to accept that this was happening. I do not mean to underestimate England's autonomous sense of itself, which, as Pocock has often said, was vigorous, historically consistent, and coherent on its own terms. But if we accept the premise that the peoples of Britain share a mutually constituted history, then we cannot accept the premise of "insularity" — or, at least, expect historiography derived from this premise to lead to anything like a full account of "Britishness"

in the legal history of the period. For that, we will need to look scrupulously for the places where a more-than-insular consciousness emerged—if
it did—and consider carefully the conditions under which this emergence
became possible, however briefly and contingently that may have been.
And there is also a political point to this search. It is Pocock himself who
asserts, "'British' . . . history . . . has an ideological consequence: it reveals
the ideological falseness of the claim of any state, nation, or other politically
created entity to natural or historical unity."[93] This, presumably, includes
the "mind" of the English common law too.[94]

Thus, we might ask: how well did the coherence of the English common law mind hold up when it was transported elsewhere within Britain,
or when, for instance, it was imposed on Ireland? Because Pocock is committed to arguing that the common law mind could have been shaken in its
insularity only by a demonstration that its origins were not immemorial,
he does not consider the possibility that the juxtaposition and clash of two
contemporaneous legal systems within the British Isles could disrupt the legal
insularity[95] of at least some Englishmen. But the possibility that English
common law might be less "insular" (though not more British) than Pocock
argues has certainly occurred to others; controversy attended Pocock's
claims since their first publication.[96] In a defense of his thesis, Pocock says
the common law could have been insular in two ways: "Englishmen may
have been so thoroughly insular as to know nothing whatever about law
outside their part of the island"; this, he concedes, is demonstrably false.
Or, "they could have known a good deal about other systems of law and
yet maintained the 'insular' conviction that no law but common law had
ever obtained in England,"[97] and this Pocock claims is so. But I think that
Pocock's critics were justified in insisting that English legal insularity implied more than a belief in uninterrupted custom, and further, that the
objections they raised adumbrated serious issues that Pocock himself came
later to consider. The unsettling effects of the interaction of common and
other laws were worth talking about because they implied that the English
people and their legal tradition did not exist in complete isolation from
other peoples, no matter how much the English claimed that they did. His
critics understood Pocock to be saying that not only could the common
law tolerate no contamination of its past, but it also demanded that its adherents exclude from consideration the claims other existing laws could
advance. Pocock, that is, seemed to have been positing a common law
that was synchronically as well as diachronically insular. Common law, the
claim seemed to be, was "insular" in that it was a closed system of thought,
a sealed discourse—tightly self-contained, self-referential, self-generating.

And although Pocock denies this—"the more one insists that [common lawyers] knew a good deal but rejected its significance for their own law, the less the 'common-law mind' resembles a self-explanatory closed ideology"[98]—his denial begs the sort of questions he himself would later raise in other contexts. What unacknowledged transactions *did* occur between the nonclosed "system" of English common law and other legal systems? If English common lawyers "knew" of these other systems, did they always and unambiguously fail to register their "significance"? By what devices of denial did they accomplish this? According to Pocock, the English system of law could coexist with others; its more informed practitioners could be knowledgeable about those others, and yet that system of law could be thoroughly "insular" in that it would permit no assimilation of the premises of other legal systems, no recognition whatsoever of any authority outside itself. Again, it is thanks to Pocock that we can now ask, retrospectively: how is this "multi-contextual history"[99]?

Pocock would be the first to acknowledge, of course, that the closed "insularity" of the English law can be exaggerated. Common lawyers did know of many other types of law and could accommodate jurisdictional dispute. The civil law practiced, for instance, in the courts of Chancery could be acknowledged as long as it "kept to its sphere," as Edward Coke said. The law of nations required no controversion. Natural law underlay and did not contradict common law. Common lawyers had an array of maneuvers by which they could recognize the place of alternative laws and yet maintain the common law's legal superiority. I suggest further, though, that if we want to consider English law's "insularity"—insularity, again, in the strict sense of resistance to legal comparison—we should identify circumstances in which the common law was juxtaposed with some law in the British Isles to which it had developed no compromising response, some concurrent but inherently alien legal system. This, I suggest, was English law in Ireland. There common law faced a profoundly alien and yet in some ways oddly similar legal code—native, or brehon, law. And I also suggest that Spenser's *View of the Present State of Ireland* reveals that, "insular" though the common law is, even on that island, there is a law there that cannot simply be ignored (though neither can its validity be acknowledged). The case I have to make here is narrow; it does not tell us much about the acknowledged influences on English law. But it reveals a good deal about the author of the *View* and the embattled legal terrain on which he operated. As an agent for Lord Grey and others, Spenser administered the common law. On the evidence of this work, he was widely acquainted with (though often not sympathetic to) common-law arguments. His "view," however, is demonstrably not identical with that of the legal establishment in England. Although the *View* declares itself to be an instrument of England's law, it repeatedly reveals that there are other legal perspectives in Ireland from which the "view" is quite different, and that these "other" perspectives, which are sometimes those of the more dissatisfied New English, sometimes even those of the "mere" Irish, are not totally alien to Spenser's own. It is this "twofold consciousness"[100] (as Pocock calls it in another context) that, I think, allows the *View* to disrupt tacitly the "insularity" of the common law in Ireland. In Ireland, Spenser came to have the "tangential sense of identity" that Pocock says is the sine qua non of the British point of view. "Both ethnocentrism and nationalism," he points out, "entail a high degree of commitment to a single and unitary point of view."[101] While Spenser can be said to do his obeisance to both, his own *View*, as we have seen, is anything but "unitary." Instead, it is split among many perspectives, and of necessity takes its angle from multiple places on the British Isles: from London and Dublin and Kilcolman and even the wastes beyond the Pale where the bards circulate. "Insularity," we should remember, is literally the "condition of living on an island, and of being thus cut off or isolated from other people, their ideas, customs, etc; hence, narrowness of mind or feeling, contractedness of view" (*OED*). In this sense, Spenser's text is not and cannot be merely "insular." Spenser always has more than one island in view; as he writes he is between nations. If his treatise is to succeed (as it did not), he must incorporate (if not adopt) the "views" of the New English, the Old English, the "mere" Irish, the English in England, including their "views" on the common law. Spenser demonstrates that, contra Pocock (or, at least, a certain version of Pocock), there *was* "within the dominions of the English crown or within the four seas of Britain"—that is to say, within Britain as it was then defined—"a rival system of law" which, though it could not "be seen to have radically influenced the growth of the common law,"[102] was recognized by at least this Englishman as an unsettling threat to the "insularity" of the English common law.

Spenser can testify to the complex interpenetrations of common and brehon law because, although he is an English official and administers the common law in the kingdom, he does not share in two assumptions which Pocock says were characteristic of the English legal view of Ireland. First, for Spenser, Irish law is not "the product of a wild and uncomprehended society"[103]—wild, yes, uncomprehended, no. Spenser has thought a good deal about his country of exile. He mostly loathes and fears it, but he cannot dismiss it as effectively as Pocock seems to imply was possible. "It is but even the other day since England grew civil" (67), says Irenius. When Spenser

looks at Ireland, he does not see only a barbaric wasteland. He sees a barbaric wasteland that England was, and might still be, if the queen's resolve is
not strong enough. Second, and most important for my argument, it is not
so that to Spenser brehon law "presented no striking points of resemblance,
no principles of its own which might be found embedded in the common
law,"[104] since, I will argue, it is precisely the disturbing similarity of brehon law to common law, their mutual basis in something other than royal
authority—something like custom—which leads Spenser to distrust common and brehon law together. Since neither of these assumptions has to do
with the historicity of common law,[105] that Spenser does not hold to them
must complicate, if not disprove, the notion—wherever it originates—that
the English legal mind was so shaped and constrained by its own premises
that it could entertain no doubt of its own authority on the British Isles.

"A great show of equity"

Spenser's *View*, as I have said, deviates from the imperatives of the English legal establishment in multiple ways and hints at secrets it would not
want to know. For one thing, Irenius is not as precise in his denigrations
as he should be. He allows key terms to disintegrate into ambiguity. Take
his reply to the query, "What is that which you call the Brehon law? It is a
word to us altogether unknown" (4). "It is a certain rule of right unwritten,"
declares Irenius, "but delivered by tradition from one to another, in which
often there appeareth great show of equity in determining the right between party and party, but in many things repugning quite both to God's
law and man's" (5). Almost each word here might have been interrogated.
By "certain" did Irenius mean particular, as seems likely, or incontrovertible? At stake for his readers, after all, was whether brehon law was merely a
local code, and so, as they claimed, too particular to be grounded in natural
law, or whether it might have some indigenous justice of its own, and so be
for its adherents legitimately incontrovertible. Perhaps it is this very rigor,
this capacity to close down questioning that Irenius dislikes, but would he
then criticize the similar hermetic epistemology of the common law? In
fact, he might well. As Pocock has noted, in the period, "any custom must
be the custom of those to whom it was customary, and therefore a rule
of right to them. All custom was hermetic by definition *until* the question
arose of its compatibility with the law of nature."[106] Englishmen usually
assumed, of course, that their own custom was compatible with settled
government (and thus divine law), while Irish custom was not. But Irenius
can be seen as pressing deeper, on foundational questions. If common and

brehon law share this basis in custom, and neither is identical with natural law, finally, how secure are they? The word "certain" manages to suggest conflicting lines of argument (some Irenius might be expected to adopt, some not) all intersecting in an adjective which gestures toward a notion of stable, undoubted truth, but then works against the meaning it seems to hold out. And how were official exegetes to take brehon law as a "rule of right"? Did not "rule" imply a coherent working system of law which distinguished between what was and was not "right"? For the space of four words, Irenius seems to credit native law with unexpected validity. The next word, "unwritten," deepens the confusion. As his readers knew, the common law was as much present in the customary practices of its courts and the accumulated wisdom of its practitioners as in written records. "Written laws contain[ed] no more than the wisdom of one man or one generation, whereas custom in its infinite complexity contain[ed] the wisdom of many generations."[107] Common law did not, need not, subsist in texts. If Irenius thinks to assail brehon law for its independence of records,[108] this adjective points up only one similarity between native and common law. The following clause offers another. Common law too was "delivered by tradition from one to another." That English law embodied unwritten customs and that Englishmen passed down their customs through tradition Spenser's readers thought of as characteristic common-law claims. How could they be attributed to a barbaric pseudo-law? And why does Irenius acknowledge that in brehon law "often there appeareth great show of equity"? Is it to the parties involved, the Irish themselves, that the law seems just? Or does he imply that it might seem so to English observers like Irenius himself? The justice of this law depends, apparently, on the perspective taken on it, the "view" brought to it, and that law itself is a matter of almost theatrical performance, a "great show of equity." Now, in the word "equity" Irenius had chosen a term resonating with implication. Equity not only denoted impartial justice generally, but it also meant specifically those principles of justice applied by a judge in a court of equity (the Chancery, for example) where the rigor of the common law could be abrogated in the interests of fairness and extenuations the common law did not recognize could be taken into account. It made use of a kind of justice the common law could not offer. Did Irenius mean to suggest that brehon law might claim an analogous dispensation from the common law of the realm? The implication is held out ever so briefly, then collapses. That brehon law is "in many things repugning quite both to God's law and man's" seems at first reading as rigorous an assertion of difference as could be made, but read against the rest of the *View*, it is not. As we have seen, Irenius pointedly refuses to be forthcoming about what he takes God's law to be, or how particularly brehon law might stand in opposition to it. And while by man's law it would be assumed he meant the law of nations, the law common to all, it is exactly Irenius's point that the law of nations is not common to all, not to the "nation" of Ireland. Brehon law stands outside it and, as an exception, calls into question the very attribute which lends the law of nations its authority: universality. Irenius invokes the laws of God and man, but his censure of Ireland as a place where men do not follow either law casts doubt on the codes he invokes even as he invokes them. At that point where Irenius's readers could have expected him to enforce distinctions with the greatest clarity, a crucial assertion turns itself into a definition which does not define.

Official readers could also note that Irenius's treatment of brehon law, although antagonistic, is far less dismissive then it might be. Irenius realizes, it seems, that the opposed systems of common and native law are not absolutely different. In their reliance on custom and in their vulnerability to uncertainty and manipulation, they resemble each other disquietingly. And Irenius does not seem sure that Irish custom is merely "lewd." He explains to Eudoxus that the Irish offer an elaborate legal rationale for resisting the queen's sovereignty. According to brehon custom, he says, primogeniture does not establish succession. Inheritance passes by election to "the next . . . of blood, that is the eldest and worthiest; as commonly the next brother" (7). And since a son cannot inherit his father's land, neither does he inherit his legal obligations. Consequently, some rebels claim, the submission of Irish nobles to Henry VIII upon his assumption of the kingship of Ireland could in no way bind their descendants, whose tradition of inheritance carries with it no allegiance to the English king. Irenius's account, however, does not suggest that brehon law is without reason. In contrast to Davies, who would later affirm the inherent rightness of primogeniture and attempt to enforce it, Irenius refuses to declare this to be the only legitimate form of inheritance in Ireland.[109] His response to Eudoxus's incredulous "How can they [withhold their allegiance] justly?" (6) is not to maintain that, by absolute standards, no such resistance could possibly be just, but to explicate their premises, detail their argument, and conclude, "they say . . . that they reserved their titles, tenures, and seigniories whole and sound to themselves, and for proof allege that they have ever since remained untouched, so as now to alter them they say should be a great wrong" (9). Unlike Davies' petitioners, who "seemed not unsatisfied in their reason" with official arguments once the legal "game" had turned against them, Irenius's Irishmen seem menacingly capable of exploiting legal reason on their own behalf.

What might have been especially bothersome is that Irenius persistently reveals that the Irish can maneuver within the procedural boundaries of the common law and yet escape its jurisdiction. Native custom, he points out, allows the Irish to escape into an inaccessible domain where common law does not work and treason is devised. Eudoxus wants to assume that brehon law "is not now used in Ireland, since the kings of England have had the absolute dominion thereof and established their own laws there." But Irenius assures him that even the natives who "seem to acknowledge subjection, yet the same Brehon law is privily practiced amongst themselves . . . they may do what they list, and compound or altogether conceal amongst themselves their own crimes" (5). For official readers, this could have a disturbing implication: the imposition of common law did not insure royal sovereignty, not only because there were "many wide countries in Ireland in which the laws of England were never established" (5), but also because even though every mark of adherence to English law might be apparent, the Irish could somehow withdraw into an inner precinct where only their own rules pertained. The disturbing result was that two laws were in effect at once. They were in contradiction (what was legal by brehon law was crime to the English), but the contradiction could not be eliminated because, once allowed into the legal system, the Irish had a vexing way of demanding that its rules be applied to them while covertly following their own. When Eudoxus suggests having English judges handpick Irish jurors "of the soundest disposition," Irenius tells him, "then would the Irish party cry out of partiality, and complain he hath not justice, he is not used as a subject" (23). A barbarian—by definition not a subject—is allowed to name himself as one and is permitted to appropriate a legal language and manipulate it to his own purposes. If this were a simple matter of an alien acting a bad part as something he cannot inherently be, an official reader might be horrified enough. But more, this role-playing could imply that within the system of common law there were no longer any essentially barbaric or civilized selves. Common law in Ireland had degenerated into legal spectacle. Selves slipped in and out of categories which should fix them, and the declarations of these shifting selves took on different meanings within the conventions of different legal codes simultaneously.

Consider the legal disarray which attends an Irishman's appeal to native custom in an English court. "For myself have heard," complains Irenius, "when one of that base sort which they call Churls, being challenged and reproved for his false oath, have answered confidently, that his Lord commanded him, and that it was the least thing he could do for his Lord to swear for him" (24). Whatever this man said, when he said it before a common-law bench there were two legal codes constraining and compelling him, each a set of conventions which could be invoked to determine what he should say and how it would be taken. First, the code of common law; it required him to take an oath and attached import to that oath as a guarantor of veracity. Common law prescribed the rules that were to shape his speech, and it dictated that what he said and the "truth" should be one. Common law procedure was used to rivet in place a set of rules for making and interpreting statements within the precincts of the court. They were to be what the judges could recognize as true or false. And then there was the native code of clan obligation and hierarchical responsibility, and it too dictated what the witness was to say: whatever would satisfy his lord's requirements. As he testified, he spoke within both codes at once, and, moreover, made it evident that he was speaking in both codes at once, even announcing this in Spenser's hearing. ("You do not have a secret if no one else knows you have it" [Rambuss 21].) This "churl" employed the language of English truth and the speech of Irish loyalty, and allowed the English to lose themselves in the complex question of which was which, and what—if anything—was being concealed. What he said could be heard as having two meanings simultaneously, each depending on what his listeners were capable of hearing. They could hear him make a true (or false) statement, or they could hear him demonstrate his loyalty to his lord by pragmatically declaring the truth that would serve him best. The English, of course, wanted to hear only one of these meanings. The conventions of legal interpretation they had established dictated that such testimony could be taken only as truth or deliberate inversion of truth. But Irenius, not surprisingly, is more alert to the devices of secrecy that are being employed here. Though he disapproves, he realizes that there is another way to construe that witness's declarations, one that the "churl" himself holds out to the English, knowing, perhaps, that it will be rejected. This Irishman alleges that his testimony is entirely consistent with his legal obligations under native custom. Even "false" Irish testimony can be prevarication—and something more. Irenius implies that the Irish rebel can, even standing in a common-law court where his very speech is governed, call upon quite another legal code within the rules of which his utterances take on meanings completely lost to the English, or, at least to those among the English who refuse to listen for what is "really" being said. Such officials literally do not know what the Irish mean when they speak. Since they cannot test Irish statements for veracity as they accept it, they do not know the truth when they have heard it. From an official point of view, as Irenius realizes, this undecidable testimony makes it impossible to conduct an honest trial. For the English, some kind of truth (or some consensus on what will count as truth) must be ascertainable if verdicts are not to seem wholly specious. But in Ireland, says Irenius, "were it so that the juries could be picked out of . . . choice men" guaranteed to interpret as the English would have them, still "there would nevertheless be . . . bad corruption in the trial, for the evidence being brought in by the base Irish people will be as deceitful as the verdicts . . . sure their lords may compel them to say anything." When anything might be meant by what is said, legal certainty is hopelessly absent. And if, as Eudoxus asks, "the proof of everything must needs be by testimonies of such persons as the parties shall produce; which if they shall corrupt, how can there ever any light of truth appear?" (24). Within the far too accommodating bounds of the common law, no certain verdict can be achieved.

In Ireland, Irenius reveals, the authorities cannot establish and protect official truth. They confront an interpretive problem: faced with "secretive" testimony like that of the "churl," they find it impossible to stipulate a set of rules for legal interpretation so rigorously binding that in their courts meaning will always remain fixed and their consensual truth always inviolate. Their rules themselves succumb to manipulation; others who stand outside their rules, who appear to act within them, reconstrue their precepts to serve their own alien purposes. They can follow the letter, but mock the spirit. "Now that the Irish have stepped into the realms of the English" (22), as Irenius says, they can do their work of subversive reconstrual from within. But the English cannot, from the edges of Irish culture, reach inside to reshape the customs of their adversaries. They possess their own code, brehon law, and it fashions them, gives them their purpose, and dictates the meaning of their actions and words even in an English court. As Irenius forces his readers to realize, English law does not provide the authorities procedures with which to govern testimony and to arrive at the truth. As Irenius laments,

> though they will not seem manifestly to do it, yet will some one or other subtle-headed fellow amongst them pick some quirk, or devise some subtle evasion, whereof the rest will lightly take hold, and suffer themselves easily to be led by him to that themselves desired; for in the most apparent matter that may be, the least question or doubt that can be moved will make a stop unto them, and put them quite out of the way, besides that of themselves they are for the most part, so cautelous and wily headed, especially being men of so small experience and practice in law matters, that you would wonder whence they borrow such subtleties and sly shifts. (23)

The Irish, Irenius complains, can conduct themselves within the common law all too well. They manipulate its rules; they take hold of some point of legal procedure, some quirk which the law itself authorizes, and force

English officials to play by their own rules for Irish ends. They make legal arguments, but though their conclusions seem willful evasions of the patent truth, the authorities cannot legally deny them. In short, these rebels' crime is that they abide by the common law in order to exploit it, not that they break it.

Eudoxus offers various remedies for this subversion from within, but Irenius demonstrates that none will stop Irish duplicity. Packing juries will not work; even fixed jurors, Irenius knows, will be defeated by unfixable testimony. Told that a quirk of the common law allows receivers of stolen goods to escape punishment, Eudoxus considers that "this . . . might easily be provided for by some Act of Parliament" (26). He wants to prevent the rebellious Irish from interpreting the law for themselves by appealing to a body of official interpreters whose pronouncements will organize the rules for those under them. He tries to transcend the problem by locating authority above it, but, as Irenius must tell him, he only displaces the problem upward. What Eudoxus suggests "is almost impossible to be compassed" because by law "the said parliament must consist of the peers, gentlemen, freeholders, and burgesses of that realm itself" (26)—that is, Ireland—and these are just as likely to misconstrue the common law as any of the Irish. Later, Eudoxus thinks to put his trust in another body of interpreters, the judges. Even in a doubtful case, he thinks, "the judge when it cometh before him to trial, may easily decide this doubt and lay open the intent of the law by his better discretion" (33). Eudoxus's expectation would have seemed reasonable, and Irenius's rejection of it reveals the depth of his distaste, not just for the corruption inflicted on the common law, but for that law itself. Even without a fully elaborated doctrine of judicial review, it was thought that a judge should conjecture the purposes Parliament (acting according to common law) had meant a statute to serve. The exercise of his "better discretion" was required of him. But Irenius will not tolerate the vagaries of any interpreter. The judges "are men"; their reason or will may "be miscarried"; the "sense of a law" must not be left to their discretion. Since "it was less . . . the content of the law than the judicial process itself—usage, judgement, and statute—that was immemorial,"[110] Irenius's renunciation of this ongoing elaboration of common law by its practitioners amounts to a dismissal of the common law as it elaborated itself. He rejects it precisely because its practices are ongoing instead of "steadfast . . . and unmoveable," because within it the law is not self-evidently "plain" in its sense, but must be elaborately and ceaselessly reconstructed.[111]

Once this exegesis starts in an Irish court, he implies, it does not stop. No matter where placed, behind the bench, before it, within the jury, every interpreter of the law offers his own self-interested account. Even written law will not halt this contest. Some of the kingdom's "statutes are so slackly penned, and [some] . . . so unsensibly contrived, that it scare carrieth any reason in it, that they are often and very easily wrested to the fraud of the subject" (32). They can be read to any purpose (and usually to the purposes of the authorities).[112] Their slack penning allows an unlicensed play of reading in the spaces opened up as they lose shape and definition under the pressure of rigorous but self-motivated interpretation. No amount of contrivance, however "sensible," could halt the misappropriation of these statutes. Irenius is no believer in inherent meaning. He sees that, as one official reader of his day put it, "every thinge is as yt is taken,"[113] and, in Ireland, it is possible to take a statutory text, not just wrong, but any way you want. For this misprison, Irenius condemns more than the misreaders themselves; he blames the law which allows misreading. Eudoxus wants to believe that this legal disarray "is no fault of the Common Law, but of the persons which work this fraud to Her Majesty." But Irenius replies that "the Common Law hath left them this benefit, whereof they make advantage, and wrest it to their bad purposes" (28). Ireland is engulfed (perhaps only an official poet would have thought of it this way) in a crisis of reading.

"The strait rule of right"

Spenser's sense of the complexities of reading extends to the reading he knows will be brought to bear on his own text. He anticipates and pre-empts his readers' objections to his enactment of the breakdown of English law by incorporating them into the dialectic between Eudoxus and Irenius. For those who had to pass judgment on the *View*, it may have been especially disconcerting to see the text articulating, even parodying, official counterarguments even as they came to mind, and then to see those arguments undercut. Eudoxus, the voice of truth, warns Irenius even before he can begin his critique that it is the "fear of law which restraineth offenses." Without it there is only chaos. "Therefore in finding fault with the laws I doubt me you shall much overshoot yourself, and make me the more dislike your other dislikes of that government" (3). Since this injunction expresses the limitations Spenser's readers will impose, but he himself, as we have seen, regards the law as thoroughly implicated in an epistemic betrayal of the Crown, he is forced into a contradiction. He must defend the intrinsic validity of the common law *and* demonstrate that, precisely because it has so little intrinsic validity in Ireland, it cannot be defended. This proves to be a contradiction from which he cannot escape. Eudoxus may eventually conclude that Irenius has "reasonably handled the inconveniences in the laws," (37) but, for official readers, Spenser's treatise may finally have been vitiated by Irenius's unwillingness to declare unequivocally, in an altogether "reasonable" way, the legitimacy of the English common law in the Irish kingdom.

Initially, Irenius declares the common law doctrine that law is authentic when it fits the nature of its adherents. Even in Ireland, he tells Eudoxus, "laws ought to be fashioned unto the manners and condition of the people to whom they are meant, and not to be imposed upon them according to the simple rule of right." It is not, as we see eventually, that Irenius is opposed to a simple rule of right in the colony, but that he grasps that the official readers after whom Eudoxus is patterned assume that the common law itself could provide a simple rule of right, and he must convince them that the imposition of common law alone is not enough. He argues generally that the laws of one people cannot appropriately be imposed on another; he employs a classical example. Since the Lacedemonians were warlike and the Athenians bred in the "sweet delights of learning and sciences," he states, "he that would transfer the laws of the Lacedemonians to the people of Athens should find a great absurdity and inconvenience" (11). And "if Lycurgus should have made it death for the Lacedemonians to steal, they being a people which naturally delighted in stealth . . . there should have been few Lacedemonians soon left" (24–25). Similarly, English law should not be laid upon the barbaric Irish, to whom civility is unnatural. He counsels (and it is advice like this which has misled some critics to think of Spenser as a humane legal skeptic) "regard and moderation . . . in tempering and managing of this stubborn nation," though his interlocutor "cannot see how that may better be than by the discipline of the laws of England" (11).

The resistance Irenius encounters, the dogma he must maneuver around (while appearing to concur) is, I argue, that of the common-law mind. Eudoxus's habits of thought and assumptions mark him as a type of this mentality in the act of encountering Ireland. He cannot believe that the common law would not suit the Irish because he knows full well that it has unquestionably demonstrated its fittingness for the queen's subjects by enduring within her realm time out of mind. It fits the need of his own people, and he cannot grasp that the people of Ireland might be so different that law fitted to the English might not fit them. "As for the laws of England," he says, "they are surely most just and most agreeable both with the government and with the nature of the people. How falls it out, then, that you seem to dislike of them, as not so meet for that realm of Ireland?" (10). But who does he mean by "the people"—the English, the Irish, or both?

Eudoxus knows the Irish are alien. When he asks Irenius to define brehon law, it is, he says, "a word to us altogether unknown" (4). Their very terms are strange. But, presumably because it would seem to diminish the common law's authority, he resists the relativistic implications of this sense of otherness. His law must be theirs. This inability to accept irredeemable difference is found in Davies too. He could castigate the degenerate English because they obliterate their difference from the natives; "they had no marks or differences left amongst them of that noble nation from which they were descended" (172). But when he envisioned the pacific future English hegemony would make possible, he hoped, as stated in one of the epigraphs to this book, for "no difference or distinction but the Irish Sea betwixt vs" (217). According to some arguments, Irish difference was not essential; it could always be rectified by a thorough enough application of official terror. But Irenius tries to persuade Eudoxus (and his official readers) that the Irish are so intractably other that among them the common law is made as alien as they. They fit the law to themselves. It "is not so easy" he insists, "now that things are grown into a habit and have their certain course, to change the channel, and turn their streams another way: for they may have now a colourable pretence to withstand such innovation, having accepted of other laws and rules already" (10). Paradoxically, Irenius, who is painfully aware of the groundlessness of the common law in Ireland, its inability to maintain the categories it tries to enforce, asserts the irreducible difference between English and Irish, while Eudoxus, who cannot believe that the common law is anything but a simple rule of right valid anywhere in the realm, forgets this difference as soon as it might detract from the common law's legitimacy.

So as not to appear to detract from that legitimacy, Irenius twists his arguments to accommodate Eudoxus. "The laws," he insists, "I do not blame for themselves, knowing right well that all the laws are ordained for the good of the common wealth" (3). But then he subverts his assumptions. In this sentence, the word "ordained" signals the strategy Irenius will employ against his interlocutor's common-law theory. Denying the claim that the common law's origins lie beyond the reach of memory and take their legitimacy from no primal lawgiver whatsoever, Irenius will imply that law can proceed from only one quasi-divine source: the prince. A law must be judged, he will intimate, not by how long it has endured but by how well it conforms with the royal will from which it issues. Even long-standing laws can be replaced if in the present they no longer serve the Crown; immemoriality is no criterion for validity. That a law has since time out of mind been found acceptable to the people shows only that it suits them, not their prince. And, in Ireland, the people are such that no law should be fitted to them, and no law which is can possibly be suited to official purposes. The Irish have appropriated a law founded on custom and made its conventions their own. What the government needs in Ireland is a law founded on something entirely detached from the approval of its subjects, founded on something absolute—Elizabeth's inherent prerogative. Irenius explains that, though some laws are "first intended for the . . . peaceable continuance of the subjects," they become "disannulled or quite prevaricated through change and alteration of times" (3). Each word here is calculated: laws are "intended"; they reveal a royal mind behind them, not the unreasoning consensus of numberless ages. They are made "for," not by, the subjects. And time does not sanction them, it "prevaricates" them; it turns laws into liars because they speak to conditions which no longer hold. There is no common law ahistoricism in Irenius's jurisprudence, and neither is there any appeal to statutory law, by which the common law strove to accommodate historical change. Law is subject to historical change and, just for this reason, cannot be left to history, nor to those who seek to meet its changes. It must always be remade by a monarch who, unhindered by the constraints of accumulated custom, can fit the law to present exigency.

Irenius proceeds to entangle his official readers in a contradictory but tactically evasive argument combining common law and royalist premises. He leaves at first unresolved a confusion over what he asserts, but moves with increasing clarity to a declaration that the common law is irredeemably unsound. Irenius has seemed to admit that, despite his demurrals, the common laws are essentially "good still in themselves." But now he elaborates. The common laws are good because . . . but here, within the same sentence, he equivocates. They are good because, in flat opposition to the claims of immemoriality, "William of Normandy brought [them] in with his conquest and laid [them] upon the neck of England." They were "readily obeyed through the power of the commander which had before subdued the people to him and made easy way to the settling of his will." *And*, in another clause, common law "fitted well with the state of England then being"; it suited the disposition of the nation, which "before the entrance of the Conqueror was a peaceable kingdom" (4). Does Irenius attribute the law's warrant to the royal will or the proclivities of the people?

By ambiguously invoking a theory of conquest, Irenius calls into play opposing arguments in a debate over the original authority of common law. Common lawyers heard it claimed that a Nimrod-like Norman conqueror established English law by the sword. He ruled, not with the sanction of time-tested custom, but by the prerogative the law of nature gave the victor. He obviated, at a blow, the authority of customary law, and ruled by "the inescapable authority of *jus gentium*, a form of law either Roman or natural but not English."[114] This claim could be met. As the debate proceeds into the next reign, some deny that the conquest had occurred at all; some explain that it did, but William or a successor had bound the Crown by contract to recognize preexisting common law; some assert that William had won his kingship in a battle fought according to laws that predated his coming. But, whatever the claim, it cannot be simply acknowledged that common law originated in one brutal act of royal will; its genesis in custom must be preserved. But though this debate figures a real conflict, it is, as Spenser writes, submerged. Particularly at the end of Elizabeth's reign, it is possible, useful, and crucial *not* to see a contradiction between evolving royal absolutism and the law of the realm. Quite clearly, Spenser understands his readers well enough to know this, so Irenius must, at least when he speaks of England, hedge and allow his argument to fold in on itself, making his point only obliquely. Later, he again slides in contradiction; "the positive laws," he instructs Eudoxus,

> were first brought in and established by the Norman conqueror, which were not by him devised nor applied unto the state of the realm then being, nor as it might best be (as should by lawyers principally be regarded), but were indeed the very laws of his own country of Normandy, the condition whereof how far it differeth from this England, is apparent to every least judgement. (10–11)

Besides denying what before he asserted—that English law suited the disposition of the conquered—Irenius now denies that the conqueror ever tried to insure a fit between law and people, not because, as he will later claim, it was his entire prerogative to make his own law, but because his law is already customary, rooted across the Channel in the customs of Normandy! The argument is an odd hybrid (authority shifts within the declaration from conqueror to custom and then back), but, as an approach to Irenius's readers, it accomplishes two things. It suggests that concern over suitability of law for people should be relegated to lawyers (common lawyers, of course); their preoccupation with custom is somehow improper for kings and their servants, those, that is, who truly serve them and them alone. And it implies that if those readers use their "judgement," even the least of them will see that the origins of common law are not what common lawyers claim; no unbroken continuum of custom reaches time out of mind into the altogether English past. No matter how much they had later been absorbed,[115] common legal forms were first Norman, not indigenous, and William imposed them, they did not evolve. Just what common lawyers most needed to deny, Irenius, in the midst of his contradictions, insinuates. Despite the evasion, his readers would have noticed.

But Irenius's most effective disruption of his readers' common-law assumptions follows Eudoxus's invitation to "declare your opinion . . . about the laws of the realm, what incommodity you have conceived to be in them, chiefly in the Common Law, which I would have thought most free from all such dislikes." At this point, Eudoxus licenses Irenius to display the failings of the law. As the voice of truth, he withdraws himself, and delivers the argument over to "the course which you [Irenius] have purposed to yourself: for it fitteth best, I must confess, with the purpose of our discourse." Within the text, his abandonment of the strictures of official truth marks the place at which "purpose" of its author's "discourse" becomes, to a suspicious reader, most apparent. Irenius means to demonstrate that the common law, though "of itself most rightful and very convenient . . . for the kingdom for which it was first devised" (21), was yet in itself utterly groundless. And he means to justify reestablishing common law in Ireland on royal prerogative alone.

He begins with a common-law premise. It "seems reasonable" to him that "out of the manners of the people and abuses of the country for they were invented, [laws] took their first beginning." Though even here the accent is on active invention, not communal evolution, the laws' origins do lie, it seems, among the people. "For else," Irenius thinks,

> they should be most unjust, for no laws of man according to the strait rule of right, are just, but as in regard of the evils which they prevent, and the safety of the common weale which they provide for. (21)

Irenius seems to acknowledge that fitting law to people insures justice, but he immediately vitiates the worth of that sort of justice by pointing out that it is not absolute. Irenius has taken the very criterion by which common law was validated, its fittingness, and used it to insinuate that, by absolute standards, any "law of man," any law conforming to the predilections of mere men, can only be inequitable. He uses legal absolutism tactically, invoking it only for as long as he needs to suggest that common law cannot measure up to its requirements, that it has no ultimate grounding in impartial justice, before offering another ground for justifying law, a pragmatic one: law must prevent evil in the realm.

But Irenius's example of a properly expedient law shifts his readers' notion of a political evil from "abuses to the country" to threats to the prince; he merges the interests of the monarch and the commonwealth into one.

> In the true balancing of justice, it is a flat wrong to punish the thought or purpose of any before it be enacted; for true justice punisheth nothing but the evil act or wicked word. Yet by the laws of all kingdoms it is a capital crime to devise or purpose the death of the king. (21)

Irenius now has a license for the searching of inner selves English rule demands. "Now then," he says, "if those laws of Ireland be not likewise applied and fitted for that realm, they are sure very inconvenient" (22). If the law is to be brought to bear on the mocking theater of secrecy that the Irish conduct in English courts, it must be capable of penetrating their play of impossibly undecidable acts and words. This intrusion will be accomplished only if his official readers understand that the good of the realm is bound up in the good of the prince and, within a code not entirely devoted to the protection of the Crown, it is possible to devise the death of kings and the destruction of good government. Since in the "true balancing of justice" there is no absolute ground for legal authority, law must be founded on a determination to do whatever necessary to defend its center of authority—the ruler; a commonwealth would be "more hurt by . . . loss of their prince, than such punishment of the malefactors, and therefore the law in that case punisheth his thought" (22).

To his official readers, then, Irenius offers a law which is both utterly without a foundation in customary justice and utterly justified, as justified as any law can be. He abandons the "strait rule of right," a code of absolute truths dwelling beyond the reach of his "view," because the corrupted law in Ireland convinces him that right (and truth) are nowhere to be had within public forms and legal custom. To achieve certainty, law must be founded upon an absolute will unmediated by representation and impervious to reconstruction. The law proceeding from this absolute will calls upon nothing outside itself for justification; it is justified by the sheer exigency of there being law at all. "Jus Politicum, though it be not of itself just, yet by application, or rather necessity, is made just, and this only respect maketh all laws just" (22). The only figure Irenius can imagine strong and enduring enough to make law when necessary is a prince who perceives that the law protects and extends his own will to power. Without that rigorous presence, the center opens up and legal chaos rends the "estate of things." The "tumultuous rebellions" in Ireland had once been (and might still be) obliterated, says Irenius,

> by reason of the continual presence of the king, whose only person is oftentimes instead of an army to contain the unruly people from a thousand evil occasions, which that wretched kingdom is for want thereof daily carried into:

the which when so they make head, no laws, no penalties can restrain, but
that they do in the violence of that fury tread down and trample underfoot all
both divine and human things, and the laws themselves they do specially rage
at and rend in pieces as most repugnant to their liberty and natural freedom,
which in their madness they effect. (12)

Since laws cannot restrain, but are themselves the victims of the terrible liberty of the natives, Irenius proposes to do away with all legality in dealing
with the Irish and to impose royal authority directly, "even by the sword"
(95), "for it is vain to prescribe laws where no man careth for keeping them,
nor feareth the danger of breaking them" (94). Indeed, English hegemony
in Ireland has always rested on royal prerogative. Henry II established an
"absolute power of principality" by his conquest and, since "all is the conqueror's, as Tully to Brutus saith," that king could dictate whatever "tenures,
what laws, what conditions he would over them, which were all his, against
which there could be no rightful resistance." Later, some Irish had deluded
themselves that by proclaiming the kingship of Henry VIII in their Parliament they had entered into a contract with the Crown. Now, they think
themselves "tied but with terms." But their submission gave Henry VIII
"only the bare name of a king" (9). Royal prerogative does not rest on the
willingness of the Irish to recognize it as such. Equals form contracts and
law validates them, but the English sovereign in Ireland can make what
laws he will. Without evasion, Irenius offers his readers law established far
above the confusion of licentious common law. From there, he urges, it
will be possible to remake Ireland entirely. From there, nothing is substan-
tial enough to resist the imposition of official truth; everything is bent to
fit its imperatives. "Since we cannot now apply laws fit to the people . . .
we will apply the people and fit them to the laws" (141–42). This assurance
(occurring late in the treatise) brings Irenius's premises into the open and
carries his argument to a savage conclusion. His earlier pretence that law
must conform to the disposition of people is abandoned. Irenius now needs
no custom to justify his new order. Subjects constituted by the law cannot
deny the law's claims; they cannot falsify its truth. What Irenius holds out
to his readers is law as an instrument of unlicensed power, the power to
create official truth. He offers a place outside the shaping of custom, a place
from which to shape custom. He offers transcendence.

Unhappy Ghosts

Spenser's *View* is a work of compelling but finally self-defeating ambition. Spenser means, I think, to salvage Elizabeth's Irish policy (despite her

better impulses if need be), to expose and then negate the contradictions in the royal view of Ireland. In "A Briefe Note of Ireland," another document submitted to the Council, Spenser addresses the queen directly. Her English subjects in the kingdom have suffered grievously, he says, and he wants to

> vnfould vnto your Maiestie the feeling of theire miserie and to seeke to impresse in your Princlie minde the due sence thereof whereby some meete redresse may be tymelie provided. . . . But our feare is leste your Maiestes wonted mercifull minde should againe be wrought to your wonted milde courses and perswaded by some milde meanes either of pardons or proteccions, this rebelliouse nacion may be againe brought to some good conformacion which we beseech allmightie god to averte and to sett before your gracious eyes the iuste consideracion howe that possiblie may be.[116]

In the *View*, Spenser proposes to aid almighty God in averting a royal blunder, to tutor his queen, to set before Elizabeth's very eyes the impossibility of mercy, to impress in her princely mind the confused misery which, because of her misplaced benevolence, corrupts her Irish colony. We see in this treatise a powerful literary intelligence struggling to tell the secret truth of Ireland: that truth is not to be had there. The *View* summons the queen to invest her law with her own inherent sovereignty. But in order to convince Elizabeth of this necessity, Spenser must repeatedly point up the malignant effects of her seeming absence from the legal system while never explicitly acknowledging that her legal authority is lacking at all. We need not doubt that Spenser devoutly believes that royal authority alone is capable of guaranteeing legal certainty and halting the confused play of interested judgments he castigates, but all the evidence of unregulated indeterminacy he brings forward only goes to prove that the royal authority he is invoking has failed to establish even the conditions of its own intelligibility.

Spenser thought, as he had Eudoxus say, that "the original cause of this evil" lay in England's failure to impose on Ireland what he called its "language." "For it hath been ever the use of the conqueror to despise the language of the conquered, and to force him by all means to learn his" (67). It is because he hears another speech in Ireland that Spenser wants to silence its speakers, literally taking the words out of their mouths, for "the words are the image of the mind, so as they proceeding from the mind, the mind must be needs effected with the words; so that the speech being Irish, the heart must needs be Irish, for out of the abundance of the heart the tongue speaketh" (68). Irish selves articulate their language, and their language in turn articulates them. To alter the one is to alter the other, and so the Irish must forget their tongue. Within their own language, Spenser thinks, the unreconstructed Irish achieve a different order of being. Bound up in alien words, they set themselves apart from official truth in a realm which, in its autonomy and corrupt resplendence, may have seemed to resonate with the fascination and repulsion of idolatrous art. It could not be shared; it must not be tolerated. Spenser must eradicate it for the sake of the pure truth his own self-divided treatise cannot offer. In the *View*, Spenser reaches beyond his own evasions for that principle of truth, dragging his recalcitrant readers after him, investing himself in its verities, when he can, and obliterating, when he can, whatever opposes it. But we infer from his text and conclude from his last days that he failed to achieve the final certainty of sanctioned truth. Ireland up in arms, his plantation burned, Spenser, in London, pleaded with Elizabeth in the "Briefe Note" "to receive the voices of a fewe moste vnhappie Ghostes, of whome is nothinge but the ghost nowe left which lie buried in the bottome of oblivion farr from the light of your gracious sunshine." [117] Rendered insubstantial by the failure of received truth to sustain itself or him, Spenser also presented Elizabeth, the sole unquestioned incarnation of truth left him, a treatise entitled *A View of the Present State of Ireland*. This dialogue strives to be a resolute declaration of official truth, but in it we can hear the voices of more than a few unhappy ghosts.

"An untransmuted lump of futurity"

Edmund Spenser's *A View of the Present State of Ireland*, as Rambuss notes, "wasn't published until 1633, and even then some passages did not make it past the censors" (112). Indeed, the fate of the tract continued to depend on the politics of two British kingdoms—England and Ireland—and to be negotiated between both. The original suppression of the *View* by the royal government in the one kingdom did not mean that it disappeared from the trans-island debate over Ireland. On the contrary, the *View* remained embedded in the "matter of Ireland" as what C. S. Lewis once called (with another author in mind) "an untransmuted lump of futurity," a crucial, though often half-occluded, text. "In the thirty-seven years during which it circulated in manuscript form . . . [j]udging by the twenty-odd surviving copies, the *View* must have been one of the most popular and widely known . . . contemporary treatises." [118] The *View*'s arguments were implied in many other writings on the subject, both in England and Ireland, though this was not always acknowledged. It adumbrated events in Ireland that would fulfill its worst predictions and highest ambitions, but it was never quite allowed to emerge as the central text that Spenser's perspicacity would seem to make it. Thus, we can see in the later history of the *View*'s publication (and covert appropriation) the complex dynamics of exposure/concealment that troubled its first reception. Tracing the *View* as it moves in and out of the shadows of this debate, as I will do here briefly, will also help me to delineate the history that links Spenser's treatise with the intra-British conflicts of the middle of the seventeenth century. These will be my concern in the next chapter.

In Spenser's home country, the government that banned the treatise could find no occasion to license its publication over the next three decades. Eventually, "the *View* made its typographical debut [in 1633] in a weighty volume of Irish historical tracts edited by the distinguished Dublin archivist Sir James Ware."[119] There is a sense, though, in which the *View* had been promulgated, if not actually published, in Ireland long before 1633, and in a most direct and consequential fashion. It had been suppressed, true, but the very fact of its suppression may have lent it a certain cachet. Oftentimes, it was put forward by the New English as an exemplary statement of rigorous policy toward the barbarism of the "mere" Irish and the degeneracy of the Old English. This partial, mostly tacit tolerance of the *View* is especially curious given the vigor with which the English government began to put some of its proposals into practice soon after the death of its author. During the last years of Elizabeth's reign, resistance among the Gaels was much depleted by the campaigns of Lord Mountjoy against the earl of Tyrone, and by Mountjoy's eventual victory over him and his Spanish allies at the battle of Kinsale.[120] After the ascension of James I in 1603, the royal government moved decisively and with increasing success to subdue the more recalcitrant Irish lords and to impose English laws and customs on much of the populace. Brehon law was declared null and void and extirpated wherever possible. The property of "traitors" was seized, forfeited to the Crown. In 1607, the notorious "flight of the earls"—including Tyrone himself—out of Ireland and into Roman exile gave the king's government a long-awaited chance for large-scale confiscations in Ulster. A commission was quickly appointed to oversee the earls' holdings. Its main concern, says a historian, was to maintain "tranquility and calm within the province while awaiting orders for the plantation which everyone expected, and for which the first plans were being drawn up when the earls were barely out of sight of the lands in question."[121] The settlers who arrived from England were soon ensconced in the earls' Ulster domains, where they and their descendants would remain.[122]

One of the principal architects of this Jacobean conquest was, again, Sir John Davies. As attorney general in Ireland, it was he who framed the charges against the earls, he who ordered their lands expropriated, and he who drew up plans for a mixed plantation of "British" and Irish in the province of Ulster. His sense of the threat posed by Irish resistance was, however, quite different from Spenser's. James I's military conquests made it possible to assume that the common law was now inviolate, that its authority had been established incontrovertibly. Faced with a trial in which the "proof of everything" seemed unsure, for instance, Davies fixed the rules by fixing, as it were, the trial itself. Once he "had punished one jury with good round fines and imprisonment for acquitting some prisoners contrary to direct and pregnant evidence," he wrote to a correspondent, "another jury being impanneled for the trial of others found two notorious malefactors guilty . . . both which were presently executed."[123] Davies said that he sent the "law . . . [to] make her progress and circuit about the realm under the protection of the sword . . . until the people have perfectly learned the lesson of obedience and the conquest be established in the hearts of all men" (109). Like Spenser, this official had the largest ambitions for legal (and thus cultural) reform in Ireland. But, unlike Spenser, who often despaired of reaching the alien hearts of the Gaels, Davies was sure that common law, properly enforced, could be brought to bear upon inner Irish selves and their hearts fashioned into those of true subjects. His confidence amounted to a certainty that English law would secure the hegemony of English truth in the Irish kingdom. Davies administered a brutal military government, but his conquest, as he envisioned it, was finally epistemic. "Whereas the greatest advantage that the Irish had of us in all their rebellions," he wrote,

> was our ignorance of their countries, their persons, and their actions, since the law and her ministers have had a passage among them, all their places of fastness have been discovered and laid open, all their paces cleared, and notice taken of every person that is able to do either good or hurt. It is known, not only how they live and what they do, but it is foreseen what they purpose or intend to do. (216–17)

Now, rebellious Gaels sequestered within a code of alien law could be reached, observed, and, above all, known. Law passed among them, separating and categorizing, assigning every Irishman a niche within the official scheme. Fixed in place by the English "State," every Irish intention was open to Davies' surveillance and coercive refashioning.

Nicholas Canny has suggested that Davies' *Discovery* was pervasively, if not explicitly, indebted to Spenser's analysis and proposals in the *View*. Like Spenser, Davies was convinced, says Canny, that " 'the principal mark and effect of a perfect conquest' was the extension of 'laws to a conquered people' . . . like Spenser, he did not think this development was possible until the people had first been brought to subjection through military means."[124] The relation of the *Discovery* to the *View*, though, is not simply a matter of straightforward influence or shared premises. As we have seen, Spenser's views on Ireland could be notably unstable, vacillating from near despair over the intractable incivility of the kingdom to a determination to rectify that incivility utterly. Or he may veer quickly from loathing for the country to an urgent desire to appropriate it wholly and finally. He expressed the first inclination in his *View* when he reported that many Englishmen "wished . . . that all that land were a sea pool, which kind of speech is the manner . . . of desperate men far driven." He expressed the second inclination (in fact, on the same page) as he began to put forward his plan by which Ireland might be "mastered and subdued, since the poet says that the wise man shall rule even over the stars, much more over the earth" (2). In Spenser, as with others among the English, Ireland stimulated dreams of vast corruption and of vast power. At times in his argument the one requires the other: because the kingdom is absolutely deleterious to all good rule, absolute rule must be imposed. Davies, by contrast, picks up only the latter rhetorical emphasis in the *View*. His sense of the Irish problem and its historical antecedents is acute, but he approaches this problem with a certain naive pragmatism; he is convinced it is solvable. For example, Spenser bemoans the "degeneracy" of the Old English, and Davies does too, charging that they "metamorphosed like Nebuchadnezzar, who, although he had the face of a man, had the heart of a beast; or like those who had drunk of Circe's cup and were turned into very beasts, and yet took such pleasure in their beastly manner of life as they would not return to their shape of men again" (171). What Davies lacks, however, is Spenser's paradoxical sense of the predicaments of "difference" in Ireland. Spenser knows that the radical "otherness" of the English and the Gaels makes antagonism between them inevitable and probably irresolvable. He also knows that this opposition is always in danger of collapse, and that with that collapse might come the "degeneration" of the very identities this "otherness" sustains. Spenser, whose *Faerie Queene* had treated endlessly of the theme of transformation (and who, at the end of book 2, had meditated on the Circe exemplum Davies employs), realized better than the attorney general that the problems of English and/or Irish and/or "degenerate" identity were and would continue to be intrinsic to the conflicted kingdom of Ireland. Davies, by contrast, was confident that "Ireland" and all the conundrums it implied could be, in effect, abolished. Davies looked forward to the day, he told James I, when "the whole island from sea to sea hath been brought into His Highness's peaceable possession, and all the inhabitants, in every corner thereof, have been absolutely reduced under his immediate subjection"

(224). On that day, as, again, one of the epigraphs to this book states, "we may conceive an hope that the next generation [of Irish] will in tongue and heart, and every way else, become English, so as there will be no difference or distinction but the Irish Sea betwixt us" (217). But as hardly needs to be said, events did not bear him out.

Davies' *Discovery*, then, is an official reading of the *View* that in a way does the work of Elizabeth's Privy Council all over again. His sense of Spenser's deliberately convoluted argument is so powerfully selective that it obliterates its most disturbing implications. And when the *View* was finally published in 1633 in a volume dedicated to Thomas Wentworth, the new Lord Deputy of Ireland, the revisions continued. The text was printed together with tracts of Meredith Hanmer and Edmund Campion in *Two Histories of Ireland*.[125] "As for his worke now published," said Sir James Ware, the volume's editor,

> although it sufficiently testifieth [to Spenser's] learning and deepe judgement, yet we may wish that in some passages it had bin tempered with more modera- tion. The troubles and miseries of the time when he wrote it, doe partly excuse him, And surely wee may conceive, that if hee had lived to see these times, and the good effects which the last 30. yeares peace have produced in this land, both for obedience to the lawes, as also in traffique, husbandry, civility, & learning, he would have omitted those passages which may seeme to lay either any particular aspersion upon some families, or generall upon the Nation.[126]

He proceeded to do just that, "silently but systematically purg[ing] Spenser's text of all its more offensive blemishes, omitting whole sections in places and changing the sense of argument in others."[127] For instance, Ware leaves out the *View*'s allegation that, since the coming of St. Patrick, Ireland's "religion" had been "generally corrupted with . . . Popish trumpery. There- fore, what other could they learn than such trash as was taught them, and drink of that cup of fornication, with which the purple harlot had then made all nations drunken?" (84–85). Other editing is more subtle and re- veals a shrewd political intelligence at work. As Willy Maley has pointed out, Ware's *Two Histories* was published at a "volatile moment in Anglo-Irish affairs . . . coincid[ing] with an upsurge in English Protestant propaganda," but his collection itself laid out a range of political views, and "comprised both Old and New English positions."[128] Ware's revisions, thus, are di- versely conciliatory. In Spenser's original manuscript of 1598, for example, Eudoxus is shocked to learn "that the English Irish [in the kingdom] should be worse than the wild Irish" (151). In Ware's text of 1633, Eudoxus is cha- grined instead to hear "that any *English* there should be worse then the *Irish*." Ware's Eudoxus, like Spenser's, follows this with: "Lord how quickely

doth that countrey alter mens natures!"[129] But this denunciation of mutability in Ireland itself covers a "mutation" that has taken place between one
version of the *View* and the other. Ware deflects the author's exact criticism
of the degeneracy of the Old English—"English Irish"—onto "any" of the
"English" and briefly allows Eudoxus to suggest that the claim of "English"
degeneracy itself is fantastic. Just who these "English" might be he leaves
vague, while even the "mere" Irish are permitted a degree of civility. They
are no longer "wild."

The calculated obscurity of such lines is striking, and especially since,
as I have said, it has been argued that the first edition of the *View* was meant
to serve precisely the interests of a very specific group in the colony—the
New English.[130] These émigrés, says Nicholas Canny, took Spenser as their
exponent even after his death, and the *View* can be "regarded as a syn-
thesis of [their] opinions"[131] in the following decades. "Recent [English]
arrivals . . . saw the usefulness of the opinions of Spenser . . . when they
sought to defend themselves against the barbs of their Old English adversaries."[132] Longtime inhabitants charged the newcomers with corruption,
disruptive "innovation," and excessive, counterproductive brutality toward
the Gaels. Spenser's denigrations of the Old English could be cited in response. Spenser could also have been used, says Canny, to advance the claim
of the New English that they should be "treated [by the Crown] as special
subjects . . . [the *View* reiterated] the importance of their civilizing function
in Ireland."[133] The *View*'s vehement denunciations of Gaelic barbarism implied the required contrast between the New English and most of the king's
other subjects there—the Old English and the Gaels. However, we should
note that Ware's changes play down Spenser's abuse of just these two groups
in the colony, which suggests that the first edition of the *View* had more
than one purpose to accomplish and was not meant to bolster only the New
English. Sometimes Ware even included lines that were directly critical of
these interlopers. Just after the editorial "mutation" I have mentioned, for
instance, he permits Eudoxus to draw the conclusion, as he did in 1598,
that "it is not for nothing (I perceive) which I have heard, that the Coun-
cell of England thinke it no good policie to have that realme reformed or
planted with English"; they might well become as treacherous as the Gaels
and much more dangerous.[134] The New English needed to discredit rival
groups in Ireland, certainly. They also sometimes needed to placate them,
as Ware's tactful revisions may show. These, after all, were the peoples they
lived among, and later events would prove the value of politic discretion.
It may be that the ambiguities of Ware's changes, his silent reinscription
of the categories prevailing in Ireland, correspond with the ambiguities of

the position of the New English themselves. Isolated among the Gaels and
the Old English and separated from the English as such, the New English
needed to denigrate the island's other inhabitants while implying that their
own continued presence on the island would be its salvation. Throughout
the early seventeenth century, Spenser's *View*—or, at least, a version of it—
allowed the New English to remind a distant royal government that was
increasingly skeptical of their achievements in the kingdom, and resentful
of the wealth they were accruing, that they alone were well placed to bring
that "savage nation" into eventual conformity with true order and religion.
And, even when Spenser's text itself was not called on to legitimize such
claims, his name was. An anonymous author took on the initials "E. S." to
present *A Survey of the Present Estate of Ireland, Anno 1615* to James I.[135]

Appropriations of Spenser's *View* would continue well into the seventeenth century. In the next chapter, I will consider the reaction of an English poet, Andrew Marvell, to Oliver Cromwell's triumphant return from
Ireland in 1650. The "Horatian Ode," as we will recall, celebrates a conqueror whose glory it is to have made the rebellious Irish "ashamed

> To see themselves in one year tamed:
> So much one man can do,
> That does both act and know. (73–76)[136]

I should point out here, though, that the Cromwellian victories that Marvell celebrates—with great ambivalence, as we will find—were widely
thought of at the time as a realization of and a vindication of Spenser's
harsher proposals in the *View*.[137] Events in the century after Spenser's death
only deepened the animosity most English felt toward the Irish. Around
1670, someone's marginalia to James Ware's prefatory comments claimed
that "the rebellion of Oct. 23. 1641 justified Spencers wisedome and deep
insight into that barbarous [Irish] nation."[138] Indeed, in the eyes of some,
Cromwell's invasion of Ireland in 1649 and the subordination he then imposed on it were so patently Spenserian that the *View* became, in effect,
official policy.[139] Now, the history of official ambivalence toward Spenser's
treatise vanished as if it never was. Canny points out that "in 1652, when
plans were already being laid for the Cromwellian confiscation of Ireland,"
a writer "recommended that he who would advance the plantation in Ireland could hardly find better hints than in 'Mr. Ed. Spenser his *View of the
State of Ireland*, published,'" this person asserted confidently, "'almost three
score years ago, 1596.'"[140] The *View*, which Elizabeth's government could
not countenance, was in retrospect granted full authorization—and publication!—under the aegis of Oliver Cromwell's conquest. That Ireland was a

savage nation, one that must be subdued and governed "even by the sword," Cromwell knew as well as any of his royal predecessors. "For," as Spenser had declared, "all those evils must first be cut away with a strong hand before any good can be planted" (95). Whatever critique the Privy Council may have found "secreted" in *A View of the Present State of Ireland* in 1598, by the 1650's it had become a sharp instrument in a war between nations.

CHAPTER 3

British Poetics

ANDREW MARVELL'S "AN HORATIAN ODE UPON CROMWELL'S RETURN FROM IRELAND" AND "THE LOYAL SCOT"

"More normal and less random"

The "question of [Andrew Marvell's] political sincerity"[1] has been persistent. In his own day, and especially his later years, Marvell (1621–78) was dogged by rumors and accusations. The brief against him was mainly this: that he was a man of no settled principles or partisan loyalties. He was a "coward," said his chief antagonist, Samuel Parker, willing to ally himself with whatever regime was in power at the moment and disposed to justify himself, speciously, later.[2] "He was made Undersecretary to *Cromwell's* Secretary," said Parker, "But the King being restor'd, this wretched man falling into his former poverty, did, for the sake of a livelihood, procure himself to be chosen Member of Parliament for a Borough," although even there Marvell was "an enemy to the King's affairs . . . vent[ing] himself with the greater bitterness, and daily spew[ing] infamous libels out of his filthy mouth."[3] Marvell's critics were not deterred by his insistence that he "never had any, not the remotest relation to publick matters" during most of Cromwell's rule, or that the employment he eventually took was "the most innocent and inoffensive toward his Majestie's affairs of any in that usurped and irregular government."[4] More recently, readers have recognized that the charges against Marvell are, as stated, if not totally untrue, then so unnuanced as to be almost useless in accounting for the subtleties of his investments in the politics of mid-seventeenth-century England. But they have not had to credit them entirely to see that there is something crucial about this poet's changing loyalties that needs explaining. What *were* Marvell's ultimate civic allegiances, they have wanted to know? How was he able to change his adherence so quickly and, it appears, without much feeling of inconsistency? What allowed him to reconcile the very different demands that succeeding regimes imposed on him? If no man can serve two masters, how much less three—two Stuart kings and one regicide! Yet, Marvell did so, and in the midst of the internecine turmoil of his day. Was he then an "opportunist," as some have said?[5] "The problem," as John M. Wallace put it succinctly a quarter of a century ago, "is to define, as well as one can, a context which will not only make Marvell's early political judgments and decisions intelligible, but which will help to make his subsequent development appear more normal and less random" (67).

Perhaps the most elegant and historically informed attempt to rescue Marvell's reputation has been made by Wallace himself, who argues for an underlying continuity among his shifting stances. Wallace, in effect, locates a position that cuts across the spectrum of mid-century English politics; this allows Marvell to adopt whatever loyalties he must while remaining true to his core principles. " 'Turn-coat', 'collaborator', and their synonyms are grotesque distortions for the kind of changing allegiance that Marvell typifies," he asserts. Marvell, like many thousands of others, could "turn . . . [his] coat . . . with the times and follow . . . with a clear conscience the changes of regime between 1649 and 1688" because he was a "loyalist" in a specific and then well-recognized sense: he was one who "defers the transference of his allegiance until after the death of his former sovereign" (4–5). What appears to be Marvell's opportunism, says Wallace, is actually a reluctant submission to the dictates of Providence as events reveal them, and so a form of higher "loyalty" to those dictates. In "An Horatian Ode upon Cromwell's Return from Ireland" (1650), for instance, Marvell is declaring that it is "providence" itself that has "ruined a great work of time." "The people of England, like the poet, must learn to forget themselves and their prejudices, and to mark the signs God had given" (105). As the divine mandate passed from Charles I to Cromwell, and then later to Charles II, Marvell obediently accepted each dispensation in turn, and then shaped his politics to serve a new ruler.

Wallace observes that "loyalism was created from chaos, in those moments of desperation when the only conceivable action is the performance of the daily routine" (41). As Charles I went to the block, no response was possible but a stunned acceptance of the inevitability of this divine fiat. A constraining "loyalty" to still barely understood imperatives had to be improvised. This emphasis on the *provisionality* of such loyalism is what I find strongest in Wallace's account, and it helps to explain Marvell's apparent ability not only to shift between opposed frames of reference but also to operate so adroitly within them. Marvell's lifelong preference for covert action and oblique expression must indeed have had a good deal to do with his sense that fashioning a political commitment was, inevitably, the work of a discrete moment. (Marvell "was on occasion devious and often wrote anonymously,"[6] his editors have said. In the early 1660's, he involved himself in several back-channel missions abroad, and was under government surveillance at the time of his death.) And perhaps it was Marvell's loyalism that made it possible for him to adopt a certain "internal distance" from his ostensive politics. For the most part, Wallace avoids reducing Marvell to a polemicist of one sort or another. But he does not always do justice to his own insight that loyalism was "created from chaos" and thus answers to quotidian demands that can never be entirely reduced to a set of principles. To say that Marvell was a "loyalist" of this stripe does not really do much to diminish our sense that he is something other than completely "loyal" in his day-to-day affairs, and especially in his poetic practice. The "Horatian Ode" is the obvious example, both of Marvell's techniques of misdirection and the limits of Wallace's approach. In this notoriously ambiguous poem, Marvell both praises Cromwell and yet has managed to leave many convinced that he was a sub-rosa royalist. Wallace, however, insists that "as a response to a particular event which had confirmed Cromwell's power . . . the ode is not ambiguous at all." He acknowledges that the "Ode" "would have been impossible to write in 1649" (70), and that the very "matrix of Marvell's political thought . . . lies in the months between the King's death and the writing of the ode. Everything else, I believe, follows naturally from the commitment which was the upshot of his cogitations during that period" (68). But rather than reading the "Ode" in light of the "events" of those decisive months, he elects to unfold the contradictions of what he calls Marvell's "decided political stand" (71). His contradictions, says Wallace, are those of "loyalism" as such. And, in places, it can seem that Wallace wants to say that these contradictions are really no contradictions at all: "There was no confusion in Marvell's mind about the way in which [Cromwell] should be greeted on his return from Ireland" (72).[7] Wallace can claim to have established that in Marvell's time there was a credible position—"loyalism"—by which, in retrospect, we can reconcile the poet's diverse "loyalties." He does not thereby help us to decide what "loyalty," if any, is implied by a given political poem written at a given historical moment. By Wallace's own argument "loyalism" in this period was a longterm strategy by which one accommodated but did not deny the contradictions forced on one by changes at the top. But it is often in those very contradictions, and in their subtle manipulation, that Marvell's politics can be detected. In a sense, they *are* Marvell's politics. Typically, Marvell's poetry insinuates, as he alters stance from line to line, tacit alliances that are much more complicated than adherence to any single "position," even one as flexible as "loyalism." And, as readers of his poetry have long realized, it is these discrepancies that must be accounted for, and so seldom can be. Thus, it may still be true that, as Annabel Patterson declared in 1978, "few people argue nowadays about the shape of Marvell's political convictions, taken as a whole."[8] That they continue to argue about Marvell's apparently conflicting loyalties in certain poems suggests that it is precisely taking Marvell's politics "as a whole" that does not work as a reading strategy. Quite possibly, Marvell himself never took his own politics "as a whole," nor, given the exigencies of his day, could he.

In this chapter, Marvell's "loyalism(s)" will be my subject, but I will not try to pinpoint Marvell's exact allegiances, nor will I (always) be looking for covert affinities. Instead, I will locate my reading at specific points in his much interrupted and dislocated political career when he was invested in a certain set of unresolvable problems: the interisland conundrum that I have called the question of Britain. Of course, the field of British politics does not totally subsume the "machinations" of Andrew Marvell. How could it? But its own persistent ambiguities make it a good place to look for them at work. In two of his poems, one written in 1650, the other around 1670, Marvell can be observed thinking through the issues in the debate over a British union at that moment. How can England establish dominion over the two islands? By what means—cultural, legal, military—is Britain now being produced? What loyalty is due the ruler who is, or might be, capable of effecting this union? What sort of nation is implied by the establishment of Britain, and who belongs to it? What unites (or severs) the Briton from other Britons? To set Marvell's works within this ongoing controversy is not to try to "make his . . . development appear more normal and less random." That would be to attribute to Marvell a consistency that, I have claimed, is just what his politics lacks. On the contrary, we will see that Marvell's two interventions in this debate are often internally inconsistent and are radically incompatible with each other. But it may be that we come closer to the shifting heart of Marvell's mid-century politico-poetic maneuverings if we do not look for obvious continuity, if we consider a Marvell, that is, who is *less* "normal" and *more* "random" in his "development."

The two works to be treated here, the "Horatian Ode" and "The Loyal Scot" (c. 1670), are both imbricated in British events and controversies. The

first was composed (but not published) during the reign of Oliver Cromwell; the second was written during that of Charles II (and variously published some 25 years later).[9] My reading of the "Horatian Ode" is, inevitably,
a rereading, although what I offer is less another survey of that poem's many
ambivalences than a new way of framing those ambivalences within the
fraught circumstances of 1650. In the "Ode," an English poet lauds an English conqueror as he passes from one periphery, the land of "the Irish" (73),
to another, the Scottish country of "the Pict" (105). The itinerary Cromwell
traces itself implies a certain version of Britain. But while Marvell praises
Cromwell for his demonstrated puissance, his sway over the disparate corners of his domain, I will say that the "Horatian Ode" is by no means a
polemic for British union. Instead, it is an investigation into the question of
Britain at a highly charged moment in the history of three island kingdoms.
On the other hand, "The Loyal Scot," which Marvell wrote at the end of
his poetic career and near the close of his life, does seem to be just such a
polemic. A paean to Archibald Douglas, a handsome young Scotsman who
died in flames defending Britain, begins the poem. In the discourse that
follows, Marvell argues against the divisiveness of certain Scotch presbyters
and for the benefits of an amalgamation that would abolish all cultural and
national differences between the Scots and the English. These are trivial in
any case, he asserts. What is needed is "One king, one faith, one language,
and one isle, / English and Scotch, 'tis all but cross and pile" (260–61). I will
suggest, however, that this poet's proclamations here are not only or simply
polemical. The charge that Marvell was a "coward" was often leveled along
with the allegation that he was a "sodomite." If it is hard to locate the truth
of this claim, it may be because the sensibilities of Marvell's day allowed his
erotic "loyalties" little more than an oblique expression. But, more likely,
this is because in Marvell's work erotics and politics are almost always inex-
tricable. We rarely find an expression of his "sexual" affinities that does not
at the same time imply and entail other, more overtly partisan allegiances.
His commitments are varied, but not discrete. What, then, do the erotics
of "The Loyal Scot" have to do with its announced project—the creation
of a British state? In this poem, what stands at the nexus between "that
utterly confused category"[10]—"sodomy"—and the vexed question of Britain? More generally, what does it tell us of the politics of Britishness among
men (or between men, to echo the title of Eve Kosofsky Sedgwick's classic study[11]) and the "nation(s)" that may (or may not) have been emerging
among them in the late seventeenth century? I will turn to these questions
in the latter sections of this chapter.

   In other hands, Edmund Spenser's for instance, the question of Britain received a much more systematic treatment than we will find in these occasional poems of Marvell. What is crucial here, though, is that these *are* ephemeral pieces, making brief and mostly inconsequential interventions in a fluctuating politics. The "Horatian Ode," as I have said, went unpublished during Cromwell's reign, and, predictably, was canceled from almost all of the copies of Marvell's *Miscellaneous Poems* in 1681. "The Loyal Scot" addresses the issues of an abortive political episode, and has been mostly ignored within Marvell studies. However, it is because Marvell's way with these issues is not systematic (nor could it be, given the ambiguities of his politics) that investigating the permutations of Britain in this verse is worthwhile. It is because these poems are so very much of their respective times that they can help us to rethink the discontinuity—and, equally, the continuity—between Marvell's "loyalties" from reign to reign.

As I have said, Marvell's encounters with the question of Britain were keyed to the exigencies of 1650 and 1670 in specific. However, Marvell's preoccupation with that question itself (if not the "answers" he arrived at) persisted throughout his several meditations on it, even though a lasting British union was never achieved in the seventeenth century. Cromwell, as we will see, proved uninterested in taking up the imperial title and dominion that many of the English thought was his due, and the Commonwealth he established during his Protectorate, declared to include England, Scotland, and Ireland, collapsed with the Restoration. "In 1660 the parliamentary unions with Scotland and Ireland were dissolved: not until 1801 were the three legislatures again to be united."[12] Charles II's own attempts to bind Scotland and England in 1670 foundered, as usual, on the unwillingness of the two nations to surrender their separate prerogatives. But it is important to remember that what was usually not called into question during this divisive period was England's hegemony over its British neighbors. The creation of an Anglocentric union out of the disparate kingdoms of the islands was a project that was not only (though it was usually) royalist. It was a project whose fulfillment also seemed to be promised by the ascendancy of Oliver Cromwell. It was a project whose possibilities were also very much Marvell's concern when Cromwell was gone and the house of Stuart had come again. The dream of Britain endured under very different English governments, and Marvell recognized that dream of power in its larger outlines. If, as seems plausible, among the virtues that Marvell most admired in an English leader was a demonstrated capacity for truly British rule, then one reason that Marvell may have been able to serve otherwise irreconcilable rulers was that he had a continuing commitment to the unifying possibilities that Cromwell and Charles II seemed to hold

out at certain times in their reigns. And it may have been this possibility of
an overarching sovereignty in both of them that made Marvell's contradictory "loyalty" to each of them sustainable.

Thinking Supranationally?

An acknowledgment of the indeterminacy of the "Horatian Ode" is
now almost mandatory for reading the poem, and has become a reading in
itself. Frank Kermode and Keith Walker remark that "there has been a great
deal of interpretation, some of it of high quality, but the poem remains
resistant to decoding"; indeed, "it is baffling to anyone who wants simply
to know where the poet stood with Cromwell in 1650." [13] David Norbrook
notes that critics have debated almost every shading of its notoriously enig-
matic lines, but that the enigma of those lines has only increased with the
exegesis devoted to them. Once the "Horatian Ode" was praised by for-
malist readers, he says, for its "balance between Charles and Cromwell, between the arts of peace and war, between feudal and bourgeois orders, and
so on." But "as critics have begun to situate the poem more closely in its
historical context, that 'balance' has become harder to locate." The "Ode,"
as he puts it, "is grim, witty, exuberant, explosive, savage, elliptical, elegiac,
[and] apocalyptic" [14] all at once. Since each of Norbrook's adjectives would
have been taken to imply a certain politics in 1650, a distinct stance toward
the events of recent years, that the poem can encompass each one of them
would seem to make it, finally, an undecidable poem. "Baffling apparently
it will remain," predicts Thomas Greene, "despite the most earnest herme-
neutic footwork." [15]

Part of the problem, as I have said, may be with the "historical context"
in which readers have been "situat[ing]" the poem. Which history? Which
context? More than most of Marvell's poetry, the "Ode" might seem to lend
itself to a reading of its British ramifications. It was written when something like a Britain had begun to seem plausible, and largely because of the
triumphs of the figure Marvell eulogizes, Cromwell himself. As Derek Hirst
has said, it was "in the middle of the seventeenth century [that] England
came close to experiencing a genuinely British moment." [16] "In the Republic" that Cromwell came to dominate, Hirst says, "conquest and forcible
union brought the relations among what had been the more or less discrete
political units of Britain unavoidably into the view of politicians, of news-
book readers," and especially, of course, "those in the way of the marching
armies." [17] No doubt, in 1650 this Britain was also becoming apparent to
Andrew Marvell, who was then employed in the household of a parlia-

mentary general, Lord Fairfax. Before that year, the creation of an island-girdling Britain had been an ideal to be championed by some members of the English political nation. This vision had been often invoked among them, but was never fully realized. With Cromwell's successes, Britain became as real as the pikes and muskets of his soldiers could make it. And if these were not sufficiently convincing, his government had other forms of control. In 1656, the Venetian secretary in England wrote his superiors that

> In Ireland we hear of some rising against the government plotted by the Spaniards and just now encouraged by King Charles. The people there were working secretly but with great activity to put their plans into execution. Men in disguise travelled throughout the country to rouse the people and incite them to rebellion. But their plans became known here and the Protector immediately took steps to check it at its birth and not allow matters so prejudicial to his authority and seat to get a start. Instructions have accordingly been issued for the arrest of some of the most mutinous and for a strict and thorough surveillance of everything.[18]

Cromwell's invasion of Ireland left in place a network along which not only intelligence could pass, but reportage as well. Wallace notes that Marvell's "Ode" undoubtedly responds to "reports that filtered back to London and were reported in the weekly newspapers," and, moreover, that "from the start, the government had been anxious to publish accounts of submission from all over the British Isles, and Ireland was no exception" (85). To which can be added that it was these very accounts that helped to create the sense that the Isles were indeed British. What Benedict Anderson has claimed of nation formation in a later period was also true, to an extent, of the creation of that nebulous polity, Britain, in the midst of the seventeenth century: "the development of increasingly rapid communications . . . made it possible for rapidly growing numbers of people to think about themselves, and to relate themselves to others, in profoundly new ways."[19] In the early 1650s, Britain emerged, briefly, as a construct out of the simultaneous imaginings of disparate peoples who suddenly found themselves forced to consider their propinquity to others on the islands. If nothing else, what they had in common was subjection to the government of Oliver Cromwell. Ironically, the associations among the British peoples that had been vigorously asserted by royal polemicists such as Francis Bacon during the reign of James I were now made visible during the regime of his son's executioner.

This is the "historical context" that makes the "Ode" a peculiarly British work. It is enabled by the emergence of a Britain during the period of Cromwell's interisland conquests; it participates in the controlled flow of information that gave rise to the notion of such a unified polity. And it both

announces and celebrates the conditions of its own inscription. It is Cromwell's ability to fashion a loyal Britain out of its rebellious Irish, Scottish,
and English nations that, in part, makes him worthy of Marvell's calculated
adulation. "What may not then our isle presume," asks the poet,

> While Victory his crest does plume?
> What may not others fear
> If thus he crown each year? (97–100)

His lines locate the glory of Cromwell's triumph in England, but only because this "Caesar" (101) has circulated out beyond its boundaries to achieve
the neoimperial dominion over "others" which sustains the security, and
perhaps even the identity, of "our isle." It is also this "historical context"
that makes it impossible to reduce the poem's politics to any one strand of
English controversy, no matter how provisionally held or how entangled
it might be in other such strands. What some historians have argued generally of the mid-century "English" "Civil War" can be said specifically of
Marvell's "Ode": at every point, it entails the affairs of three kingdoms, and
implies an ongoing interplay of political events among them.[20] I do not
mean to say that the perplexities of the "Ode" can be "explained" by expanding its "historical context." Rather, I suggest that the problems of the
poem itself, its famously intractable difficulties, *are* those of its "historical
context," specifically those adumbrated by Cromwell's Irish campaign of
1650. Marvell's "Ode" serves as both a commentary on and an instance of
the question of Britain in that year.

Most critics of Marvell's tribute, though, have concerned themselves
with its significance for the kingdom that Cromwell was returning to in
1650 rather than the one he was coming from, and, before I continue with
what I think of as a more British reading, I want to suggest that they have
had good reasons for doing so. It can happen that a British historiography
(like that which informs this study) can minimize the very real insularity
that the English managed to create for themselves throughout most of their
history. "We may think we know what the term 'Britain' means," Hirst has
also said, "but we should pause a little—as successive rulers were forced to
do—before requiring our forebears to think supranationally."[21] The debate
over union during Cromwell's regime was complicated by a persistent distrust of the royalist antecedents of the project, as well as by a perennial reluctance among Englishmen to accept non-Englishmen as compeers. Even
for Cromwell himself—"God's Englishman"—"the concept of 'Britain'
[was] an unwelcome intrusion associated with the ambitions of the Stuarts
and the convenanters which threatened England's identity."[22] The possi-

bilities of the British moment may have been newly apparent to most of the English in 1650, but they were certainly not always welcomed. In fact, these possibilities could and did elicit a kind of general indifference that was not that far from outright hostility. Hirst notes that in the years leading up to the Protectorate, a "complacent Anglocentrism,"[23] as usual, pervaded England's dealings with its island neighbors. These others had little to do, it was alleged, with defining England's culture or polity. As contrasted to the Scots, for instance, says J. G. A. Pocock, "Englishmen were more 'insular,' more 'ethnocentric,' more 'provincial' in their refusal to admit 'cosmopolitan' components in their national life and history" because they felt that they "possessed 'sovereign' and 'absolute' power over themselves" by virtue of their exclusive heritage of immemorial law. This sense of English singularity was not weakened but bolstered by the ascendancy of a man who had ousted a king in the name of that law, and who saw "the Stewart monarchy . . . as a menace to the unity of [the] English realm."[24] During and after the war of the three kingdoms, "Anglocentric complacency" did not modulate into a dawning recognition of the Irish and Scots, but into a greater insistence on the preeminence of Englishness.[25] While it is true, as Marvell and many others registered, that Cromwell's rise to power implied an apparently more British dominion, it is also true that he advanced the claims of his government against Charles I in the name of a legal tradition that, by 1650, had come to regard the Scottish—that is, in a sense, British—dynasty on the English throne with abhorrence. Nor did the dynamics of English politics under the Protectorate allow the British moment Cromwell had precipitated to come to fulfillment. As Hirst notes, "No reminder is needed that Cromwell passed by the opportunity to link his name, and a new style, with the new Britain; more remarkable is the failure of the republic in general to make more of the ideological and propaganda openings that its British conquests had created."[26] Britain, as it turned out, was not really on the agenda, neither for Cromwell nor for the English Parliament.

This is why, as we will see, in his "Ode" Marvell is able to be so equivocal about the Britain that he also does so much to promote: he enters into the ambivalence that Englishmen generally felt in 1650 about the prospect of merging themselves with peoples whom they had ignored or vilified for many centuries. In the "Horatian Ode," Marvell answers to, and manipulates, contradictory imperatives: he both upholds the British union Cromwell is effecting and he hints at instabilities that would vitiate the effectiveness of that union. Consequently, the Britain Marvell imagines in the "Ode" is in danger of being dismantled almost as soon as it is constructed, and the poem is an uncertain vehicle for the promulgation of British consciousness.

To his English readers, Marvell proclaims the advent of a conqueror who will do away with the geopolitical limits that have circumscribed the reach of English power. Cromwell will rule from Dublin to Glasgow to London, and, as Marvell would later say of Charles II in "The Loyal Scot," teach his subjects the "last secret": "how to make them one" (265). But the borders that Cromwell will do away with also, of course, inscribe crucial differences; they make his English readers who they are. There can be something deeply threatening about being told that you are about to become "one" with those whose unlikeness to yourself has ensured your own identity and, if truth be told, your superiority. Thus, like other poets of Britain before him, Marvell offers a vantage point from which Englishness can be seen as mere particularism, to be superseded by allegiance to a higher destiny—in 1650, that of Oliver Cromwell. " 'Tis madness to resist or blame / The force of angry heaven's flame" (25–26). But, at the same time (and, again, like other poets of Britain before him), Marvell works against (as he also accommodates) an intense, though tacit, resistance to precisely that project of transcendence among those same English readers. The "Ode" imagines the abolishing of a localized identity—Englishness—but does not forget, since its readers cannot forget, that it is the very fixity of this identity, its refusal to even acknowledge a relation to others, that keeps it intact.

Predictably, these British/English tensions in the "Horatian Ode" are irresolvable, although perhaps we can make too much of even this ambivalence. "It was not just bloody-minded ethnic chauvinism which moved the English in their dealings with associated peoples," as Pocock says; "it was also the intensity of their own problems and the need to settle them among themselves."[27] In this real and crucial sense, Marvell *is* English, and so is his poem: it assumes an exclusively English readership and makes no overt gestures beyond the confines of the English nation. Nor, whatever its uncertainties, did the "Ode" offer Marvell's English contemporaries a more "cosmopolitan" understanding of the cultural politics of 1650. It has been said in another context that "to feel that one is from an origin is not a pathology. It belongs to that group of grounding mistakes that enable us to make sense of our lives. But the only way to argue for origins is to look for institutions, inscriptions and then to surmise the mechanics by which such institutions and inscriptions can stage such a particular style of performance."[28] In the "Horatian Ode," Marvell seems to have decided to integrate his poetry into the operation of one such institution, Cromwell's war machine. Like the "forward youth," he will "leave the books in dust, / And oil the unused armour's rust" (5–6), and submit his verse to the imperatives of Cromwell's martial strategy. But he does so at a time when the invasions staged by this conqueror were reconfiguring the borders of the English kingdom. As Cromwell the republican put royalist theories of union into military practice, England became England plus Ireland, and then threatened to become England, Ireland, and Scotland—and maybe Britain. Triumphant as Marvell's Cromwell is, the England he claims to serve is also a zone whose borders have been rendered porous by his relentless drive to establish a hegemony that transcends (and incorporates) England itself. Thus, the English "origins" that Marvell stages in the poem as his own are always jeopardized by the very "mechanism" that produces them. And the question of how Marvell "thinks" about all this, whether it be "supranationally" or otherwise, is not one that can be answered simply or finally. The "Ode" is a poem by an Englishman who glimpses the potential for more-than-Englishness that Cromwell's victories seem to imply, but who is keenly aware that more-than-Englishness is a condition fraught with its own complement of paradoxes.

"The ordinary sepultures of the 'British' nation"

If Marvell's "Ode" needs to be understood against the backdrop of Cromwell's Irish campaign of 1650, that campaign itself needs to be understood against the backdrop of events that took place in Ireland in 1641.[29] On October 23 of that year, leaders of the Gaelic aristocracy, with some support among Old English landowners, rose up against the royal government and its policies. Sir John Temple's *The Irish Rebellion* (1646), a hostile account, later stated that the "main points" of the rebels' demands, "insisted-upon [by] them . . . were, 1st, the restauration of the publick profession of the *Romish* religion; 2ndly, the restitution of all the plantation-lands unto the natives; and, 3dly, the settlement of the present Government in their hands. All the remonstrances from several parts, and that came out of the several provinces of the Kingdom, do concur in these propositions, with very little or no difference."[30] Initially, the conspirators launched their assaults against royal strongholds in both Dublin and Ulster. The first of these attempts failed, but not the second, and rebellion quickly spread through the province, and then throughout the north of Ireland generally. In the early stages of the insurrection, which eventually engulfed the entire island and concluded only in 1643, about four thousand English Protestant settlers were killed.[31] Many of them, said outraged Englishmen later, were killed quite horribly. Temple's account, a litany of atrocities, is typical: "What shall we say to a Child boiled to death in a Cauldron?" (94). "Alas!" he exclaims, "Who can comprehend the fears, terrors, anguish, bitterness and

perplexity of [the English], the despairing passions and consternations of
their minds! . . . to hear the base, reviling, speeches used against their Country and their Countrymen; some loudly threatening that all should be cut-
off and utterly destroyed, that had one drop of *English* blood in them" (98).
From 1641 until now, this uprising has been, understandably, a charged and
polarizing topic. As Pocock has argued, though, the "Irish rebellion of 1641
was no archaic affair of Gaelic warriors charging out of the mists, but the
complex response of Old English and Old Irish populations to the threats
that renewed English and Scottish settlement and intensified royal control
presented to their position in the polity."[32] What precipitated the uprising
of 1641, that is, was the displacement of more than one British enclave into
territory historically claimed by others. Like Cromwell's later campaign, it
occurs at a nexus of trans-island forces.

In what follows, I will be using *The Irish Rebellion* to show how two
larger issues—the problem of knowledge in Ireland and the question of
Britain—had come to be framed in the years after 1641. For my purposes,
Temple's treatise is useful less as documentary evidence of Irish atrocities
than as an index of the ways in which Irish Protestants decided to represent
the uprising. As T. C. Barnard has argued, these "massacres were distinguished from . . . other [episodes of violence in Ireland] by the thorough
and effective methods by which they were publicized."[33] Temple's book in
particular would express and justify Protestant outrage for decades to come;
"it exerted a strong and baleful influence."[34] The politics of Marvell's "Ode"
will become somewhat more distinct, I suggest, when the poem is placed
at the end of a chain of concatenating events: the revolt of 1641, sparked by
the influx of English and Scottish settlers into Ireland; the Irish Protestant
response, promulgated by the Temple's *Irish Rebellion*; Cromwell's invasion
of 1650, itself a response, in part, to the propaganda war being conducted
by polemicists such as Temple; and, finally (for our purposes) Marvell's own
"reading" of that invasion, offered up to the conqueror in the "Horatian
Ode." In order to show how intricately entangled this poem is in the problems of Britishness in the 1650's, I will trace the chain that links Temple's
treatise to Marvell's verse.

Initially, Temple's book seems to deny the very possibility of a "Great
Britain." The term "British" often figures in *The Irish Rebellion*, but not as
an inclusive trope. For Temple, it means only English and Scottish settlers,
"Protestants within this Kingdom of Ireland."[35] Pointedly, the Irish are
not included in this grouping. Indeed, the only hope for the reformation
of their country is that it "comes to be re-planted with British Inhabitants, and settled in peace again" (4). After the rebellion, says a deposition

from which Temple quotes, "multitudes of men, women, and children were found drowned, cast into ditches, bogs, and turf-pits"; these became "the ordinary sepultures of the *British* nation" (92). Their bodies, strewn indiscriminately over the landscape, emblematize the lack of proper distinction that has been Ireland's fatal flaw. Like many Englishmen before him, Temple bewails the "kind of mutual transmigration into each others manners" that has occurred between settlers and natives, "many English being strangely degenerated in Irish affections and customs; and many Irish, especially of the better sort, having taken-up the English language, apparel, and decent manner of living." "Their intermarriages were frequent, gossipred, fostering, (relations of much dearness among the Irish,) together with all other forms of tenancy, neighbourhood, and service, interchangeably passed among them" (23). Temple's solution, in the aftermath of the massacre, is entirely as radical and rigorous as Spenser's was half a century earlier. There must be a "wall of separation set-up betwixt the Irish and the British" (4) — cultural and political apartheid, that is, militarily enforced. But while, as we saw, Spenser's disdain for the Irish went together with a tacit appreciation, even appropriation, of their "subtle evasion[s],"[36] in the aftermath of 1641 Temple can find no way to recognize the natives as anything but "aliens" and "enemies" (16). The partial acknowledgment that Englishmen such as Spenser were earlier able to extend to the Gaels is a casualty of the revolt; the problem of Irish secrecy remains, but is now so exacerbated that resolution is impossible. This, in fact, becomes one of the organizing problems of Temple's treatise. The effect of the "wall" he erects between Britishness and Irishness is to conceal from him the true causes of the rebellion he castigates, and he knows it. Besides a testament to the horrors visited upon the English settlers in 1641, his treatise is an investigation — a blocked investigation, finally — into the inscrutable Irish malice that could have inspired them. His purpose, he says early on, is "to draw truth." By relying on trustworthy material, recorded statements, and the like, "we may well hope to arrive at the true knowledge of the main particular passages of this late Rebellion" (5). Yet, shortly he is noting "in the nature of the Irish, such a kind of dull and deep reservedness, as makes them, with much silence and secrecy, to carry-on their business" (25). He must then begin his inquiry by confessing that "I cannot yet determine who were the very first contrivers, where the first Debates were entertained, or who first sat in Council about it" (63). In about the middle of the treatise, he is driven to confess that "my intelligence fails me, and I am able to deliver no more" of the intent of the conspirators, other "than appears in the bloody effects and horrid executions acted in the first beginnings of their Rebellion" (78–79).

Thereafter, most of his book is taken up with cataloguing the atrocities committed against the English, an inventory of outrage that must speak for itself because Temple has less and less to say. The absolute otherness of the despicable Irish—"a blind, ignorant, superstitious, people" (64)—is left as both the cause and the "bloody effect" of the rebellion, a sine qua non that must suffice as sole explanation. Perhaps, for Temple to declare more than that the plot was "mysterious and obscurely laid" would be to detract from the revulsion he means to elicit. But this mystery doubles back on the "clear and unquestionable probabilities of truth . . . [that] I have here set-down" (5). As he says of the rebellion itself, his "wall" of separation, "as all other works of this nature, [has] its foundation laid in the dark" (63).

Interestingly, however, the "wall" Temple constructs around Englishness is slightly eroded at some points. Without making much of this, Temple seems to allow for English affinities with the Ulster Scots, who, he says, were duped during the revolt. To "keep-off the Scots from giving [the English] any assistance, [the Irish] openly professed to spare, as really they did at first, all the Scottish nation; and pretended they would suffer them . . . to live quietly among them" (44). The Irish rebels are depicted as enemies to all their British neighbors. Any Gael who gave alms to "any *Scot, Englishman,* or *Welchman,*" the "*Irish* Metropolitan" (79) supposedly declared, would be excommunicated. Of course, the British polity as Temple understood it was still divided by intractable differences, mostly religious. He could not imagine a Britain in which "evil-affected Irish Papists" (29) might be included. The problem all along had been that these Irish had been dispersed among those from whom they are intrinsically different. They had been "living promiscuously among the British in all parts" (43). One of the surest signs of the enmity they bear the British around them was their desire *not* to be different from them. Temple quotes the rebels' demand "That all marks of National distinctions between *English* and *Irish* may be abolished and taken-away by Act of Parliament" (75). We can guess why this horrified Temple: he knew that it was merely a ploy by which Englishness would be transformed into its barbaric opposite. "Resolved universally to root all the *British* and *Protestants* out of *Ireland,*" he says, the rebels not only "would have penalties inflicted upon those that spake *English,*" but would "have all the *English* names of places changed into the old *Irish* denominations" (79). For Temple, English identity in Ireland remained precarious, and he was ferocious in his insistence on maintaining the necessary contrasts. All the same, Temple must note, and with approval, "A new Colony of Protestant British Inhabitants, chiefly from Scotland, [which] is planted . . . in the Province of Ulster" (21).[37] In the same Ireland across which Temple wants to lay his "wall," interisland migrations have the effect of generating a rather more expanded sense of what it means to inhabit the multipartite domain of Charles I. Inscribed in the prose of Temple's *Irish Rebellion*, we can observe a dialectic that, as we will see, is also at work in the verse of Marvell's "Horatian Ode": on the one hand, a rigorous separation of Englishness and Irishness, and, on the other, a more incipient Britishness to which this dialectic tentatively gives rise.

To some extent, Cromwell's invasion of Ireland was launched as a reaction to the conditions there—at least, as Temple and others had defined them. A historian has claimed that Cromwell's campaign against the Irish reveals nothing other than English xenophobia at work. "In all we know of Cromwell's attitude to Ireland and the Irish . . . there is not sign of any distinctive outlook, any special insights into the Irish problem. He simply shared the attitudes of most Englishmen. Ireland had to be reconquered, as historically subordinate to England, as a potential strategic threat, and as the home of barbarous papists whose crimes must be punished, whose religion must be suppressed."[38] Cromwell's speech and actions in Ireland largely bear this out. When he arrived in Dublin on August 15, 1649, he assured the gathered crowd that he and the three regiments he had with him were there "to restore them all to their just liberty and property," and that "all those whose heart's affections were real for the carrying on of the great work against the barbarous and bloodthirsty Irish, and . . . for the propagating of the Gospel of Christ . . . should find favour and protection from the Parliament of England."[39] Like most Englishmen, Cromwell was incensed by the brutalities, both real and concocted, of the uprising of 1641, and he was not inclined to be lenient. His victories at Drogheda and Wexford were followed by massacres in both towns. These, he declared, had been intended to prevent further defiance: "truly I believe this bitterness will save much effusion of blood, through the goodness of God."[40] Particularly telling is a state paper he issued to refute the allegation that he meant to "extirpate" Catholicism from Hibernia. At a Conventicle in Clonmacnoise, Irish prelates had assembled to declare themselves joined "against a common enemy." "Who is it that created this common enemy?" thundered Cromwell in return. "I suppose you mean Englishmen. The English! Remember, ye hypocrites, Ireland was once united to England." Here, Cromwell speaks to the issue that preoccupied Temple—the alterity of the barbaric Irish—but shifts to the opposite pole of this vacillating sense of difference. While Temple could regard the Gaels only as absolutely other, Cromwell must insist, just as implausibly, that they are absolutely the same—or could be. This conqueror did not see in the long history of English/Irish engagement the working out of the many differences between these nations. Nor did he believe that by invading Ireland he was creating a "union" between two peoples where none had been before. Rather, Cromwell held that such a "British" polity already existed, and that it was more or less identical with the circuits already laid down by the jurisprudence of England. For Cromwell, as for Sir John Davies at the turn of the century, "English presence in Ireland was in large part a matter of property rights, triable at law," [41] and these, he considered, had pertained on both islands since time out of mind. "Englishmen had good inheritances which many of them purchased with their money; they or their ancestors, from many of you and your ancestors," he reminded the "Archbishops, Bishops, and Prelates." "They had good leases from Irishmen for long time to come; great stocks thereupon; houses and plantations erected at their cost and charge. They lived peaceably and honestly amongst you." [42] There is no historical specificity to Cromwell's narrative of supposed coexistence, but that is just the point. To tell a story of two nations at odds would imply, at the very least, that they both existed, and Cromwell did not accept that. Cromwell, rather, held to the opinion that was later articulated in the Irish Parliament presided over by his son, Richard: the Irish were "all English" [43] and always had been. They were "united" with other Englishmen under one common law—until, of course, their shocking propensity to deviate from their borrowed Englishness ruptured the unmarred continuum of Anglo-Irish (actually English) legal history and created the need for a conquest such as his own. "You broke this union!" he assails the Irish clergy. "You, unprovoked, put the English to the most unheard-of and most barbarous massacre (without respect of sex or age) that ever the sun beheld." For Cromwell, the threat from Ireland would be done only when the island was "in perfect peace" [44] —in effect, when it was not Ireland, but some (properly subordinate) version of England.

Cromwell marched into Ireland, then, not only to ensure doctrinal uniformity within his realm, and not only to prevent that island from being used as a base of operations against his newly established government, but also to solve Temple's epistemic riddle for him, and so to fulfill a project that official England had envisioned since the eleventh century—the "final" resolution of the Irish question. And this, it seemed in 1650, was a goal he had achieved. By June, his success in Ireland had driven the king-in-exile, Charles II, to form an alliance among the Scottish covenanters, and it had been decided that Cromwell should march on Scotland to forestall any planned invasion. When this general arrived back in his home country in May, "the back of Irish resistance was clearly broken," [45] and most Englishmen were once again confident that their ancient relation to the Gaels—contemptuous indifference on their side, hostile subordination on the other—had been restored.

"He secrecy with number hath enchased"

Now, how did Marvell introduce himself into this fractured epistemic field in the "Horatian Ode"? Is his relation to the Irish like that of Temple? Is he obsessed with but baffled by Gaelic otherness and the "mystery" that it adumbrates? Or is his stance more like Cromwell's? Does he deal with the Irish problem by eliding the Irish difference? It is not surprising that, in a tribute to an English conqueror, Marvell's treatment of the Irish is mostly an elaboration on the tropes of hegemony that Cromwell's victories implied. The "Ode" itself is very concerned with the problem of knowledge that Ireland entailed for the English in the 1650's. This concern is marked in the famous lines:

> And now the Irish are ashamed
> To see themselves in one year tamed:
> So much one man can do,
> That does both act and know. (73–76)

Cromwell, Marvell says, acquired his power in Ireland not only by "[u]rg-[ing] his active star" (12) "through adventurous war" (11), and so defeating the Irish, but by "know[ing]" as he acted. In Ireland, what Cromwell knows appears to be almost as absolute as the power he achieves. Indeed, Cromwell's power/knowledge are fused and mutually sustaining. The Irish come to know themselves as Cromwell's subjects, and to be "ashamed," because "one man," a "greater spirit" (44), who can "both act and know," has a pervading knowledge of their actions and their thoughts. And this "one man" reshapes them. As Blair Worden says, the Irish speak "like men who know they deserve what has come to them."[46] They have come to know themselves, that is, as Cromwell knows them. A single impulse toward total English control over the recalcitrant kingdom of Ireland thus seems to drive Marvell's "Ode," as it sometimes drove texts we have previously considered: Shakespeare's *Henry V*, Spenser's *View*, Davies' *True Discovery*, and so on. The royalist project that these turn-of-the-century Englishmen tried to advance has found its culmination, it seems, half a century later. When Marvell's "Ode" asserts that the Irish have fully succumbed to "one man . . . That does both act and know," it promulgates a fantasy of epistemic dominance of long standing in official English circles.

Still, I do not think that the frustrations of (not) knowing, so intensely troubling to English governance of Ireland, simply disappear from the "Ode" with the seeming incorporation of the Irish into Cromwell's cognitive mastery. Nor are the perplexities that Temple condemned there altogether absent from this poem. Again, the epistemic problems of Ireland are the very problems of Marvell's Cromwellian poetry, the problems for which these texts are now so well known. Cromwell's return from Ireland in 1650 provided Marvell not only with the occasion for an ode, but with a structure of difficulties, both political and poetic, around which his ongoing meditations on Cromwell could coalesce. These have to do mostly with the complexity of sorting out national identity in the aftermath of Cromwell's trans-island campaign and with the quandaries that result. It is true that toward the Irish Marvell appears to adopt an attitude of dismissive superiority that is modeled on Cromwell's own. But the problems of knowing that Ireland represented to the English are not resolved thereby. Instead, as we will see, they become implicit in Marvell's relation to Cromwell himself.

Take, as a brief first example, Marvell's treatment of that other British people appearing in the "Ode," the Scots. With Cromwell on the way to England's northern border to quell resistance among the covenanters, Marvell predicts that

> The Pict no shelter now shall find
> Within his parti-coloured mind,
> But from his valour sad
> Shrink underneath the plaid:
> Happy, if in the tufted brake
> The English hunter him mistake,
> Nor lay his hounds in near
> The Caledonian deer. (105-12)

Certainly there is a claim for epistemic control being made here. Like the Irish, the Scots will find that their "parti-coloured mind[s]" yield to the sway of their conqueror's more single understanding. And there appear to be no discernable limits to Cromwell's intellectual regime; the Picts will not find "shelter," even within the recesses of their own consciousness. But the passage itself also draws us into questions that disrupt the hegemony it seems to assert. The very suggestion that the Scotsman might try to hide his thoughts from Cromwell's knowing reminds the English reader that his mind is not "ours," and that it is divided up—or "parted"—differently from "our own." In one sense, then, the resistant Pict does *not* disappear from the poem at this moment. Instead, his presence is foregrounded, and precisely by the erasure that Marvell seems to promise. Then, too, even as these English/Scottish distinctions are being emphasized, they are also being eroded. "Our" feeling for just what is and is not "ours" is disrupted here. Whose mind is this, finally? As Thomas Greene points out, the "Scot clearly *doesn't* want to appear." He seems almost to hide within the poem. And so, says Greene, "an analogy might be drawn between his self-concealment in the shadowy brake and the reticence of a text that doesn't want to give itself away too facilely." [47] If the Pict does not want to yield up his idiosyncratic meaning to Cromwell, neither, it may seem, does Marvell, whose celebratory poem is notoriously resistant to just the kind of reduction that Cromwell's rule imposes. And, if the Pict's mind, like his plaid, is "parti-coloured"—diverse, counterwoven—it is hard to know what adjective would better describe the "Ode" itself. We find ourselves wondering not only what Marvell means, but from where it is, as it were, that he means it. His lines hint at shifting associations that place him on every side of every border in the war that Cromwell is prosecuting. The "forward youth" who steps out to announce the advent of Cromwell's suzerainty over Britain is also implicated in a poem that implies all of the distinctions among the British peoples that Cromwell would have ignored.

"They can affirm his praises best"

Just after he claims that "the Irish are ashamed / To see themselves in one year tamed" (73–74) by Cromwell's active knowing, Marvell enlists those same defeated Irish into the chorus of praise for their conqueror:

> They can affirm his praises best,
> And have, though overcome, confessed
> How good he is, how just,
> And fit for highest trust. (77–80)

As I return to this Irish crux, I want to expand the scope of my questions, and to ask not only what is it that Marvell's Cromwell knows, and how does the poet participate in that knowledge (if he does)?, but also what is it that these Irish say, and how does the poet participate in that saying (if he does)? Marvell's "Ode" gives a voice to one sort of English national snobbery and helps to enforce it. But he also quite deliberately introduces into his poem the voices—or what are alleged to be the voices—of the Irish objects of this contempt. As he emerges from the "shadows" to "sing" (3) of Cromwell's victory, what are the consequences of this ventriloquism for his own poetic annunciation?

Critics have often taken an apologetic tone over these lines, which seem to be callously indifferent to the aspirations of the Irish of Marvell's day and to elide the severity of Cromwell's campaign. According to Wallace, we should keep in mind that this operation was, by seventeenth-century standards of warfare, or even our own, fairly well restrained by a "gentlemanly code" (85). The Irish, he says, might actually have hailed Cromwell for his benevolence. Newspaper accounts reaching England in 1650 were claiming that, in Cork for instance, " 'the generality of the Townsmen [were] wel affected to the English, and enemies to the Irish' " (86). At worst, Marvell was "guilty of [no] more than a mild exaggeration, the purpose of which the poem explains." In any case, to the properly informed reader, "the rhetorical intention of the Irish testimony is not obscure" (85). "The ode . . . is not about Ireland, and the satisfaction of her people is plainly recalled to witness Cromwell's fitness for another task," that of the rule he must take up as "Governor of England and Supreme Head of the Commonwealth" (88). The "Ode," Wallace means to say, was occasioned by the triumphant return of Cromwell from Ireland, and the acquiescence of its people is invoked to celebrate and justify that triumph, but it is not "about" Ireland, he holds, because it is mostly "about" English politics. Cromwell had gone to Ireland to establish a primacy that only seemed to require Irish acknowledgment. "The irony of these lines may be less keen than we suppose." Blair Worden has also suggested. Cromwell's massacres at Drogheda and Wexford, "which have troubled the English [!] memory, seem to have disturbed few consciences at the time."[48] He too points out that the English were reading what purported to be Irish praise of Cromwell in their journals. One such document declared that his victories exceeded those of Alexander the Great and other stalwarts. These explanations are compelling. Wallace and Worden attribute Marvell's disdain for Irish autonomy and dignity to the cultural politics of his milieu. To put this another way: they do not require Marvell to "think supranationally." They accept that this English poet was invested in a sense of English cultural superiority, and that along with that investment went a necessary indifference, even a hostility, to the claims that the Irish might make for themselves. If the Irish are "disappeared" by and from the "Ode" so that Oliver Cromwell may be aggrandized, this is no more than we should expect.

Yet, our uneasiness over the seizure of these Irish voices persists, as critics—often the same critics—have also attested. "We remain surprised to hear [the Irish] talking like men who know they deserve what has come to them," observes Worden.[49] "It is disturbing to find a poem that celebrates national emancipation simultaneously endorsing Cromwell's brutal repression of Irish resistance," says Norbrook.[50] The obvious rejoinder—that the "national emancipation" that the "Ode" "celebrates" is emphatically not that of Ireland, but another nation altogether that can realize its own liberation only at the expense of these subjected Irishmen—does not quite allay our disquiet either. "A question mark remains and keeps the poem open."[51] The "Ode" is assuredly an act of expropriation, but notice also that the poem

calls our attention to that expropriation, and does so far more pointedly
than most of the English invective directed at the Irish during the period,
which makes no attempt whatsoever to consider what they might or might
not have to say "for themselves." The poem's manipulation of the Irish capacity for language is, if nothing else, remarkably overt, and means that
Ireland cannot simply be ruled out as one of the sites that impinge on the
scene of its writing. But how does Ireland, and the problems it implied for
the English, make its presence felt?

How this happens is hinted at, I think, in Worden's acute observation
that the "Irish introduce the encomium of Cromwell, but they fade from it,
so that we cannot be sure at what point the poet resumes his own voice."[52]
Against Worden's remark that "we are surprised to hear [the Irish] talking"
in voices that do not sound like their own, we can set this other assertion
that the voices they do speak in sometimes cannot be distinguished from
Marvell's, and to consider the implications of this. Although the "Ode"
itself seems to be, and is, vigorously Anglocentric, the poet's voice does not
always issue from that center. Neither the English poet nor the Irishmen he
imports into his poem can be rendered distinct enough to tell apart, always,
and this gives rise to a kind of modulation within the several cultural registers that intersect in the "Ode": English, Irish, Scottish . . . "British." Finally,
the tonal shifts in Marvell's drifting voice make it impossible to locate him
on the map of Britain that the "Ode" projects. If we could "place" Marvell,
of course, then it might also be simpler for us to pin down the antagonisms
that the poem suggests. But the "Ode" is famously not susceptible to just
this kind of determination.

Consider the consequences of this dislocation in the lines that immediately follow the Irish praise. Cromwell, we are told, is

> Nor yet grown stiffer with command,
> But still in the Republic's hand:
> How fit he is to sway
> That can so well obey. (81–84)

If the Irish are saying this, as Worden implies they might be, then it could
seem that they comment on their conqueror's fitness to rule by comparing
his obedience to the Republic to their own obedience to him. As they acquiesce in Cromwell's triumph, Cromwell yields to "the Commons" (85),
with the result, somewhat paradoxically, that he is now able to "sway"
both his kingdoms, the one he has mastered and now "presents . . . for
his first year's rents" (85–86) *and* the one to which he returns. It has often
been noticed that key passages in the "Ode" can, if pressed, yield a royalist

interpretation. Clearly, overweening ambition could be read into the in-sinuation that the model for Cromwell's government in England might be the military regime that he had established in Ireland. Many of his oppo-nents insisted that he intended just such a rule. In 1649, before the Irish campaign, Clement Walker declared that

> in order to [establish] *Government by the Sword, Cromwel* is voted *to go into Ire-land with his own confiding Officers and Army, with all power Civil and Military for three years*; what doth this import less than that he is to be K[ing]. of *Ireland*? there to practice the first rudiments of Kings-craft, and when he hath in-ured those Semi-barbarians to a *Military Government*, he shall return with his *Janisaries*, and subdue the *English* to the like obedience.[53]

But the English/Irish ambivalence in the voicing that Worden identifies at this point complicates our sense of what position Marvell is taking in mid-century controversies. Is Marvell promoting a Cromwellian government or not by putting these insinuations (if he is) in the mouths of the ostenta-tiously, maybe too ostentatiously, loyal Irish? How do these voices calling from the margins register in England, and with whom?

If we step back to view the "Horatian Ode" as a whole, we can see that it has been set from its beginning on a terrain that is not that of England alone, but is precisely that of the war it commemorates, the war *between* kingdoms. This conflict took Cromwell to an enemy whose language may or may not be echoed in this poem, and then back again to "our isle" (97). From the first lines, in which the "forward youth that would appear" (1) almost, but not quite, steps forward for (as?) the poet, the exact "author-ship" of the "Ode" is in question, and so too is the author's involvement in Ireland. "To what degree," Greene asks in a nuanced reading of the poem, "is the youth to be identified with the twenty-nine-year-old Marvell?" This half-hesitant figure seems ready to

> leave the books in dust,
> And oil the unused armour's rust:
> Removing from the wall
> The corselet of the hall. (5–8)

In these lines, he appears to announce his own willingness to forsake his juvenile love lyrics, as Greene notes, and also to recognize that the con-queror he eulogizes has made a similar renunciation and emergence. "So restless Cromwell could not cease" (9). But "the parallel between the youth and the poet" (and then Cromwell), on which Greene remarks, hints at equivalences that strain our sense of who each of these figures is and what each represents. "Marvell doubtless had no way of knowing," says Greene, of "the ancient Irish use of the word *lorica*, latin for breastplate, the generic term for the apotropaic spells produced by Old Irish culture." Whether or not Marvell could have known this, Greene's etymology indicates the cross-cultural currents that run through just this piece of terminology, and the displacements they might entail. If Marvell, as, say, the youth, takes up a "corselet" to make what Greene calls his "defensive preparation,"[54] and this same item is laden with Irish connotations, is the poet implying that some sort of Irishness accrues to himself? Or that his relation to Cromwell somehow covertly mimics that of the general's Gaelic enemies? Surely not, just as it cannot be that Marvell is hinting at an even more unlikely association between, on the one hand, Cromwell, who (like the youth/poet) girds himself in certain (Irish) armor in preparation for "adventurous war" (11) in Ireland, and, on the other, his Irish enemies and their "defensive preparations" in that same country. None of these linkages is necessary, or even especially plausible. As Greene goes on to point out, the Latin word *lorica* alone can intimate that poet and youth (and perhaps conqueror) are alike engaged in defensively shielding themselves before battle. The resources of language that Marvell and his classically educated English readers had at their command were more than enough for him to accomplish this subtle bit of cross-identification between himself and his poetic subject. Still, as Greene implies, to read the "Ode" in the context established by seventeenth-century English and its burden of Latin terminology may not be enough. Latin had passed into the linguistic heritage of the Gaels too, and had taken on its own meanings there. We cannot know if Marvell knew enough about Gaelic to hear such resonances. In a way, what he did or did not know of this language is not to the point: *lorica*, with all its Latin/Gaelic connotations, is lodged together with "corselet" in the lines he wrote. And perhaps Marvell and his contemporaries did know of this juxtaposition and what it could imply. Since the borders that separated language use in and between the two kingdoms of England and Ireland were, in the nature of their relation, constantly blurred by the comings and goings between them, the reading that Greene so delicately holds out would, I suspect, have been at least a potential exegesis for some in the seventeenth century as well. "Propinquity if nothing else related Ireland and England. Travel between the two islands was quick, cheap and regular."[55] The intermingling of the English and the Irish could produce unexpected hybrids of language: as here, perhaps, one word may bear two distinct senses, or not, or all at once. A verbal crosshatching such as this presents itself to us in the "Ode" as one more poetic crux, one more indeterminacy in a work that already resists reading. We do nothing to "solve" the difficulties of this poem by pointing out that "Ireland" may have been insinuated into its mysteries; it becomes, in a way, more unreadable. But we do expand the cross-cultural range, the "Britishness," if you will, that its mystery encompasses.

To claim this is not to claim that in the "Horatian Ode" Andrew Marvell achieved anything like "authentic" Irish or Scottish voicing. The reading I have offered here militates against the notion that on the British Isles there could be fully "authentic" "national" voices. Moreover, it should be stressed that Wallace is right to say that the "Horatian Ode" is not "about" Ireland. Marvell was not much concerned with representing that country or the speech and sentiments of those who lived there. Despite what English newspapers of the time alleged, we can assume that the Irishmen who "are ashamed" are almost entirely simulacra designed to aid Marvell in lauding a newly great Englishman. However, such ambiguities of national identity do help to explain why the "Ode" cannot be read as an unequivocal paean of praise for Cromwell's conquests on the two islands. True, he brings England subject kingdoms as his "rents" (a word whose implications might give us pause). Ireland is won, and soon Scotland. "And to all states not free / [he] Shall climacteric be" (103–4), ushering in a new reign of English dominance. But this promised British empire comes accompanied by all the anxieties and perplexities that the "Ode" intimates. These can make themselves known by the (re)appearance of a single letter. Cromwell, says Marvell, had "lived reserved and austere" (30) in "his private gardens" (29), and yet he

> Could by industrious valour climb
> To ruin the great work of time,
> And cast the kingdom old
> Into another mould. (33–36)

This is the "fate" against which "justice" "complain[s]" (37), impotently. In the *Miscellaneous Poems* of 1681, as here, Cromwell "cast[s]" one "kingdom old / Into another mould." He disrupts the royal line, and his transformations are confined to his own country. A manuscript exists, though, in which it is "kingdoms" that he reshapes.[56] This conqueror, who has already dismantled the accreted edifice that was "England" and fashioned it anew, is now at work on other principalities as well, tearing them down and recombining them into something else—something "British"—for which the "great work of time" may not have prepared the English.

"The first emperor of Great Britain"

It seems likely that the emergence of this sense of "Britain" in the "Horatian Ode" was despite and not because of Oliver Cromwell. As we saw, the "peace" this general went to Ireland to impose was to be purely English. Cromwell himself had little tolerance for the distinctions a British union would have to accommodate. It may be, though, that it is in its intimations of Britishness that Marvell's "Ode" expresses most powerfully of all the implications of the invasion of Ireland in 1650. Cromwell's campaigns among the British Isles in that year may not have been meant as empire building. Cromwell may not have thought of himself as an emperor. But to many in England and abroad, his victories presaged just that.[57] The "Horatian Ode" is so unavoidably a British poem because the man it lauds was so often regarded as a British conqueror. In September of 1654, an observer in Cologne wrote: "Here is a common report . . . that the protector went into the parliament-house, and there had his peroration for an houre; and that after, the parliament with unanimous consent called his highness emperor; and his title they have written thus: *Oliver, the first emperor of Greate Britaine, and the isles thereunto belonging, allways Caesar, Etc.*"[58] In Venice that same year, Secretary Lorenzo Paulucci had heard that Cromwell "will now assume another title and . . . style himself Emperor of Great Britain."[59] And, from Essex, Edward Hyde speculated in May that Cromwell's title would be *Oliverus Maximus, Insularum Britannicarum Imperator Augustus.*[60] These expectations were not unique to 1654. Two years before, Thomas Manley had addressed a panegyric, *Veni, Vidi, Vici*, to the English Caesar, whom he hailed as the "Lord Generall of Great Brittaine."[61] Nor did they cease after that year. In 1656, George Wither would nominate Cromwell "Lord, of the noblest of all Soveraign Stiles, / Of Britain's Empire, Provinces, and Isles."[62] But the ambitions they attribute to Cromwell were not realized. "First emperor," "allways Caesar"—Cromwell was never to adopt these titles. He was still the "Lord Protector" when he died in 1658. Nonetheless, the phrasing of these titles reveals what Cromwell's ascendancy had come to signify to many of his contemporaries. In Cologne, they were sure that England's ruler would restore Britain to a classical dignity it had not known since Caesar, its Roman conqueror. Yet, he would be the "first" to do so. He, and he alone, would be the one by whose conquests "Greate Britain" would finally be established in the "isles thereunto belonging." The Lord Protector is called upon both to fulfill and obliterate the British history his title invokes, as it reaches for a precedent to give a new name to a form of sovereignty that many believed was now Cromwell's destiny. Cromwell himself resisted the imperial style and the emblems of British dominion. For a time, though, his conquests made something like a "Great Britain" seem splendidly inevitable.

Marvell, for his part, would continue pondering Cromwell's epistemic and political mastery over the British Isles—and beyond—throughout his reign. In the "Horatian Ode," Cromwell knows enough, in England, to delude Charles I into fleeing his palace at Hampton for the Isle of Wight:

> And Hampton shows what part
> He had of wiser art,
> Where, twining subtile fears with hope,
> He wove a net of such a scope,
> That Charles himself might chase
> To Carisbrooke's narrow case (47–52)

Before Cromwell subdues the three kingdoms, he forces his royal predecessor onto a journey that can look like only a feeble, prefiguring parody of his own campaign. In the next Cromwellian poem, "The First Anniversary," Marvell once again celebrated the supremacy that the conqueror's overwhelming knowledge had garnered him among his own British people, but here too Marvell's praise is subtly ambivalent. The poet again presents Cromwell as an Orpheus bringing the English into a civil order that is coextensive with the reach of his own mind:

> The Commonwealth then first together came,
> And each one entered the willing frame;
> All other matter yields, and may be ruled;
> But who the minds of stubborn men can build?
>   (75–78)

Who but Cromwell? This ruler does not deny conflict within the "frame" of his nation, but that is because it poses no threat whatever to his mastery: "The crossest spirits here do take their part" (89). Just as buttresses thrust from contrary directions to support a roof, "the resistance of opposed minds, / The fabric (as with arches) stronger binds" (95–96). Such a reign of certainty, says Marvell, benefits the English, who achieve their own dominion through Cromwell's power. Specifically, it keeps them from devolving into "the ancient Pict" (318). All manner of menacing interlopers—"Sorcerers, atheists, Jesuits possessed" (314)—may try to entice the English into false readings of the Scriptures, but their "king" (311) spits them out, and by protecting doctrinal purity, ensures their national purity as well. As Cromwell's knowing becomes the principle that holds English identity together on the British Isles, it also protects England against foreign threats by producing an effect of "unknowing" in those who are not English. "Is this," an alien prince is imagined to ask,

> the nation that we read
> Spent with both wars, under a captain dead,
> Yet rig a navy while we dress us late,

And ere we dine, raze and rebuild their state?
What oaken forests, and what golden mines!
What mints of men, what union of designs! (349–54)

To this potentate, whom Marvell summons into his poem much as he invokes the pacified Irish, all that stands between England and his own designs
on it is Cromwell's single purpose and the mysteries he provokes in others.

The nation had been ours, but his one soul
Moves the great bulk, and animates the whole.
He secrecy with number hath enchased. (379–81)

As Pierre Legouis notes, what Marvell "means in plain English [is] that
[Cromwell] has begun hostilities with great armaments without declaring
war," which he was then doing as he launched an attack on Spain's possessions in the West Indies.[63] However, the effect of the lines is not to
create the sense that what is English—as language or nation—is plainly evident. To be English (and thus, presumably, to be able to read this poem)
is not, or not entirely, to belong within certain borders. More powerfully,
it is to be drawn within a circle of knowingness centering around the
magisterial figure of Oliver Cromwell. From outside this circle, England is
un"read"able, but amazing in its unity and its martial prowess. From inside,
England is a shared secret, "enchased"—ornamented—by Cromwell with
"number." And Cromwell is not the only Englishman who works in secrets
here. "Number," of course, has more than one significance. It is the precise
quantification imposed on affairs of state by Cromwell. It is also, I suggest, the "numbers" of this very poem, offered up by Marvell (who, in the
"Ode," refuses to leave "His numbers languishing" [4]). Marvell implies that
Cromwell's numbers and his own are linked; the poet "seems to have privileged information of the Protector's design, still wrapped in mystery."[64] To
read and grasp that design is to read and grasp the poem. Alternatively, to
be baffled by the one is to be baffled by the other, and so to be uncompre-
hending, un-Cromwellian, un-English.

Our reading of the "Ode" compels us to ask, though: is Marvell claiming for himself an absolute unity with the mysteries of Cromwell's governance? Or is the Marvellian voice also heard in the plaintive speculation of
the foreigner, pondering Cromwell, "riddle of the wise" (383)? The poem
ends ambiguously:

Pardon, great Prince, if thus their fear or spite
More than our love and duty do thee right.
I yield, nor further will the prize contend,
So that we both alike may miss our end. (395–98)

As in the "Ode," the most copious praise of Cromwell is placed in the mouths of subordinated aliens. "Our love and duty" seem almost suspect, as if the fearful devotion that these others attain by "fear or spite" is not altogether possible for Cromwell's more ostensibly "loyal" English subjects. And this English poet? With whom has he been "contend[ing]" in his verse? With these aliens? To praise (or to dispraise) Cromwell? Is his "end" in some way at variance with the Lord Protector's? Marvell's poems to Cromwell exalt the knowing power of the British ruler he serves. In "The First Anniversary," as in the "Ode," Marvell conceived of a ruler whose supremacy over several nations arose from a splendid certainty in which his own poetry could take part. But whether Marvell always means to promote such power, and do only that, and whether he always is, or can be, at one with that power are questions that his verse never quite forecloses.

"Love adds its intimate note"

In the years just prior to 1670, a union of England and Scotland was once again proposed, this time to ameliorate economic problems that had arisen between the two kingdoms after the Restoration. Although Charles II had been quick to abolish the Anglo-Scottish union that Cromwell had put in place, he was now keen for such a consolidation under his own auspices, much like his grandfather at the turn of the century. In September of 1670, a gathering of Scottish and English commissioners convened, and the "articles [the king] submitted for discussion were in fact precisely the ones that James I had drafted when he first formulated a plan for union."[65] Eventually, this proposal, like its predecessor, would be rejected by the nations it was meant to bring together. Negotiations came to a halt when the English commissioners refused to countenance the Scots' demand that all members of their own estates be admitted to a proposed joint parliament.[66] More than legal technicalities prompted their objections, however. English merchants were loath to forgo the trading advantage that separation between the kingdoms gave them, and many Englishmen simply "hated and despised the very name of Scotland."[67] Writing in 1670, one especially virulent pamphleteer abused the country itself, which, he said, was "full of Lakes and Loughs, and they well stocked with Islands; so that a Map thereof looks like a Pillory Coat bespattered all over with Dirt and rotten Eggs, some pieces of the Shells, floating here and there, representing the Islands."[68] Its people, he said, were "proud, arrogant, vain-glorious Boasters, bloody, barbarous, and Inhuman Butchers. Couzenage and Theft is in Perfection amongst them, and they are perfect *English* haters; they shew their Pride in exulting themselves and depressing their Neighbors." To join with Scotland, he insisted, was to cede cultural superiority and, especially, political prerogative. "When the Palace at *Edinburgh* is finished, they expect his Majesty will leave his rotten house at *Whitehall*, and live splendidly among his nown countrymen the *Scots*; for they say, That *Englishmen* are very much beholden to them, that we have their King amongst us."[69] No more than at the turn of the century could those who were British in name conceive of themselves as united in fact.

It was in the midst of this controversy and surrounded by invective of this sort that Andrew Marvell lifted from his own "The Last Instructions to a Painter" (1667) a lingering, 48-line tribute to a brave, beautiful soldier from Scotland who had died for England and put that passage at the beginning of a poem advocating a British union of the two kingdoms. Around 1644, John Cleveland had penned a famous satire, "The Rebel Scot," excoriating the covenanters who crossed the Tweed to aid the English Parliament against the Crown. Now, Marvell imagined him among "the Elysian glades" (2), forced by the ghosts of other poets to praise this Scottish youth, and so to do penance. Cleveland limns an attractive portrait of Archibald Douglas:

> on whose lovely chin
> The early down but newly did begin;
> And modest beauty yet his sex did veil,
> While envious virgins hope he is a male. (15-18)

If Douglas seems oblivious to his own beauty, others in the poem are not:

> His shady locks curl back themselves to seek:
> Nor other courtship knew but to his cheek.
> Oft as he in chill Eske or Seine by night
> Hardened and cooled those limbs so soft, so white,
> Among the reeds, to be espied by him,
> The nymphs would rustle; he would forward swim.
> They sighed and said, 'Fond boy, why so untame
> That fliest Love's fires, reserved for other flame?' (19-26)

This paragon, who in actuality was something older than a boy and married, had been the commander of a Scottish company during England's recent war with the Dutch, and had died upon the deck of HMS *Royal Oak*. As the enemy retreated down the Medway in 1667, they had fired his ship, and although Englishmen had fled, Douglas chose to burn to death "rather than live to be reproached with having deserted his command."[70] "[W]onder[ing] much at those that run away," says Marvell, Douglas

> Like a glad lover the fierce flames . . . meets,
> And tries his first embraces in their sheets.
> His shape exact, which the bright flames enfold
> Like the sun's statue stands of burnished gold.
>
> . . .
>
> But when in his immortal mind he felt
> His altering form and soldered limbs to melt,
> Down on the deck he laid him down and died,
> With his dear sword reposing by his side:
> And on the flaming planks so rests his head
> As one that hugs himself in a warm bed. (43–46, 51–56)

For Marvell, Douglas's courage demonstrates both the "glories of his ancient race" (39) and his touching dependence on the approval of his superiors. "[S]ecret joy in his calm soul does rise" to know that George Monck,
his English commander, "looks on to see how Douglas dies" (41–42).
Douglas does not disparage his own Scottishness, nor does he aspire to the
Englishness of the Duke of Albemarle. Rather, he achieves a better condition, Britishness, that a properly respectful observer like Monck must recognize. Both Douglas's demise and his own poem, Marvell implies, make
the same argument: distinctions between the two kingdoms should be acknowledged, but are ultimately meaningless and must give way to a union
that transcends them. "[A]t thy flame," the poet predicts,

> Our nations melting, thy colossus frame,
> Shall fix a foot on either neighboring shore,
> And join those lands that seemed to part before.
>
> (71–74)

Douglas's immolation melds the Scots and English together, and his flam-
ing body comes to emblematize the text in which he is celebrated:

> Fortunate boy, if e'er my verse may claim
> That matchless grace to propagate thy fame,
> When Oeta and Alcides are forgot
> Our English youth shall sing the valiant Scot. (59–62)

The erotic overtones of this encomium are hard to miss, but difficult to
characterize. Marvell is at pains to present Douglas as a beauty—his "lovely
chin," his "limbs so soft, so white"—but not to make it especially clear who
finds him beautiful. Douglas withholds his "modest beauty" from women,
fleeing the "nymphs" who set themselves "[a]mong the reeds, to be espied
by him." They desire his "hardened and cooled" body, but the very hair
on it, "[h]is shady locks[,] curl back themselves to seek." This is the only

"courtship" that he knows. Does Marvell mean to imply by this merely that Douglas is virginal, or, perhaps, that his appeal is rather to men? In one of the few readings of "The Loyal Scot," Diana Trevino Benet neatly sidesteps this issue. She urges us to see Marvell's poem as "a personal and a personally significant version of the Narcissus myth." Douglas, this reader insists, "appeals tremendously to women," but he also has what she calls a "self-reflexive bent." "The virginal youth is not interested in seeing girls."[71] He is instead an unsexed "androgyne,"[72] embedded in "timeless psychic structures," of which narcissism is one. He is devoted solely to "himself as an object of admiration."[73] It has been argued recently, though, that claims for the "androgyny" of the erotics of seventeenth-century English poets often work to mask the queerness of the pleasures they offer.[74] Douglas is appealing and pointedly shuns women, and it might seem that he is implicitly meant for other admirers who will be equally delighted by the limbs, the locks that Marvell delineates. Douglas is "not interested in seeing girls," but might it be that boys want to see him? Even this supposition, however, that the erotics of "The Loyal Scot" are indeed homoerotics, is complicated because Douglas, as Marvell describes him, is not (yet) male or female, and the erotics of the poem, thus, can be neither fully "hetero" nor "homo." They are something else, something that cannot be reduced to either of these binaries. The categories that would have to be in place for us to guess at the "sexuality" intimated here are oddly displaced, falling, as it were, both "before" and "after" the moment when such identity is assigned to one of (only) two genders. At first, Douglas is virginal, but also prepubescent, his "lovely chin" adorned with "early down" so faint that the "envious virgins" who pine for him cannot be sure that "he is a male": "modest beauty yet his sex did veil."[75] And later, when Douglas does lose his virginity, and thus when he achieves a kind of "sexuality," it is not to one of the nymphs who desires him (or anyone else who might do so), but to the consummating fire that envelops him on the deck of the *Royal Oak*. "Like a glad lover the fierce flames he meets / And tries his first embraces in their sheets" (43–44). Marvell seems to be asking us to imagine a type of sex (and of "sexuality") that becomes possible only at a specific, politically fraught moment: when national identity gives way to something higher, and the body is caught up in a delightful disintegration that signals the "union" of "ancient race[s]." "Round the transparent fire about him glows" (47), "His burning locks adorn[ing] his face divine" (50). What Marvell offers in "The Loyal Scot" is not just a sexual politics, but politics *as* sex, and of an especially rigorous kind. "His altering form and soldered limbs . . . melt[ing]," Douglas becomes, not the woman he might once have seemed, and not even a generic man, but a Briton, "warm" and in bed. William Empson found these lines on the martyred youth "disgusting, and all too likely to well up from the worst perversion."[76] His is a virulent reading, but it is more responsive to the passage than Benet's. Crudely, he registers the intense, disturbing politico-erotic pleasures of this burning British boy.

Now, does it help us to understand the opening of "The Loyal Scot" to know that in his later years Marvell was frequently denounced as a "sodomite"? ("Six pamphlets attacked the [author of] the First Part of *The Rehearsal Transpros'd* and most of them accused [him] of . . . sodomy."[77]) And further, is there a sense in which "The Loyal Scot" is a "sodomitical" text? I think not, if by "sodomitical" we would refer, quite simply and ahistorically, to Marvell's "sexuality," and specifically to his "homosexuality." The argument made by Michel Foucault is by now commonplace[78] but still irresistible: this category emerges late in the nineteenth century, which rules out the hypothesis that such a term might apply to Marvell in 1670. Nor do I think we can say that this poem was "sodomitical," if by that we refer to "a more radical gender undecidability"[79] that critics of the period, influenced by queer theory,[80] have begun to discern in the (homo)erotics of certain poets. As Eve Sedgwick has noted, and as we have seen so far in "The Loyal Scot," "the sexual context of [the early modern period] is too far irrecoverable for us to be able to disentangle boasts, confessions, undertones, overtones, jokes, the unthinkable, the taken-for-granted, the unmentionable-but-often-done-anyway, etc."[81] Marvell's poem insinuates an erotics that *might* be homoerotic, and is obviously not "heteroerotic," but still is something different (if not entirely so) from either. We need a new term, or, if not, and "The Loyal Scot" is a "sodomitical" text, then we need to be clear on precisely how it is so. Now, in fact, I do think the term "sodomitical" applies to this poem. "The Loyal Scot" relies tacitly, though not solely, on homosocial male-male affinity among Britons. At every point it interinsinuates the political question of late-seventeenth-century Britain with the questions of its *eros*. But it does this in ways that are specific to the moment of the poem's inscription.

We can locate this historical moment with the help of Alan Bray. He has argued that "if one looks at the place homosexuality occupied in English society during the century and a half from the close of the Middle Ages to the mid 1600s, there is little discernible change and little sign that there ever would be." But "if we move only fifty years ahead, to the close of the seventeenth century, the picture is radically different."[82] In 1650, the "sodomite" was still an abstract type. However often this abominable figure was castigated, "he" could rarely be located. So unimaginable were "his" violations of the divine order that, whatever Englishmen and women of the time were doing, they rarely thought of it as anything so opprobrious as "sodomy." Fifty years later, a great change had taken place. By 1700, says Bray, it had become possible to conceive of the "homosexual" as a distinct "individual," one who was aberrant from society but not beyond its ken. This man, known as a "molly," belonged to a defined subculture with its own gathering places and "its own distinctive conventions: ways of dressing, of talking, distinctive gestures and distinctive acts with an understood meaning, its own jargon."[83] By 1700, one might even "be" this man, though to do this was to take on an identity that was, according to Bray, truly unprecedented. Within the half century that separates the regime of the "sodomite" from that of the "molly," Bray locates a radical break. "There is a gap, a profound discontinuity" between these two.[84] So sharp is this cleavage that "there is no linear history of homosexuality [in these years] to be written at all."[85] English society changes, says this historian, and with it "homosexuality" "itself."

What Marvell's "The Loyal Scot" suggests is that this rupture was rather less clean, and was more interestingly messy, than Bray allows. Written (or rather, assembled from various pieces) around 1670, this poem falls just in the middle of the "gap" that opens in Bray's account, and, as we might expect, the "sexuality" that it intimates conforms entirely to neither of the two "homosexualities" he describes. This is a text for which we need to conceive of a "sexuality" that partakes of both these and can be reduced to neither, a "sexuality" of the gap, as it were. By accusing Marvell of "sodomy," his enemies were clearly trying to bracket him within the older regime, whose virulence still lingers in 1670. But, discomfiting as these attacks may have been for Marvell, they led to no legal action against him, and his membership in the political nation of his day can hardly be questioned. Moreover, the affinities that "The Loyal Scot" seems to imply lack any sense of the strenuous defiance that Bray detects in, for instance, the earlier declarations of Christopher Marlowe, whose "thorough-going rejection of the intellectual climate of his time" was a "radical and dangerous solution to the generally shared disapproval of homosexuality."[86] Such an extreme stance must be taken when the "sodomite" can barely be comprehended, much less tolerated. But neither does "The Loyal Scot" call upon the not yet emergent subculture of the "molly," with its developed conventions and "understood meanings." This, apparently, was not a poem that could anticipate a readership that would quickly recognize it as its own. "The Loyal Scot" is instead a work in search of a "sexuality" around which and within which it can articulate itself. With the regime of "sodomy" vaporizing and the regime of the "molly" not yet in place, Marvell can ground his poetics in neither. If this is "sodomy," it is the "sodomy" of a period that has outlasted this term and has yet to find another with which to appall itself.

A Usefully Confused Category

Questions about Marvell's alleged proclivities are not new. They figured in the commentary on him in the seventeenth century, and they are echoed to this day: "Was he quite alone there, with only a servant-boy?"[87] Sometimes these echoes are faint. In 1965, for example, Pierre Legouis claimed that when the poet was in his thirties he had "developed gradually not only admiration but love for [Oliver] Cromwell,"[88] and, moreover, that this was a "love" he kept "in his heart all his life long." Even after the Restoration, said Legouis, when Marvell found himself serving a royal master, he always "oppos[ed] England's greatness under 'Old Noll' to her abjection under Charles II." Legouis thought that he could trace the "curve of [Marvell's] feelings" in his poems on Cromwell. He drew an arch from the early panegyric of "An Horatian Ode upon Cromwell's Return from Ireland," which expressed "admiration in the Latin meaning," through "approving admiration" in "The First Anniversary of the Government under His Highness the Lord Protector," to the funeral elegy of "A Poem upon the Death of his late Highness the Lord Protector," where, at last, "love adds its intimate note."[89] And sometimes the echoes are resounding. In 1978, William Empson suggested that Andrew Marvell was queer. He didn't put it that way, of course. "Many readers of [Marvell's] love-poetry feel that he has an uneasy relation to the girls addressed," Empson opined; "he is intensely interested, readily fascinated, but he does not seem to like them much." And what about his "Damon the Mower," in which the poet "has praised the smell of a farm hand"?[90] How obliquely Empson phrases his allegation, and how attuned he is to the cadences of the abuse that Marvell heard in the seventeenth century! Marvell's proclivities, said Empson, "must have occurred to a number of people who kept tactfully silent about it, but," he hazarded, "it has a relevance."[91] Then, in a later essay, Empson elaborated on his speculations. By the mid-1670's, he thought, Marvell may have had a few sexual experiences "with young men." Eventually, he arranged a secret marriage to Mary Palmer, his housekeeper, in order to fend off suspicions that he was a "sodomite" or, perhaps, impotent. "When men get drunk together they often become affectionate," Empson pointed out, but, he was quick to add, they "do not want to make love, only to boast about their successes with women." Now, Marvell had something to boast about, having discovered that "his reactions in bed with Mrs Palmer were entirely nor-mal." And so, Empson concludes in a sentence that nicely houses both the denials and insinuations that he has been making, Marvell "felt equipped to get drunk with men, and thus coax them into doing what he wanted."[92]

Both of these critics come close to considering "sodomy" in a political register, but without fully doing so. Their claims, though, raise questions that become more perplexing the more they are pressed upon. Legouis's comments, for instance, are crucial for what they suggest of the imbrica-tions of "love" and politics in the work of this poet and polemicist. He is right, surely, to imply that there must have been some affective burden to Marvell's engagement with the man he once addressed as "great Crom-well," "Angelic Cromwell," "great Prince,"[93] and that this was a regard that went beyond mere political expediency. And he is also right to imply that this regard should be considered together with, and perhaps should be con-trasted to, Marvell's relations with Charles II. But how was Marvell's "love" for Cromwell—or is it "admiration"?—articulated in the "Horatian Ode," a poem whose seeming ambivalences toward the returning hero are so well known? And what does Marvell's portrayal of Charles I "bow[ing] his comely head / Down as upon a bed" (63–64) in the same poem suggest of "love"? What, after all, *does* he mean by "love"? Or Empson, for that matter? Empson acknowledges that Marvell was "a politician with unscrupulous enemies,"[94] but he shows little interest in scrutinizing the "secrets about business and politics" he must have possessed; "these would be fairly easy to keep."[95] Instead, it is what he calls Marvell's "sexual constitution"[96] that exerts the fascination of the open secret. It becomes the enigma that can explain—though the critic will not say exactly how—the poet's perplexing career. It is the mystery that isn't, "tactfully" concealed (as in Empson's own writing) by sympathetic contemporaries who were in the know, openly proclaimed, very untactfully, by his enemies.

That neither of these critics considered Marvell's supposed "sodomy" in more explicitly political terms is all the more jarring because in this period this charge was almost always leveled together with other accusations of civil disruption. As Bray has shown, earlier in the century the category of "sodomy" "covered . . . hazily a whole range of sexual acts, of which sexual acts between people of the same sex were only a part. . . . But it differed . . . fundamentally [from current notions of 'homosexuality'] in that it was not only a sexual crime. It was also a political and religious crime, and it was this that explains most clearly why it was regarded with such dread."[97] Sodom-ites were lumped together with an alleged cabal of others who "threatened social stability—heretics, spies, traitors, Catholics."[98] Conversely, all such miscreants were assumed to be (at least potentially) sodomites. As an omni-bus term of vilification, "sodomy" designated not only proscribed sexual practice but an egregious offense against the social order itself. Did this opprobrium attach itself to Marvell? And if not, why? Criticism of Mar-vell, which mostly ignores the charge that he was a "sodomite," also ignores these questions, or evades them, decoupling accusations that in the poet's own time could scarcely *not* be heard together.

Hearing them together now, and taking them seriously, may give us a better sense not only of the slurs directed at Marvell, but of his (tacit) rejoinder to them. If a certain kind of sex has political implications, how might politics be used to imply a certain kind of sex? Jonathan Goldberg has done the most to restore the term "sodomy" to the critical lexicon, and here his thinking can help to point up what Marvell's alleged "sodomy" may have entailed in 1670, and what its relation to the British politics of the day may have been. The early modern "concept of sodomy," Goldberg argues generally, was at once null and overdetermined. On the one hand, it often corresponded to nothing except the period's own revulsions, and named only the empty category of the unassimilated, entirely abjected "Other." On the other hand, there was also a good deal of "work that the term [was] able to do—and continues to do—precisely because [it] remains incapable of exact definition. Always mobilizable because of its confusions, it is also always capable of deconstruction." [99] Implied, though not fully developed here, is a complex sense of how "sodomy" could have become a nexus for politico-erotic controversy. Suppose we grant, as we must, that even in 1670 it was the very "bankruptcy" of the term "sodomy" that made it such an effective instrument of slander and accusation. Since it had little to do with clearly defined sexual practices—and still less to do with any "alterna-tive" sexual identity that might have been derived from those practices—it could be used to vilify almost anyone for transgressions alleged or actual, and thus to exclude him from sanctioned community. Goldberg reminds us that "many people died . . . under the label." [100] This is the "work" that the category of "sodomy" could still do in Marvell's time, and, presumably, as I have said, some of it was being done in the accusations directed against him by Samuel Parker and his cohort. But is this all the "work" that the category could do? And, especially, is this all the "work" the category could do at this time, as it was slowly losing coherence and plausibility? Goldberg is unclear about *who*, at any time, could exploit the "confusions" of "sodomy," who, that is, might have been able to "mobilize" its many and various implica-tions, and in what ways. Was it only and always the "sodomite's" antago-nist who could manipulate this labile category for his own purposes? Or, could the vagaries built into the "concept of sodomy" sometimes also be seized upon by those who were more ambiguously positioned—like Marvell, evidently—to imply affiliations that escaped or exceeded those which were authorized? That the term "sodomy" "remains incapable of exact definition" now makes such critical investigations as Goldberg's possible and necessary. That it was just as incapable of exact definition circa 1670 may have made it possible for "sodomy" to be "deconstructed" from a number of sites within the existing apparatus of "sexual" identity, and not always the predictable ones. Moreover, it may have been possible for "sodomy" to be *reconstructed* there too—but to what extent?—from those sites, so that it could hint at alliances that had no ready articulation outside what could be fashioned ad hoc from the nebulous vocabulary of a still unspeakable "love." Perhaps, the "concept of sodomy" was, or at some times could be, a usefully confused category, and not only to those whose only use for it was denunciation. The capaciousness of this term, and its capacity for slippage and misprision, should alert us to the likelihood that within the penumbra of what could be called "sodomy" there came to be implied relations that had no exact analogue in the available understandings of male-male bonding, even those of "friendship" or "patronage."

Now, what Marvell has done in "The Loyal Scot," I think, is to seize upon an ongoing controversy in order to imply just such a relation. The controversy that he took hold of in 1670 was the recrudescent debate over Britain. The poem that he found the occasion to (re)write in that year seems to have been meant to elicit two responses from its audience: first, they will join with the assertively loyal poet in upholding the British union that Charles II has recently been advocating, and, second, they will accept Archibald Douglas as an ideal embodiment of this coming together of the king's divided peoples. In life and death, this comely young man dedicated himself to the glory of a greater Britain. By his demise, he adumbrates an eroticism that escapes (or is indifferent to, perhaps) the conventionalities of heterosexual love. This is a "sexuality" that is emerging *between* regimes, a "homosexuality"—to use Bray's anachronism—that is not the "sodomy" of the recent past, nor yet its successor. Instead, the "sexuality" of "The Loyal Scot" is that of a discrete moment. The highly ambivalent, erotically charged "union" the poem offers would be quite unthinkable without the (already shifting) framework of political tropes around which it is fashioned. Conversely, while Marvell's poem is couched in the rhetoric of Britain, it also infuses Britishness with newly emerging, not yet fully "sexual," possibilities. Indeed, Marvell may well have acquired a reputation as a "sodomite" in the late seventeenth century in part because he partook in this way of the "confusions" that the term "sodomy" was supposed to police, and increasingly could not. We may hesitate to call Marvell's verse "sodomitical." But if we hesitate, remember that there were those among Marvell's contemporaries who did not. His enemies claimed to know that he himself, at least, was a "sodomite." And maybe he was, and in the sense they meant. But if he was that, he was not only that. In 1670, he could not be.

"No more discourse of Scotch or English race"

The overt politics of "The Loyal Scot" can seem polemical and dogmatic, and indeed they are so. Its text is mostly devoted to attacks on Scottish bishops whose presumptuous bickering over theology divides the "nation" (131), blocks a union, and detracts from the dignity of the English king. "Does Charles the Second reign," Marvell asks, "or Charles the Two?" (197). Does his royal domain have one head, or is it like "that Scotch twin-headed man" who had "a single body," but was "two-necked" (186–87)? This freak stands as a grotesque counterpart to the radiant, transmogrifying body of Archibald Douglas. "Well that Scotch monster and our bishops sort" (198); they split the nation that the enraptured youth brings together. To oppose these clerics, Marvell conjures up an encompassing vision of Britain. Interestingly, this union denies much that was implicit in Marvell's own "Horatian Ode" of twenty years before. The poet was bound to respond, of course, to the imperatives of a new regime in government and a new climate of intellectual opinion. Still, "The Loyal Scot" also looks remarkably like a retrospective self-commentary—and self-censure. If Marvell had reread the "Ode" in 1670 and then sat down to write another poem refuting all of the insinuations of the first, "The Loyal Scot" could be that poem.[101] As we would expect, there are continuities between the poems. A similar impulse toward a transcendent union appears to animate both. Charles II will assume the mantle that Cromwell refused. *He* will be *Insularum Britannicarum Imperator Augustus.*[102] The first poem, however, provokes and sustains the most searching questions about the plausibility and consequences of a British union. The second seems not to do much more than proclaim its obvious virtues. Indeed, "The Loyal Scot" is assertively skeptical that there are or ever were any real distinctions among the British peoples. The Tweed River, says Marvell, does not divide Scottish vice from English virtue. The world contains only two "nations": "The good, the bad, and those mixed everywhere" (237). The uneasy "supranationalism" (to use Hirst's phrase) of the "Ode" becomes an out and out universalism that is

"British" only on the way to superseding nationality altogether. "Nation is all but name as shibboleth," asserts Marvell,

> Where a mistaken accent causes death.
> In paradise names only Nature showed,
> At Babel names from pride and discord flowed;
> And ever since men with a female spite,
> First call each other names, and then they fight.
> Scotland and England! (246–52)

A new community, that of "rational men" (256), knows how to avoid intra-British conflict by speaking as one, and in one clear, seamless discourse that is pointedly the rhetorical antithesis of the linguistically overdetermined "Ode." The poet whose verse in 1650 was ambiguously saturated by the linguistic drifts of the British Isles desires in 1670 a language that elides verbal and national distinctions altogether. "Say but a Scot," says Marvell, "and straight we fall to sides, / That syllable like a Pict's wall divides" (254–55). In these lines, he manages both to traduce national identity and exploit its categories. Not only does Scottishness inhere in a mere "syllable" which might just as well be discarded, but even the tendency to make distinctions such as "Scottish" *is* Scottish—or at least "Pictish"—and therefore as uncivil as the wall "they" boorishly attempt to erect across the island. "Prick down the point (whoever has the art)," Marvell demands,

> Where Nature Scotland does from England part.
> Anatomists may sooner fix the cells
> Where life resides, or understanding dwells:
> But this we know, though that exceed their skill,
> That whosoever separates them doth kill. (75–80)

Marvell derides the achievements of the "Nature"-dissecting "anatomist," yet his own thinking betrays the influence of the "new science" of his day, with its disdain for localism and linguistic particularity. "Experimental philosophy," said Robert Boyle, the chemist, "gave me so much aversion and contempt for the empty study of words, that not only I have visited divers countries, whose languages I could never vouchsafe to study, but I could never be induced to learn the native tongue of the kingdom, I was born and for some years bred in."[103] (That kingdom was Ireland. Gaelic was the language Boyle would not speak.) In a similar vein, Marvell disparages both the very idea of distinct places in the British Isles, and argues that, in any case, all that distinguishes them is the distortions marked in "empty words." But Marvell does not look for the establishment of a universal language, which many of those who championed "experimental philosophy" were advocating. He grounds his project elsewhere. For the political might, the certainty that can "extirpate from each loyal breast, / That senseless rancor against interest" (258–59), Marvell places his hopes on the man who heads England's government, as he had done in the 1650's. All Britons, he declares, must join in acknowledging the ruler in whom and by whom a union may truly be accomplished:

> Charles, our great soul, this only understands
> He our affection both and will commands.
> And where twin sympathies cannot atone,
> Knows the last secret how to make them one. (262–65)

Marvell, like Shakespeare before him,[104] has recourse to an entomological metaphor:

> Just so the prudent husbandman who sees
> The idle tumult of his factious bees,
> The morning dews, and flowers neglected grown,
> The hive a comb-case, every bee a drone,
> Powders them o'er, till none discern their foes,
> And all themselves in meal and friendship close;
> The insect kingdom straight begins to thrive,
> And each works honey for the common hive. (266–73)

The Britain that Marvell promotes is a uniform country where every difference has been obliterated by the epistemic mastery of Charles II: "One king, one faith, one language, and one isle" (260). It is inhabited by eminently reasonable, entirely unequivocal men who all talk and think like one rather opinionated Englishman, Andrew Marvell.

"The Loyal Scot" begins to look less dogmatic, however, and less obviously polemical, when we consider not only what it declares but how Marvell may have meant its declarations to be received. The poet is vociferous on behalf of his king's dream of British union, but as events would soon prove, the audience he was addressing could not, finally, overcome the "senseless rancour against interest" that split "One king, one faith, one language, and one isle" into many discordant parts. The unanimity that Marvell professes to desire could not be sustained. For much of this poem, Marvell writes as if he believed that the unified Britain that he champions truly existed at that moment, as if his readers were even now de facto members of that "nation," and as if his only task was to bring them to recognize their mutual obligations as Britons. But, given the anti-Scottish animus of many of the English in that period, Marvell must have realized that his rhetorical task was more complex than that. Consequently, it seems,

"The Loyal Scot" also accommodates the more skeptical—and more know-ing—reader. It tacitly acknowledges the tenuousness of the strictly political union Marvell promotes, and at the same time it intimates the possibility of a "nation" of another (though related) kind. Marvell accomplishes the first by disturbing his readers' relation to Charles II, the monarch who is supposedly the guarantor of British union. While Marvell seems to have appointed this king to be Cromwell's successor as Britain's epistemic over-lord, his treatment of him in that capacity is no less ambivalent than in his paeans to the Lord Protector. Cromwell, as we recall, was the ruler who "enchased" secrecy with "number." Here, Charles II "knows the last secret." Both achieve their grandeur by establishing a rule of personal wisdom over their obstreperous subjects, knowing better than they do what "makes them one." But are these subjects "one" in truth, or is it only in the king's mind that they come together? The poem both suggests that this is a false dis-tinction, and then reinscribes it. Charles is "our great soul," says Marvell, and thus "our" sense of division among "ourselves" is illusionary. "We"—as Englishmen or Scotsmen—do not signify except as are included in the body politic that "we" make up. As "our" animating "soul," Charles *is* Brit-ain, and so then are "we" because he knows that "we" are, whatever "we" may think. But, possibly, there are limits to what this king understands. In fact, the lines can be read as implying that *all* Charles understands is that he can "command" (demand, but perhaps coerce?) "our" affection and will. Marvell, admittedly, does not make clear what falls outside of the royal understanding, but this residuum does not vanish with the announcement that the king knows the "last secret." The husbandman-king looks over his hive, and, seeing the "idle tumult of his factious bees," "[p]owders them o'er, till none discern their foes." Are the bees as deceived as Marvell seems to say, though, or just the beekeeper? (To ask this question another way: would readers of this time, whether English or Scottish, have been convinced by Marvell's claims of British uniformity, and, if not, would they have found this metaphor at all compelling? Could they have regarded it with anything but irony? Did Marvell expect them to do otherwise?) Moreover, what be-comes of the national differences that are "powdered o'er" by the Crown? This tincture of Britishness seems a flimsy way for Charles to bind the "fac-tious" peoples of the island together, since it requires a deliberate blindness to conflicts that lie, as we often say, "just beneath the surface." Perhaps Mar-vell means to suggest that denying conflict in this way actually could create a sense of inclusiveness among the king's diverse subjects. Or perhaps he means to suggest that this denial is merely a royal convenience, a requisite obfuscation; the more knowing reader will acquiesce. Or perhaps he means to align himself with a reader who is more knowing than the king himself. But, as in his poems on Cromwell, Marvell does not allow us to settle such questions easily. We do not know for certain what Charles knows or how much of his knowledge we are meant to share. Instead, as in the "Horatian Ode," Marvell's verse leads us into epistemic problems that are keyed to the "twin sympathies" of Britishness, and that leave "us," the very readers who are supposedly "one," more conscious than ever of what divides us from "ourselves" and among "ourselves."

The appeal to national belonging in Marvell's final poem is thus curiously refracted: it insists that the reader acknowledge his loyalty to a British nation that has the authority of Charles II's royal will behind it, it subtly disrupts that kingly authority, and it intimates a belonging in some sort of community housed within Britain. There is a sense in which this poem is written to no one, at least no one whose overt politics were exactly those that seem to be implied, and who did not need to be instructed in precisely those allegiances that the poem may seem to take for granted. In part, the project of "The Loyal Scot" is to create this reader, and so too the Britain to which he might belong. Marvell, it seems, would poetically fashion a subject capable of imagining a polity under Charles that includes both himself and the people on the "other" side of the Tweed whom he has learned to think of as aliens. But, at the same time, the poem also gestures toward an association that is not named here openly, perhaps because in the latter decades of the seventeenth century it cannot yet be named. Manifestly, this poem is intended first of all for the reader who can peruse its lurid, egregious, and disturbing opening and then work out the relation between his or her own responses to its hypereroticism and the argument for British union that Marvell is making. The rhetorical structure of the poem, from encomium to polemic to peroration, dictates that no one can come to the burden of the poet's appeal for a unified domain without first coming to recognize—or refusing to recognize—the appeal of young Douglas. Membership in *this* "British" "nation" requires an appreciation for the overdetermined "sexuality" that is so enticingly represented in the young Scottish officer. It is inevitable, moreover, that as the reading progresses, questions about the "gender" of Douglas—male? female? something else?—will become involved in the questions about his nationality. Is he "Scottish"? "English"? something else? something "British"? Marvell invokes both these categories only to trouble them, and by doing so he implies a Britain that might tacitly exist, or might need to be collectively envisioned, in which men come together in one shared acceptance of what binds them politically (under Charles II) and aesthetically (in their regard for Archibald Douglas, and, of course, the poetry of Andrew Marvell). If this community is not "homosexual"—and it cannot be—it is certainly "homosocial." "[M]en with a female spite," says Marvell, "first call each other names, and then they fight." Marvell calls for a Britain without specious naming, without gratuitous conflict—and, noticeably, without women.

Marvell assertively couches "The Loyal Scot" in the rhetoric of the British nation-state, but he also hints at the presence within the polity of those whose loyalties are not entirely those of it, nor entirely distinguishable from it. If this subcommunity is itself a "nation," it is of a very specific and transitory sort, one that was not so much "imagined"[105] but implied, and that in the lines of a minor poem written to promote a failed political initiative. In the years around 1670, none of the forms of association Marvell promoted, not a British union, not the more-than-British bond he also implies, could be fully realized. Both, of course, are almost entirely hypothetical in that year—truly "imaginary," that is to say, and not yet imagined communities. It may be, though, that Marvell aligned himself with Charles's proposal *because* it is as yet unrealized and, as the politically savvy Marvell probably knew well enough, unrealizable. The events of the day presented him with an opportunity to meditate upon same-sex affinities that were just emerging into categorical definition. The astute reader of "The Loyal Scot" adheres to a Britain of Marvell's unique but perhaps prefiguring imagination. Goldberg has said that "relations between men . . . in the period provide the sites upon which later sexual orders and later sexual identities could batten."[106] This poem, it may be, locates one such site.

Marvell's poetic exploitations of the question of Britain in the poem also show why any attempt to have him adopt a given politics, however tacit and complicated, will fail. "The Loyal Scot" restates the long-standing problem of his "loyalty." It is not that Marvell eschews commitment here, but that what he commits himself to cannot itself be reduced to much fixity. We have learned to distrust the term "sexuality" and to resist its reductions. In a strict sense, as Goldberg points out, there is no inquiry into "sodomy," only "sodometries," that is, "relational structures precariously available to prevailing discourses."[107] In "The Loyal Scot," Marvell insinuates just such a "sexual" relation, and does so within the terms set out by one political "discourse," that of Britain. But is this latter "discourse" any more stable than that of "sodomy"? Marvell has located himself at a switch point between two fluctuating and as yet incoherent "discourses." In this period, what it meant to be "British" was somewhat more clear than what it meant to be a "sodomite," but not much. In 1670, both "discourses" were still structured as sets of problems, ongoing *questions*, although, historically, they were both moving toward a kind of resolution. Linda Colley has observed that early in the next century and following, "a sense of British national identity [would be] forged, and that the manner in which it was forged has shaped the quality of this particular sense of nationhood and belonging ever since."[108] Bray has said that "in marked contrast to the circumstances that prevailed in England up to the last quarter of the seventeenth century," there was by 1700 "a continuing [homosexual] culture to be fixed on and an extension of the area in which homosexuality could be expressed and therefore recognized."[109] As Marvell writes "The Loyal Scot," though, both of these "nations" have yet to coalesce (if, indeed, they ever did as fully as these writers imply). Neither of them is "available" to him as a "prevailing"—widely recognized and thus incontrovertible—starting place. Instead, in this poem as in the "Horatian Ode" of twenty years before, Marvell practices the kind of poetics at which he excelled. He introduces himself into the terms of a debate in order to deploy himself among its uncertainties. He achieves the effect he desires by juxtaposing his diverse loyalties. When is Marvell not between nations?

Coda

Britain receives one of its best-known invocations in book 2 of Edmund Spenser's *The Faerie Queene*.[1] In the house of Temperance, in a chamber "hangd about with rolles, / And old records from auncient times deriu'd" (IX.57.6–7), the knights Arthur and Guyon peruse the "antique Registers" (IX.59.4) that Eumnestes, "an old oldman" (IX.55.5), and Anamnestes, his factotum, keep in shabby disarray. "There chaunced to the Princes hand to rize, / An auncient booke, hight *Briton moniments*" (IX.59.5–6). While Guyon traces his own lineage in a volume "hight *Antiquitie of Faerie lond*" (IX.60.2), the "Briton Prince" reads of his kingdom's past, from its beginnings as a "saluage wildernesse, / Vnpeopled, vnmanurd, vnprou'd, vnpraysd" (X.5.3–4) to the "Deare countrey" (X.69.3) that he knows as his own. "[N]ation" (X.15.1) supplants "nation" on Albion; its kings and queens butcher, conquer, and betray one another reign after reign. If this seems an unedifying history, Arthur does not take it so. "At last quite rauisht with delight, to heare / The royall Ofspring of his natiue land," he "Cryde out":

> O how dearely deare
> Ought thy remembraunce, and perpetuall band
> Be to thy foster Childe, that from thy hand
> Did commun breath and nouriture receaue?
> How brutish is it not to vnderstand,
> How much to her we owe, that all vs gaue,
> That gaue vnto vs all, what euer good we haue.
> (X.69.1–9)

Clearly, what Spenser presents here is an apotheosis of Britain, and it can be claimed with considerable justice that what "we and Arthur read is the Tudor view of history, the progress and triumph of British nationalism in the full heat and patriotism of the late sixteenth century."[2] And that there could be such an allegiance in Spenser's day is worth keeping in mind. As I said at the beginning of this study, when Spenser wrote these lines, a polyglot entity that had been "kingdom," or more precisely, a consortium of "kingdoms," was modulating into a more cohesive polity, one that we now could call a "nation." A British "nationalism," even a British "patriotism," was far from unthinkable in the "late sixteenth century." In this passage, the prince's adulation reaches back into a "remembrance" of Britain's past, and he finds in the succeeding reigns of his ancestors the "perpetuall band" that links both him and his readers to their sustaining origins. By summoning up that "remembrance" and rehearsing its signal catastrophes and triumphs in canto after canto, Spenser involves the reader in the imagined community that a sense of "commun breath and nouriture" can produce. Here, the intra-British tensions that Spenser and his readers knew so well are collapsed, and a higher unity is exalted over them. The episode is informed by the drive for transcendence that animates the larger political project of *The Faerie Queene*. As has been argued, the "Britain" that Spenser calls up is never meant to be coincident with the "nation" figured in the poem itself, but must be located outside of it. Britain is an imperial ideal, and can be exemplified only in the royal personage to whom Spenser dedicates his epic. This is "Gloriana," Elizabeth I, whom the poet nominates as the "Empresse" of England and Ireland (among other locales), claiming all of the British Isles for her own. "The perfected form into which British history is prospectively or prophetically gathered is a vision of the 'body politic,' the corporate sovereignty of England as personified in the monarch."[3] The overarching "nation" which Spenser conceives is intrinsically incapable of manifesting itself in anything less splendid than his queen. Perhaps this is what we and Arthur are meant to "understand" if we are to be "British" and not merely "brutish."

Nonetheless, we would also do the subtle rigor of Spenser's "nationalism" an injustice if we do not see that the Britain he promotes is not always, or even usually, the Britain that he thinks can be realized. Spenser's "British nationalism" is an amalgam of unwavering idealism and shrewd realpolitik. Most of the problems that trouble the very idea of a Britain in the early modern period are adumbrated in this episode. The Britain of *Briton moniments*, like the Britain that Spenser and his readers inhabited, is fragmented and tenuous. If *The Faerie Queene* itself implies the possibility of a more stable polity than the one it chronicles, it also implies that this Britain is attainable only in and by an act of political faith that the text does not quite support. Arthur offers up his loyalty, we note, simply to a "countrey," and the British history that is rehearsed for him is more episodic and less teleological than a "progress." As we have seen in these pages, it was a rare moment in the English literature of this period when the attempt to conjure up Britain was not beset by pervading uncertainties and self-created contradictions. And, as is well known, this episode in *The Faerie Queene* was not that rare moment. Indeed, Spenser himself seems to insist on the difficulties of invoking Britain, as if he did not mean for us to arrive at the reading that might bring it forth without first learning the labor, perhaps the hopeless labor, that an appeal to such a unifying "nation" entails.

Where in the history that Arthur reads and that we read with him are we to locate the Britain that he eulogizes? It is not any one of the kingdoms that has existed on the British Isles, although it is in the accumulated annals of these kingdoms that Arthur finds his sense of Britishness. Harry Berger Jr. has pointed out that this "Briton chronicle is a chronicle of kings." Some are atrocious; some show "great good" (X.46.3), but none of these all too fallible monarchs can be said to embody the ideal polity that this history summons up. "No one ruler is seen to be the hero. The hero is Britain itself insofar as it triumphs through divine assistance over the evils of physical and moral nature."[4] But *which* "Britain itself" can plausibly serve as the episode's "hero"? It is not, it seems, the Britain of the poem's narrative present, at least not the recent present. Just before Arthur arrives at his own era in the chronicle, he reads of the emperor Constantine, whose realm was beset by "Those spoilefull Picts, and swarming Easterlings." Although he "Long time in peace his Realme established," he was

> Yet oft annoyd with sundry bordragings
> Of neighbour Scots, and forrein Scatterlings,
> With which the world did in those dayes abound
> (X.63.2–5)

Like other Britains that we have charted here, this kingdom is nebulous at its borders, and this ruler—who is himself "forrein," of course—must contend with hosts of aliens, "swarming," scattering "borderers"[5] who menace his territory from without (and within), and threaten to dislocate his domain from the margins. Nor, when book 2 was first published in 1590, could the heroic Britain be that of the historical present, when such "borderers"

were still daunting. As if to remind his reader of contemporary incursions
into British unity, Spenser has Arthur and Guyon achieve the house of
Temperance only after driving away "A thousand villeins":

> Vile caytiue wretches, ragged, rude, deformd,
> All threatening death, all in straunge manner armd,
> Some with vnweldy clubs, some with long speares,
> Some rusty kniues, some staues in fire warmd. (IX.13.2, 4–7)

Their resemblance to marauding Irish kerns would have been obvious
enough to Spenser's first readers (as it has been to later critics) and becomes
unavoidable when the poet compares these knaves to "a swarme of Gnats at
euentide" which "Out of the fennes of Allan do arise" (IX.16.1–2). Within
the poem, Arthur can come to know Britain only after seeming to vanquish
those among the "British" who remained quite unvanquished in 1590.

   Thus, in this episode, a gesture toward a transcendent British nation is
made together with, and blocked by, a gesture toward the very contingen-
cies that had beset and would continue to beset that polity. As Berger also
notes, "there is a muddiness, a residue of meaninglessness, in the historical
facts which disappoints the reader seeking allegorical clarity or instruc-
tion,"[6] and this muddiness prevents the reader from seeing the queen of
England as transparently also the empress of a unified Britain. The history
of chaotic and corrupted Britishness that makes the reader British—"how
much to her we owe, that all vs gaue"—is also the history that persists into
the present and keeps the reader from moving "beyond" that history to the
transcendence that the poem seems to promise. Finally, we are left to wonder whether there is any reading that can produce "Britain itself," except,
maybe, as an ideal state nowhere present in the chronicle that Arthur pon-
ders or in the epic that we construe.

   Moreover, Spenser has written this predicament into the text that
we are reading. Famously, Arthur's ravishment follows upon an "vntimely
breach" (X.68.6) that has riven the book he holds. Just as the chronicle
reaches Uther Pendragon, his own father,

> Succeding There abruptly it did end,
> Without full point, or other Cesure right,
> As if the rest some wicked hand did rend,
> Or th' Authour selfe could not at least attend
> To finish it (X.68.2–6)

What author is this if not Spenser, and, even, what hand is this if not
Spenser's?[7] Since Britain is not permitted to emerge authoritatively from

the brutish history that has been unfolding, Arthur is suspended between desire to celebrate the past that makes him who he is and exasperation that the chronicle does not seem to culminate where it should. The rupture

> The Prince him selfe halfe seemeth to offend,
> Yet secret pleasure did offence empeach,
> And wonder of antiquitie long stopt his speech.
> (X.68.7–9)

One critic has said that "the moment *in which* Arthur reads emerges from *what* he reads."[8] But also, the moment in which Arthur reads is disrupted in its coherence by the troubling incoherence of what he reads—and so too, therefore, is the reader, Arthur himself. The history he has been perusing is fragmented and incomplete; it does not arrive at the nation it heralds. The "Briton prince" who emerges from this chronicle of division is prototypically British but alienated from the figure a British history renders him. Indeed, Spenser seems to imply that it is just this self-division that makes Arthur the Britisher he now is. It is the "Prince him selfe," the line hints, who "halfe seemeth to offend" . . . himself. Is there a "secret pleasure" to be taken from this interrupted history? If so, it is the pleasure of a chronicle that, despite its "antiquitie" and the "wonder" it elicits, cannot reach into the more embattled present. Arthur finds his Britain not despite but within the "vntimely breach" that opens up and truncates the narrative of his origins. He is the "Childe" of a Britain that disappears just as it is about to conceive him. He is British; he is between nations.

Reference Matter

Notes

Introduction

1. Pocock, "British History," p. 603. I should stress that in what follows I am hardly doing justice to the multifaceted and far-reaching argument of "British History," nor to that of its companion piece, "The Limits and Divisions of British History," which, between them, manage to comment suggestively on Britain from its prehistory to its present. In particular, the expansion of British history beyond what Pocock calls its "archipelagic" stage to its "Atlantic" and "global" stages is beyond the scope of this Introduction, but see "British History," pp. 617–21, and "Limits and Divisions," pp. 329–34. In wide-ranging discussions of "Europe" as a formation, Pocock has been considering the past and present effects of British expansion on his native New Zealand. See "History and Sovereignty" and "Deconstructing Europe."

2. Between 1801 and 1922, Scotland, England (and Wales, which England had subsumed in 1536), and all of Ireland were denominated the "United Kingdom of Great Britain and Ireland." After the partition of 1922, and until the present day, this domain has been known as the "United Kingdom of Great Britain and Northern Ireland."

3. Pocock, "British History," p. 606. Pocock dubs these islands "the Atlantic archipelago — since the term 'British Isles' is one which Irishmen reject and Englishmen decline to take seriously." For the sake of familiarity, however, I will use "British Isles" throughout this book.

4. Elton, *The Tudor Revolution in Government*, p. 3. More recently, Elton has said that the "English . . . emerged from the Middle Ages very definitely as a nation, self-consciously aware of that identity and always ready to assert it across a spec-

trum of behaviour that ranged from kindly superiority to embittered chauvinism";
this "despite . . . the contributory streams of Welsh, Danish, Norman and Gascon
blood" (*The English*, p. 111). As he has done before, Elton here locates the emergence
of an English nation-state in the 1530's, the decade, he claims, in which Thomas
Cromwell inaugurated sweeping administrative reforms and consolidations. "One
thing that Cromwell positively achieved was the absorption of all England in his
concept of a unitary state," says Elton. Wales was assimilated through the "so-called
Union of that country with England in statutes . . . [that] in effect put Wales under
English law" (p. 137); in Ireland, Cromwell "succeed[ed] in establishing English
rule . . . from London over the Pale and the great lordships," though he too could
"chalk up Ireland as the main failure of his policy" (p. 139). For a comprehensive
and critical reconsideration of Elton's claims for Cromwell's innovations, see *Revolution Reassessed*, ed. Christopher Coleman and David Starkey.

    5. Greenfeld, *Nationalism: Five Roads to Modernity*, p. 6. Emphasis Greenfeld's. For
a brief critique of the "circularity" of Greenfeld's definitional argument, by which
"nation and nationalism become indistinguishable" and "nationalism becomes the
only story that can be told" of "national identity," see Carla Hesse and Thomas Laqueur, "Introduction," pp. 1–3.

    6. McEachern, "*Henry V* and the Paradox of the Body Politic," p. 35. McEachern
cites Benedict Anderson, *Imagined Communities*; Ernest Gellner, *Nations and Nationalism*; and E. J. Hobsbawm, *Nations and Nationalism Since 1780*, whose title itself implies early modern England's non-nation-ness. Anderson's well-known linkage of
the rise of the "nation" to the formation of "print-as-commodity" represented, for
him, by the novel and the newspaper, would seem to exclude the England of this
period, with its less than ubiquitous print culture, from "nationhood." (Nonetheless, Anderson's formulations have proved powerfully suggestive for the study of
many other sorts of "nationalism," including the one that will be addressed here.)
Gellner, somewhat similarly, ties the emergence of the nation properly so called
to the development of "industrial society." "The *nation* is now supremely important, thanks both to the erosion of sub-groupings and the vastly increased importance of a shared, literary-dependent culture" largely maintained and supervised by
the state. "The citizens can only breathe conceptually and operate within [a cul-
tural/linguistic] medium, which is co-extensive with the territory of the state and
its educational and cultural apparatus" (pp. 63–64, emphasis Gellner's); clearly, this
was not so in early modern England. And Hobsbawm, in turn, states that he uses
"the term 'nationalism' in the sense defined by Gellner. . . . [The 'nation'] belongs
exclusively to a particular, and historically recent, period. It is a social entity only
insofar as it relates to a certain kind of modern territorial state, the 'nation-state,'
and it is pointless to discuss nation and nationality except insofar as both relate to
it" (pp. 9–10). Classic introductory treatments of nationalism include Hans Kohn,
The Idea of Nationalism, and Anthony D. Smith, *Theories of Nationalism*.

    7. Breuilly, *Nationalism and the State*, p. 2.

    8. Ibid., p. 4.

9. Marcu, *Sixteenth Century Nationalism.*

10. Breuilly, *Nationalism and the State*, p. 5.

11. Benedict Anderson, for instance, would presumably place early modern England *after* the time of the "pre-modern empires and kingdoms," when dynastic "legitimacy derives from divinity, not from populations" (*Imagined Communities*, p. 19) and yet also *before* the emergence of the "national" community enabled by "print-as-commodity." At the end of Chapter 1, I elaborate on the implications of this "between" status for one early modern text, *Henry V.*

12. Pocock, "British History," p. 614.

13. Pocock, "Limits and Divisions," p. 316.

14. Ibid., p. 320.

15. Ibid., p. 316.

16. "I practice English history a good deal, and I have no great anxiety to see that subject radically transformed; but I am arguing that 'British history' needs to be reinvested with meaning, both because it contains areas of human experience which it would be beneficial to study, and because I have come to believe that we are doing harm to our understanding of ourselves by not studying it. But I have called it a 'new subject,' and it should be clear from what I have said that I envisage it as existing alongside English history as an old one." Pocock, "British History," p. 613.

17. Ibid., p. 614.

18. Ibid., p. 611.

19. Trouillot, *Silencing the Past*, pp. 48–49. Trouillot's argument takes Haiti as its prime locus.

20. Pocock, "Limits and Divisions," p. 316.

21. Pocock, "British History," p. 610.

22. Ibid., p. 605.

23. Ibid.

24. Pocock, "Limits and Divisions," p. 317.

25. See "nation" in the *OED*. Roughly contemporaneous definitions include: "an extensive aggregate of persons, so closely associated with each other by common descent, language, or history, as to form a distinct race or people, usually organized as a separate political state and occupying a definite territory"; but also "in mediaeval universities, a body of students belonging to a particular district, country, or group of countries, who formed a more or less independent community"; "a country, kingdom"; "the peoples of the earth"; "the whole of a country, freq. in contrast to some smaller or narrower body within it"; but then too "a family, kindred"; "the native population of a town or city"; "a particular class, kind, or race of persons." Most relevant for my argument: "an Irish clan."

26. Pocock, "Limits and Divisions," p. 311.

27. Pocock, "British History," p. 603.

28. Pocock, "Contingency, Identity, Sovereignty," p. 293.

29. S. Ellis, "'Not Mere English,'" p. 42. Among the earlier works that responded to the call for a British historiography were R. S. Thompson's *The Atlantic*

Archipelago, and Hugh Kearney's *The British Isles*. Note also Kearney's brief essay on contemporary Britishness, "Four Nations or One?" For the constitution of Britain in the medieval period, see *The British Isles 1100–1500*, ed. R. R. Davies, and Robin Frame, *The Political Development of the British Isles 1100–1400*. A recent history that impressively imbricates the politics of multiple kingdoms at the midpoint of the seventeenth century is Conrad Russell's *The Fall of the British Monarchies 1637–1642*. See also Russell, *The Causes of the English Civil War*, "The British Problem and the English Civil War," and "The British Background to the Irish Rebellion of 1641." Linda Colley's *Britons* locates the emergence of a British consciousness in a later period, but its analysis of this formation has useful analogues in the early modern. See also Colley's "Britishness and Otherness." *Strangers Within the Realm*, ed. Bernard Bailyn and Philip D. Morgan, places an expansive Britain within the history of what Pocock called the "Atlantic archipelago." For an overview of the emergence of the field of British historiography in the present, see Pocock, "Contingency, Identity, Sovereignty." Articles which treat the emergence of a notion of Britain in the early modern period, and specifically during the Union of England and Scotland attempted by James I in 1603, include Pocock, "Two Kingdoms and Three Histories?" and Jenny Wormald, "The Creation of Britain," "James VI, James I, and the Identity of Britain," and "One King, Two Kingdoms." It is a testimony to the vitality of this emerging field that, since the bulk of this study was written, four collections of essays informed by British historiography have been issued: *Three Nations—A Common History?*, ed. Ronald G. Asch; *Conquest and Union*, ed. Steven G. Ellis and Sarah Barber; *The British Problem, c. 1534–1707*, ed. Brendan Bradshaw and John Morrill; and *Uniting the Kingdom?*, ed. Alexander Grant and Keith J. Stringer. The last two volumes include papers presented at conferences on British history, held in 1993 and 1994, respectively. Besides these meetings, much of the ongoing discussion of the issues arising from a British historiography has been taking place in yearly seminars at the Folger Institute Center for the History of British Political Thought in Washington, D.C. So far, the volumes that have emerged from these seminars are *The Varieties of British Political Thought 1500–1800*, ed. J. G. A. Pocock; *Scots and Britons*, ed. Roger A. Mason; and *A Union for Empire*, ed. John Robertson. Other volumes are planned.

For reservations from historians about the implications and methods of the British historiography, see Nicholas Canny, "Irish, Scottish, and Welsh Responses to Centralization, c. 1530–c. 1640" and "The Attempted Anglicization of Ireland in the Seventeenth Century"; also Keith M. Brown, "British History."

30. S. Ellis, "'Not Mere English,'" p. 42.

31. Beckett, *The Making of Modern Ireland 1603–1923*, p. 82.

32. Pocock, "British History," p. 605.

33. See n. 29. Specifically, Russell's study deals with the intersecting politics of events leading up to the "Civil War."

34. Pocock, "Two Kingdoms and Three Histories?" p. 293.

35. Wormald, "The Creation of Britain," pp. 184–85.

36. Pocock, "Two Kingdoms and Three Histories?" p. 293.

37. Shuger, *Habits of Thought in the English Renaissance*, p. 11. Shuger is quoted in Richard Helgerson, *Forms of Nationhood*, p. 18. Helgerson notes that his own "focus on England respects [those] national boundaries," although it is written "in opposition to them" too; he means to "point out the ideological function of [such] lines."

38. Bhabha, "Introduction," p. 4.

39. Helgerson, *Forms of Nationhood*, p. 18.

40. Bhabha, "Introduction," p. 4. Emphasis mine.

41. Pocock, "Limits and Divisions," p. 335.

42. Pocock, "Contingency, Identity, Sovereignty," p. 300.

43. Spivak, "Acting Bits/Identity Talk," p. 781.

44. Wormald, "The Creation of Britain," p. 194.

45. Pocock, "British History," p. 612.

46. The Latin version, *hiberniores ipsis hibernis*, is often used to describe the cultural assimilation of the early modern English in Ireland, but see Art Cosgrove, "Hiberniores Ipsis Hibernis," on the emergence of the phrase only in the eighteenth century.

47. Pocock, "British History," p. 607. Pocock called this a "difficulty largely coterminous with the problem of nationality," meaning, I take it, that this problem will no longer be a problem when the nation stops being one too.

48. Ibid., pp. 612–13.

49. Ibid., p. 603.

50. Pocock, "Contingency, Identity, Sovereignty," p. 300.

51. Pocock, "British History," p. 613.

52. Hadfield, *Literature, Politics, and National Identity*, p. 11.

53. Pocock, "Limits and Divisions," p. 320.

54. This territory, it may be, was something like what Mary Louise Pratt has recently called a "contact zone": a "space in which peoples geographically and historically separated come into contact with each other and establish ongoing relations, usually involving conditions of coercion, radical inequality, and intractable conflict" (*Imperial Eyes*, p. 6).

55. Pocock, "British History," p. 620.

56. Trouillot, *Silencing the Past*, p. 49.

57. Pocock, "Contingency, Identity, Sovereignty," p. 300.

58. Ibid.

59. See, for instance, Steven Mullaney's "The Rehearsal of Cultures," pp. 60–87.

60. What I will say in these pages about the early modern English nation could be said of "the new historicism" as well: it has an apparent unity, but, when closely regarded, it shows itself to be made up of diverse groups (and persons) with often conflicting interests, some of whom will acknowledge this name as their own, some of whom will not, and all of whom coexist in a state of negotiated flux. Like Louis Montrose, I opt to "place [such phrases as 'the new historicism'] inside quotation marks to indicate my resistance to [the] now-conventional representation within

critical discourse [of this movement] as a fixed and homogeneous body of doctrines and techniques" ("New Historicisms," p. 392).

61. But see Leah Marcus's informed discussion of the projected British Union of 1603 and its bearing on Shakespeare's *Cymbeline* in *Puzzling Shakespeare*, pp. 118–48. And for an intriguing application of the problematics of Britishness to questions of literary history, see a series of articles by Willy Maley: "Rebels and Redshanks," " 'Another Britain'?," and "Spenser and Scotland."

62. Helgerson, *Forms of Nationhood*, p. 8.

63. Ibid., pp. 299–300.　　　　　　64. See ibid., p. 4.

65. Ibid., pp. 3–4.　　　　　　66. Pocock, "British History," p. 616.

67. Helgerson, *Forms of Nationhood*, p. 301. Cf. Pocock, "Limits and Divisions," p. 335.

68. Helgerson, *Forms of Nationhood*, p. 301.

69. Ibid., p. 300.

Chapter 1

1. Unless otherwise noted, all citations will be from William Shakespeare, *Henry V*, ed. Gary Taylor.

2. Goldberg, "Shakespearean Inscriptions," p. 119.

3. Akrigg, *Jacobean Pageant, or the Court of King James I*, p. 49.

4. Ibid., p. 3.

5. *The Political Works of James I*, ed. Charles H. McIlwain, p. 272.

6. "A Proclamation concerning the Kings Majesties Stile, of King of Great Britaine, &c.," vol. 1 of *Stuart Royal Proclamations*, ed. James F. Larkin and Paul L. Hughes, p. 96.

7. Willson, "King James I and Anglo-Scottish Unity," p. 51.

8. Levack, *The Formation of the British State*, p. 189. Levack's is perhaps the best of the histories that treat the politics of union in the early modern period. See also Levack, "Toward a More Perfect Union" and "The Proposed Union of English Law and Scots Law in the Seventeenth Century." Bruce Galloway's *The Union of England and Scotland 1603–1608* provides an excellent critique of received opinion on union, including that of D. H. Willson (see n. 8). See also Keith M. Brown, *Kingdom or Province?* Wallace Notestein, *The House of Commons 1604–1610*, includes an account of the debate over union in 1603–4 that hews closely to the parliamentary record. Also useful are Gordon Donaldson, "Foundations of Anglo-Scottish Union," and R. C. Munden, "James I and the 'Growth of Mutual Mistrust.' " For obvious reasons, the proposed Union of 1603 has drawn the attention of those interested in thinking through its implications for a British historiography. See the essays collected in *Scots and Britons*, ed. Roger A. Mason, but especially J. G. A. Pocock, "Two Kingdoms and Three Histories?" in that volume. Also stimulating are Jenny Wormald, "The Creation of Britain," "One King, Two Kingdoms," and "James VI, James I, and the Identity of Britain."

9. This occurred under Oliver Cromwell's Protectorate and was imposed on the Scots. An "Ordinance of Union" was issued by Cromwell's Council of State in 1654; the requisite parliamentary act was passed in 1657.

10. Pocock, "Limits and Divisions," p. 322. For a model of British history organized by a contrast between the march, a "zone of war," and the domain, a "zone of law," see pp. 321–23. For an innovative treatment of the politics of the march in the early sixteenth century, see Steven G. Ellis, *Tudor Frontiers and Noble Power.*

11. Bloom, introduction to William Shakespeare's *Henry V*, p. 1.

12. For standard treatments in which the English nationalist project of *Henry V* is taken for granted, see E. W. Tillyard, *Shakespeare's History Plays,* and Lily B. Campbell, *Shakespeare's 'Histories.'* For a contrasting emphasis on the heterogeneity of nations and tongues implied in the play, see Michael Neill, "Broken English and Broken Irish."

13. Campbell, *Shakespeare's 'Histories,'* p. 255.

14. Dollimore and Sinfield, "History and Ideology," p. 220. An expanded version of this essay, which also treats the "sexualities and genders" of the play, is reprinted in Sinfield's *Faultlines.*

15. Cairns and Richards, *Writing Ireland,* p. 11.

16. For a useful discussion of the opposed readings *Henry V* can elicit, see Rabkin, *Shakespeare and the Problem of Meaning,* pp. 33–62.

17. Patterson, *Shakespeare and the Popular Voice,* p. 72.

18. Colley, *Britons,* p. 6.

19. Dollimore and Sinfield, "History and Ideology," p. 225.

20. Quint, "'Alexander the Pig,'" p. 51.

21. Dollimore and Sinfield, "History and Ideology," pp. 217, 224.

22. McEachern, "*Henry V* and the Paradox of the Body Politic," p. 44. In a footnote on the following page, however, McEachern cites Brian Levack's *The Formation of the British State* and notes that "such unity would soon be a highly contested construct."

23. P. Anderson, *English Questions,* p. 10.

24. Cairns and Richards, *Writing Ireland,* p. 11.

25. Greenblatt, *Shakespearean Negotiations,* p. 56.

26. Ibid., p. 63.   27. Ibid., p. 56.

28. Ibid., pp. 65, 63, 41.   29. Ibid., p. 57.

30. Ibid., p. 43.

31. Ibid., p. 37. Emphasis mine. For a critique of Greenblatt's "monologism" aided by the theorizing of Homi Bhabha, see an earlier version of this chapter, "'Wildehirissheman.'" One way of understanding the critical investment in the unperturbed nationalism of *Henry V* is suggested in Jonathan Goldberg, *Sodometries.* Goldberg has noted that, in their readings of *Henry V*, critics in this century have often been caught up in an identification with the "virtues" this play seems to uphold, and have obscured the political and social investments in which these "virtues" originated. In particular, "most critics in this century have found it all but impos-

sible to resist the attractions" of Prince Hal, *Henry V*'s protagonist (p. 145). Goldberg argues that Henry appeals to contemporary readers, as he appealed to early modern audiences, because he presents them with an "ideal image"—"a middle-class ego ideal," that of the proto-bourgeois, purportedly heterosexual, and, of course, English man. "Shakespeare writes well before these modern regimes are in place; yet the negotiations around Hal and the path he pursues are capable retroactively of taking on the charge of the modern heterosexual male subjectivity" (p. 161). But, for Goldberg, Hal is an index of the duplicities of this modern "heterosexuality" from its early modern beginnings. Misogynistic in its contempt for women (except as they figure in a system of "patriarchal exchange" [p. 156]), homophobic in its horror of male/male sexual relations (but itself defined by male/male social relations), the "heterosexuality" that Henry embodies is a "homo-narcissism" (p. 159)—men's love for other men masking itself as untainted "admiration." In conjunction with this, I would argue that the Englishness of Hal is as much under construction in *Henry V* as the sexuality deployed through him. Goldberg notes that this "heterosexual" prince has also long been considered "the embodiment of virtues indistinguishable from Englishness" (p. 145), as the "English essence," as the very "nation" itself (p. 147). But if the eroticized identities that *Henry V* promoted in 1599 were implicated in a denial of just those revulsions that made them possible, then what burden of "abjection" (p. 154) was entailed by Englishness? Can Henry be as straightforwardly "English" as he is "heterosexual"? If not, what must have been denied and/or displaced for this national "essence" to come into mode in turn-of-the-sixteenth-century England?

32. Helgerson, *Forms of Nationhood*, p. 8.

33. Pocock, "British History," p. 603.

34. B. Anderson, *Imagined Communities*, p. 6.

35. Gurr, introduction to William Shakespeare's *King Henry V*, p. 4. Emphasis mine.

36. Bhabha, "Introduction," p. 3. Emphasis Bhabha's.

37. For a compendium of the traits typically associated with the stage Irishman, Welshman, and Scotsman in the early modern period, see Bartley's useful *Teague, Shenkin, and Sawney*.

38. Altman, "'Vile Participation,'" p. 9.

39. Hayes-McCoy, "The Completion of the Tudor Conquest, and the Advance of the Counter-Reformation, 1571–1603," vol. 3, p. 127.

40. Altman, "'Vile Participation,'" p. 12.

41. Citations from John Donne, "H. W. in Hibernia Belligeranti," in *John Donne: The Complete English Poems*, pp. 217–18.

42. Hadfield and Maley, "Introduction," p. 9.

43. William Shakespeare, *Henry the Fifth*. 1600. Reprint, Oxford: Clarendon Press, 1957.

44. Geoffrey Bullough, introduction to *Henry V*, in *Narrative and Dramatic Sources of Shakespeare*, vol. 4, p. 347.

45. Altman, "'Vile Participation,'" p. 2.

46. Ibid., p. 13.

47. Nashe, *The Works of Thomas Nashe*, vol. 1, p. 213.

48. This phrase is taken from the title page of the Quarto of 1600 and is quoted in Taylor, introduction to *Henry V* (p. 7).

49. For a list of these elisions, see Appendix F in Taylor's *Henry V*, pp. 312–15.

50. Patterson, *Shakespeare and the Popular Voice*, p. 73.

51. Taylor, introduction to *Henry V*, p. 12. See also Gary Taylor, *Three Studies in the Text of* Henry V, and Stanley Wells, *Modernizing Shakespeare's Spelling*. The former develops an earlier version of Taylor's theory on the relation of Folio to Quarto.

52. Hadfield and Maley, "Introduction," p. 11.

53. Pocock, "Limits and Divisions," p. 325.

54. Quinn, *The Elizabethans and the Irish*, p. 13.

55. Dollimore and Sinfield, "History and Ideology," p. 224.

56. Ibid., p. 225.

57. Ibid., p. 226.

58. Ibid., p. 224.

59. Taylor, Appendix F in *Henry V*, p. 313.

60. Edwards, *Threshold of a Nation*, p. 76. Edwards is responding to and elaborating on a comparison between St. Lawrence and MacMorris first made in Jorgensen, *Shakespeare's Military World*, p. 80.

61. *Letters and Memorials of State*, ed. Arthur Collins, vol. 2, pp. 130–31.

62. Hadfield and Maley, "Introduction," p. 14.

63. Patterson, *Shakespeare and the Popular Voice*, p. 80. The description is William Camden's from his *Annals*.

64. Mathew, *The Celtic Peoples and Renaissance Europe*, p. 351. There is much about this work that, as it elaborates a contrast between generalized "Renaissance" and "Celtic" sensibilities, can seem outdated. But its densely circumstantial history— "pointilliste," as Pocock has called it—conveys a rich sense of the interrelations of a British politics in the early modern period. See especially "The Welsh Aspects of the Essex Rising," pp. 336–58. For Pocock on Mathew, see "British History," p. 604.

65. Patterson, *Shakespeare and the Popular Voice*, pp. 83–84.

66. Collins, ed., *Letters*, vol. 2, p. 133.

67. Ibid., vol. 2, p. 137.

68. *Dictionary of National Biography*, p. 649. The *Dictionary* includes the only account of St. Lawrence's diasporic career, which eventually took him to the Low Countries as a mercenary, then back to Ireland and continuing trouble with the English authorities.

69. Falls, *Elizabeth's Irish Wars*, p. 232.

70. Elizabeth I, quoted in ibid., p. 239. Tyrone was the "tree" that the queen had in mind.

71. Collins, ed., *Letters*, vol. 2, p. 137.

72. R. R. Davies, *Domination and Conquest*, p. 13. The other terms Davies says could

be applied to the conquerors—"Norman," "Cambro-Norman," "Anglo-French"—indicate the heterogeneity of identity that marked the "English" nobility from 1066 on.

73. Lupton, "Mapping Mutability," p. 96.

74. Clarke, *The Old English in Ireland 1625–42*, pp. 16–19.

75. Myers, *A History of Ireland in Elizabethan England*, p. 25.

76. Renwick, ed., *A View of the Present State of Ireland*, p. 48.

77. Canny, "Identity Formation in Ireland, p. 160.

78. Jorgensen, *Shakespeare's Military World*, p. 80. Perhaps it was this policy which led St. Lawrence to complain, when directed "to return to his Charge . . . that he had but a poore Command there" (Collins ed., *Letters*, vol. 2, p. 137).

79. Jorgensen, *Shakespeare's Military World*, p. 79.

80. Collins, ed., *Letters*, vol. 2, p. 137.

81. Myers, introduction to *A Discovery of the True Causes Why Ireland Was Never Entirely Subdued [And] Brought Under Obedience of the Crown of England Until the Beginning of His Majesty's Happy Reign*, p. 172. Oscar Bergin says that in "English documents of the period the family name is written both in its Norman-French form Fitzmaurice (or Fitzmorris) and in its Irish form MacMaurice or Macmorris (= Mac Muiris)," and states definitively that in "this latter form it is used by Shakespeare in *Henry V* for his Irish character, or rather lay figure, Captain Macmorris. The name might easily have reached Shakespeare's ears, for the Lords of Kerry, like the rest of the Geraldines, were Irish chiefs who never lost their connection with England and the continent." He holds, though, that "to suppose that Shakespeare had any individual in mind were to consider too curiously of the matter. A medley of national characteristics, real or imaginary, a little broken English, and a good Irish name were enough for his purpose" (*Irish Bardic Poetry*, p. 53).

82. Taylor, introduction to *Henry V*, p. 67.

83. Greenblatt, *Shakespearean Negotiations*, p. 59.

84. Ibid., p. 57.

85. Edwards, *Threshold of a Nation*, pp. 75–76.

86. Cairns and Richards, *Writing Ireland*, p. 10.

87. Goldberg, "Shakespearean Inscriptions," pp. 118–19.

88. Jorgensen, *Shakespeare's Military World*, p. 78.

89. See the paraphrase of W. J. Craig quoted in Edwards, *Threshold of a Nation*, p. 75.

90. Ibid., pp. 75–76.

91. Leerssen, *Mere Irish & Fíor-Ghael*, p. 95.

92. Christopher Miller, *Blank Darkness*, p. 5.

93. Leerssen, *Mere Irish & Fíor-Ghael*, p. 41.

94. Spenser, *View*, p. 67.

95. Edwards, *Threshold of a Nation*, p. 86. Though, as Pocock has pointed out, these Welshmen might mean, rather less submissively, that "they'd be glad to serve him *in Welsh*" (personal correspondence).

96. Canny, *The Formation of the Old English Elite in Ireland*, p. 4.

97. Leerssen, *Mere Irish & Fíor-Ghael*, p. 25. Emphasis mine.

98. Edwards, *Threshold of a Nation*, pp. 248–49.

99. Greenblatt, *Shakespearean Negotiations*, p. 57.

100. Leerssen, *Mere Irish & Fíor-Ghael*, p. 87.

101. Jorgensen, *Shakespeare's Military World*, p. 60.

102. Ibid., p. 79. The comparison between MacMorris and these ferocious Irishmen is Jorgensen's.

103. Edwards, *Threshold of a Nation*, p. 76.

104. Leerssen, *Mere Irish & Fíor-Ghael*, p. 39.

105. Rackin, *Stages of History*, p. 113.

106. Nashe, *The Works of Thomas Nashe*, pp. 212, 213.

107. Ibid., p. 211.

108. Barton, "The King Disguised," p. 105.

109. Pocock, "British History," p. 609.

110. Greenblatt, *Shakespearean Negotiations*, p. 63.

111. Hobsbawn, *Nations and Nationalism Since 1780*, p. 8.

112. Owen, *Wales in the Reign of James I*, pp. 6–7.

113. Levack, *The Formation of the British State*, p. 184. This process did not come to much. James gave English titles to several Scotsmen, "but the titles, instead of contributing to the cause of Anglo-Scottish union, actually worked against it. In 1621 twenty-six English peers, angered by the selection of three Scottish peers to lead the procession of earls at the opening of the English parliament, drafted a protest against the Scottish invasion of the English peerage" (p. 188).

114. James I, *The Political Works of James I*, p. 297.

115. James had his own sense of the otherness of this tongue. In 1609, complaining of the translation and transcription of a work he had "written all with my own hand," James said that the copyist had "marred it quite" in "pressing" it from Scottish to English, "and made it neither, so as it is now good Britaine language or rather Welsh" (Owen, *Wales in the Reign of James I*, p. 2). Here, the king gestures toward the claims, made by some Welsh, that those of their nation had been the primordial Britons. But he also registers a disquiet with the strangeness of the Welsh tongue. Language that has been mangled, that has slipped away from the royal hand that writes and has taken on some meaning altogether unintended, cannot be "British." Writing that alien must be "Welsh."

116. Glanmor Williams, *Renewal and Reformation*, p. 11. I am indebted to Williams's superb history of late medieval and early modern Wales throughout this section.

117. Glanmor Williams, *Renewal and Reformation*, p. 8.

118. Brendan Bradshaw claims that "by the time of Henry VIII's death the crown's control of . . . Wales was no longer a critical problem, though the work of consolidation was far from complete. The principality had been quietly absorbed into the kingdom." But he also argues that up until "the accession of Henry VII,"

well after the period that Shakespeare dramatizes in *Henry V*, Wales presented the "crown's effective jurisdiction" with a "challenge" that was just as severe as that posed by Ireland under the Tudors (*The Irish Constitutional Revolution of the Sixteenth Century*, p. 20). By returning to this period in 1599, Shakespeare could summon up a Wales whose past "challenge" had, to an extent, persisted into the present. See also Bradshaw, "The Tudor Reformation and Revolution in Wales and Ireland," and Brady, "Comparable Histories?"

119. Dollimore and Sinfield, "History and Ideology," p. 224.

120. Penry, *A Treatise Containing the Aeqvity of an Humble Svpplication which is to be Exhibited vnto Hir Graciovs Maiesty and this high Court of Parliament in the behalfe of the Countrey of Wales, that some order may be taken for the preaching of the Gospell among those people*. Further references will be given parenthetically in the text.

121. Adam of Usk, *Chronicon Ade de Usk*, quoted in Glanmor Williams, *Renewal and Reformation*, p. 10.

122. Penry Williams, "Government and Politics," p. 150.

123. R. Brinley Jones, *The Old British Tongue*, p. 42.

124. Owen, *Wales in the Reign of James I*, p. 1.

125. Glanmor Williams, *Renewal and Reformation*, p. 322.

126. See Owen, *Elizabethan Wales*, p. 175.

127. Morgan, "From a Death to a View," p. 44.

128. If Penry does not simply uphold the proud tongue of a Welsh nation, such voices could be heard in his time. In 1604, Robert Holland lauded his new sovereign, James I, and, in an epistle to a translation of his *Basilikon Doron*, told him that the Welsh were a "Nation of great antiquity, keeping their countrey, and contynuing their language so long a tyme inuiolate without change or mixture" (R. Brinley Jones, *The Old British Tongue*, p. 61). And for centuries to come, Welsh would be heard alongside English; in many places, *only* Welsh would be heard. "Even in the 1880s," as Linda Colley has noted, "some 350 years after the Act of Union between Wales and England, three-quarters of all Welshmen still spoke their own language out of choice" ("Britishness and Otherness," p. 316). Like many of the Welsh lexicographers of the sixteenth century, Penry claimed that promulgating Welsh texts was not an end in itself, but would promote the learning of *English* among Welshmen, and would thus enable political conformity. "Raise vp preaching euen in welsh, and the vniformity of the language wil bee sooner attained" (R. Brinley Jones, *The Old British Tongue*, p. 52). William Salesbury, who in 1547 compiled a Welsh/English dictionary, said that his book would enable those who read Welsh to "be bothe theyr owne scholemaysters and other mennes also, and thereby most spedely obteyne the knolege of the englishe tōge" (*A Dictionary in Englyshe and Welshe*, quoted in R. Brinley Jones, *The Old British Tongue*, p. 37). And his declared desire was to bring all Welsh "subiectes . . . vnder the obeysaunce of the imperiall diademe, and triumphant Sceptre of Englande" (*A briefe and a playne introduction* [1550], quoted in ibid., p. 36). But while the desire of this Welshman for incorporation into England was no doubt heartfelt, the obliteration of "differēce" that he championed did not occur.

Wales remained very much a separate locale for the early modern English, an "aloof and distinctive country," and precisely, as Linda Colley notes, because so many Welshmen there spoke in an impenetrable and unfamiliar speech (*Britons*, p. 13).

129. Gwyn Williams, *Madoc*, p. 32.

130. All citations from William Shakespeare, *Henry IV, Part I*, ed. David Bevington.

131. Christopher Highley, in a fine article on the involvements of other British nations in Shakespeare's *Henry IV, Part I*, notes that although Glendower "shows a civilized self-restraint" in this scene, Shakespeare also "turns the chieftain into a figure of ridicule. . . . And behind [his] preoccupation with prophecies and astrological signs we can perhaps detect a more general disdain for the superstitions that Protestant Englishmen associated with the popular Catholicism of both Wales and Ireland" ("Wales, Ireland, and *1 Henry IV*," p. 99). But we might think of this another way: Glendower's affinity for magic, when combined with his "civility," does not diminish this quality, but lends it a contradictory and lingering menace.

132. Glanmor Williams, *Renewal and Reformation*, pp. 9–10.

133. See Lloyd, *Owen Glendower*, and Glanmor Williams, *Renewal and Reformation*, pp. 3–30.

134. Pocock, "British History," p. 609.

135. Abraham Fleming, editor of the second edition of Holinshed's *Chronicles* (1587), quoted in Highley, "Wales, Ireland, and *1 Henry IV*," p. 101. For a reading of act three, scene one, in which the rebels take a maladroit leave of their wives, including Glendower's Welsh daughter, see Goldberg, *Sodometries*, pp. 164–69. Here, too, Goldberg is alert to the dynamics of gender and sexuality in this scene, but leaves aside the imbricated questions of nationality.

136. Highley, "*Wales, Ireland, and 1 Henry IV*," p. 105.

137. Owen, *Wales in the Reign of James I*, p. 12.

138. Glanmor Williams, *Renewal and Reformation*, p. 462.

139. Gwyn Williams, *The Welsh in Their History*, p. 18. See also Owen, *Elizabethan Wales*, pp. 68–70.

140. R. Brinley Jones, *The Old British Tongue*, pp. 33–34.

141. Llwyd, *Breuiary of Britayne* 60r.

142. The Welsh, for instance, were thought especially litigious. In Wales itself, court cases "had become a new way of carrying on feuds" (Penry Williams, "The Welsh Borderland Under Queen Elizabeth," p. 30). Emigré Welshmen were well represented among England's lawyers, and especially among those, said Llwyd, who "professe the Ciuile, or Canon lawes in this Realme" (*Breuiary of Britayne* 60v). Llwyd saw this too as an effect of the civilizing of the Welsh: "And like as this [Welsh] nation (as Tacitus reporteth) beyng very impacient of iniuries, was alwayes at variance in continuall warres, and slaughter within itself: so now, through feare of lawes whiche they doo very ciuilly obey: they striue in actions, and controuersies vnto the consumyng of all their gooddes" (ibid. 61r).

143. Penry Williams, "The Welsh Borderland Under Queen Elizabeth," p. 33.

144. Glanmor Williams, *Renewal and Reformation*, p. 465. See also Gwynfor Jones, "The Gentry," p. 21.

145. Bartley, *Teague, Shenkin, and Sawney*, p. 66. See also Gwyn Williams, *The Welsh in Their History*, p. 17.

146. Gwynfor Jones, "The Gentry," p. 30.

147. Ibid., p. 29.

148. Owen, *Wales in the Reign of James I*, p. 3.

149. Bartley, *Teague, Shenkin, and Sawney*, p. 48.

150. Penry Williams, "The Welsh Borderland Under Queen Elizabeth," p. 33.

151. Glanmor Williams, *Renewal and Reformation*, p. 464.

152. Ibid., p. 466.

153. Lacey, *Robert Earl of Essex*, pp. 64–65.

154. Hadfield and Maley, "Introduction," p. 7.

155. Greenblatt, *Shakespearean Negotiations*, p. 57.

156. In the Quarto, Gower *is* on the stage when the altercation begins, since he tells Fluellen, "Here a [Pistol] comes, swelling like a Turkecocke" (Quarto F4r).

157. Quarto C2v.

158. Quarto F4v.

159. Joel Altman notes that "Pistol was speaking to current affairs when he envisioned a profitable future in sturdy vagabondage upon his return from Henry's France." Not only was "a new act against vagabonds and sturdy beggars [passed] in the 1597–98 Parliament but also a proclamation authorizing summary execution of incorrigible offenders under martial law. Specifically mentioned were those 'coloring their wandering under the name of soldiers lately come from the wars,' who have 'not only committed robberies and murders upon her majesty's people in their travel from place to place, but also resisted and murdered divers constables and others that have come to the rescue'" ("'Vile Participation,'" p. 12).

160. Gwyn Williams, *Madoc*, p. 35. See also Kendrick, *British Antiquity, passim*, and Ferguson, *Utter Antiquity*, pp. 84–105.

161. Glanmor Williams, *Renewal and Reformation*, p. 452.

162. Gwyn Williams, *The Welsh in Their History*, pp. 17–18.

163. Glanmor Williams, *Renewal and Reformation*, p. 456.

164. Ibid., p. 453.

165. Gwyn Williams, *The Welsh in Their History*, p. 19.

166. Gwyn Williams, *Madoc*, p. 36.

167. Patterson, "Back by Popular Demand," p. 41. Although these "nationalist" passages are to be found only in the Folio, Patterson's argument would seem to imply that the Quarto—"a symbolic enactment of nationalist fervor"—should include them as well.

168. Benedict Anderson, *Imagined Communities*, p. 19.

169. Goldberg, *Sodometries*, p. 161.

170. P. Anderson, *English Questions*, p. 21.

171. Greenblatt, *Shakespearean Negotiations*, p. 58.

Chapter 2

1. See the "Bibliographical Note" to Edmund Spenser, *A View of the Present State of Ireland.* All further references will be given parenthetically in the text.

2. This premise has been questioned recently by Jean R. Brink, who argues that "the suppression of the *View* seems to be an invention of recent scholarship, which portrays the Elizabethan state as making extraordinary efforts to contain subversive texts" ("Constructing the *View of the Present State of Ireland,*" p. 206). In itself, the Stationers' Register does not, she says, provide definite evidence that this treatise was censored. Indeed, no finished text of the *View* exists and we cannot even assume that Spenser wrote it. (But see also Andrew Hadfield, "Certainties and Uncertainties," *passim.*) This chapter, which grows out of "recent scholarship," does in fact assume that Spenser wrote the *View* and that Elizabeth's government, or elements within it, found it unpalatable. But here I am less concerned to "prove" overt censorship than I am to account for the text's relation to the inhibitions and imperatives that governed discourse about Ireland among the English political class. Both, I argue, are keyed to a still deeper problem, that of the status of English common law within an unavoidably "British" domain. That the *View* was suppressed, as it most probably was, is a useful sign of the difficulties that it posed for English authorities, but that its severe and paradoxical argument would pose such difficulties is a judgment that we derive, finally, from reading the text itself together with the other available material, that is to say, from reconstructing the community of opinion within which Spenser sought to position himself. And the restraints that this community could impose were not always so definitive as outright silencing. As Glenn Burgess puts it in his nuanced study of absolutism in early modern English political thought, "The crucial point is that censorship did not function as an attempt to impose a uniformity of views or to prevent criticism of government policy. It was exercised in circumstances where words were likely to incite people to particular actions. We can even go beyond this and say that it was exercised against, not words as such, but words used in contexts where they could create political and social disobedience." If Spenser's *View* was explicitly censored, then we have a powerful indication of how volatile its arguments were. But even if, as is perhaps more likely, it was not so much "censored" as "disappeared," kept from publication by a collective sense, arrived at variously by the interested parties, that this text would not be convenient at the moment, then we still have to account for the objections that would, tacitly, have been raised. Burgess wonders if "censorship was even as important in shaping the *silences* in political writing and debate as a sense of *decorum*" (*Absolute Monarchy*, pp. 7, 12; emphasis Burgess's). My argument is meant to address the indecorousness of the *View*, a quality that is borne out by the difficulties that this text poses for its readers even today.

3. Goldberg, *James I and the Politics of Literature*, p. 9.

4. Brady, "Spenser's Irish Crisis," p. 22.

5. For in-depth accounts of the debate over Irish policy, both in England and

Ireland, see Bradshaw, *The Irish Constitutional Revolution of the Sixteenth Century*, and Brady, *The Chief Governors*.

6. Goldberg, *James I*, p. 9.

7. Quinn, *The Elizabethans and the Irish*, pp. 127–28.

8. Bottigheimer, "Kingdom and Colony," p. 52. Bottigheimer is quoting Canny, "The Ideology of English Colonization," p. 583.

9. Goldberg, *James I*, p. 9.   10. Yeats, *Essays and Introductions*, p. 371.

11. Goldberg, *James I*, p. 9.   12. Yeats, *Essays and Introductions*, p. 372.

13. Richard Bellings's judgment on Spenser, made around 1635, is quoted in Maley, "How Milton and Some Contemporaries Read Spenser's *View*," p. 193.

14. Rambuss, *Spenser's Secret Career*, p. 3. Emphasis Rambuss's. Further references will be included parenthetically in the text.

15. Rambuss cites Mulcaster's *Positions*, p. 269. As Rambuss notes, his approach is generally indebted to the work of D. A. Miller in *The Novel and the Police*—see especially the chapter on "Secret Subjects, Open Secrets," pp. 192–220—and of Eve Kosofsky Sedgwick in *Epistemology of the Closet*. See also an earlier essay of Sedgwick's, "Privilege of Unknowing," included in *Tendencies*, pp. 23–51, and partially excerpted in *Epistemology of the Closet*, pp. 4–8. Implied throughout much of these works is a brief, powerful meditation on speech and silence found in Michel Foucault's *The History of Sexuality*, in which Foucault urges that "silence itself—the things one declines to say, or is forbidden to name, the discretion that is required between different speakers—is less the absolute limit of discourse, the other side from which it is separated by a strict boundary, than an element that functions alongside the things said, with them and in relation to them within overall strategies" (p. 27). Lines from this passage also provide an epigraph for Rambuss's *Spenser's Secret Career*.

16. Spenser's *View*, to which I devote many pages of *Between Nations*, is not meant to stand in here for all of his poetic work. Rather, for me the polemical *View* defines an end point: Spenser in the close of his career. As readers will notice, the questions of Britain the treatise raises radiate backward throughout this author's corpus, and these questions would bear further treatment. I hope to return to them in later work.

17. For a reevaluation of the implications of Spenser's "exile," see Rambuss, *Spenser's Secret Career*, pp. 62–63.

18. Canny, "Spenser's Irish Crisis," p. 204.

19. Canny, *The Elizabethan Conquest of Ireland*, p. 45.

20. Maxwell, *Irish History from Contemporary Sources (1509–1610)*, p. 46.

21. Brady, "The Road to the *View*," pp. 41–42. Brady responded to Goldberg's *James I and the Politics of Literature* and to an earlier version of this chapter, "Some Quirk, Some Subtle Evasion," in which I argued that Spenser's *View* "insinuates the distasteful ambiguities involved in trying to recreate the verities of English law in an alien land; he argues obliquely for the incoherence of the law, the chosen instrument of official policy" (p. 152). Brady's summation of Goldberg's argument and of mine—"it has sometimes been contended that it was [Spenser's] unambiguous ad-

vocacy of naked force that provoked a response of embarrassed silence from those men of affairs whom he had hoped to influence, or more sceptically, that it was his honest declaration of the real bases of English power in Ireland that produced the same reaction" (p. 41)—seems off the mark. Who is being said to hold which position is unclear, as is the difference between advocating the use of "naked force" and declaring the "real bases of English power in Ireland." Surely, the Privy Council was aware that naked force *was* the real base of power in the kingdom. And while Goldberg does indeed draw a distinction between the "realities" of government there and some illusory sense that the *View* perhaps inadvertently punctured, my argument, in fact, went to the critique of the common law that Spenser advanced in his treatise.

Brady has elaborated his thoughts on the *View* in the course of an ongoing debate with Nicholas Canny, who argues that in the *View* Spenser represented the opinions and interests of the New English in Ireland. He meant to gain support from the Crown for this faction by denigrating the Old English and their policy of gradual assimilation of the Gaels. See also Canny's "Edmund Spenser and the Development of an Anglo-Irish Identity"; Canny's reply to Brady's "Spenser's Irish Crisis," also entitled "Spenser's Irish Crisis"; Brady's "Reply"; and Canny's "Introduction." Against Canny, Brady holds that, "far from being a clear and rational statement of some dominant political theory, or of some prevalent ideological disposition, the *View* is riddled with ambiguity. It has defeated all attempts to identify it as a contribution to English political thought concerning Ireland because it itself is a symptom of a profound crisis in the English experience of that country," as well as a product of Spenser's "personal crisis" in the late 1590's ("Spenser's Irish Crisis," pp. 33, 41). In the later stages of the debate, Canny and Brady appear to have reached some agreement, Canny accepting Brady's thesis on the *View*'s treatment of the common law (while ignoring his earlier claims for the text's incoherence), and assimilating that thesis to his own claim that Spenser was characteristically New English (see Canny, "Introduction," p. 11). For a critique of Brady's positioning of the *View* in relation to the allegedly less ambiguous book 5 of *The Faerie Queene*, see Patterson, "The Egalitarian Giant," pp. 99–102. This essay was later reprinted, with some revisions, in Patterson's *Reading Between the Lines*, pp. 80–116.

22. Brady, "The Road to the *View*," p. 43.

23. Canny, "Edmund Spenser and the Development of an Anglo-Irish Identity," p. 7.

24. Yeats, *Essays and Introductions*, p. 361.

25. Dunne, "The Gaelic Response to Conquest and Colonisation," p. 14.

26. Canny, "The Permissive Frontier," p. 18.

27. Canny, "Permissive Frontier," pp. 23–24.

28. Ibid., p. 36.

29. Beckett, *The Making of Modern Ireland 1603–1923*, p. 18.

30. Ibid., p. 15.

31. Canny, *Old English Elite*, p. 9.

32. For further discussion of the ambiguities of English mapping in the king-

dom, see my "Off the Map." For other "views" which address the *View* specifically, see Lupton, "Mapping Mutability," and Bruce Avery, "Mapping the Irish Other."

33. Sir John Davies, *A Discovery of the True Causes Why Ireland Was Never Entirely Subdued [And] Brought Under Obedience of the Crown of England Until the Beginning of His Majesty's Happy Reign*, p. 188. Further references will be included parenthetically in the text.

34. Canny, *Elizabethan Conquest*, p. 26.

35. On such marriages, which were rare, see Cosgrove, "Hiberniores Ipsis Hibernis," pp. 6–7.

36. Canny, *Old English Elite*, p. 4.

37. Ibid., p. 20.

38. Bottigheimer, "Kingdom and Colony," p. 49.

39. Canny, *Old English Elite*, p. 11.

40. Canny, "Ideology of English Colonization," p. 583.

41. Ibid., p. 588.

42. Canny, "Edmund Spenser and the Development of an Anglo-Irish Identity," p. 2.

43. Renwick, "Commentary" to the *View*, p. 182.

44. Ibid., p. 184.

45. "Both Nicholas Canny and Brendan Bradshaw write of the *View* as if Irenius were identical with Spenser," Patterson says (*Reading Between the Lines*, p. 98). For Ciaran Brady's sense that in the dialogue Eudoxus is "the relatively passive partner," the "straw man" of the piece, see his "Spenser's Irish Crisis," pp. 37, 39, 41. For Patterson, Eudoxus is rather an "independent thinker, who asserts the value of many aspects of Irish culture that Irenius means to suppress" (ibid., p. 99).

46. Gross, *Spenserian Poetics*, p. 80.

47. Ibid.

48. Goldberg, *James I*, p. 10. Goldberg employs an alternative spelling.

49. Gottfried, "Irish Geography in Spenser's *View*," pp. 134–35.

50. Canny, *Elizabethan Conquest*, p. 99.

51. Ibid., p. 55.

52. Ibid., p. 56.

53. Renwick, "Commentary" to the *View*, p. 175.

54. As John Pocock has pointed out, Spenser's readers could also have known that "County Palatine" more specifically derived from *comes palatinus*, an imperial title designating a companion of the palace who derived his authority from the prince, but by full delegation (personal correspondence).

55. "To the right Honorable the Earle of *Ormond and Ossory*," from Spenser, *Spenser: Poetical Works*, p. 411.

56. Collins, *Letters and Memorials of State*, vol. 1, p. 20.

57. Ibid., p. 47.

58. Ibid., p. 20.

59. Canny, *Elizabethan Conquest*, p. 21.

60. Ibid., p. 106.

61. Rich, *A New Description of Ireland*, p. 3.

62. *Smyth's Information of Ireland* (1561), quoted at length in Hore, "Irish Bardism in 1561," p. 166.

63. This view resurfaced recently, when Lance Morrow told the readers of *Time* that "television now hastens reality into art with a sort of Irish efficiency: when an Irish Republican Army terrorist-hero blows up a British army truck in the mid-afternoon, the deed will probably be a song in the pubs that night. Such ready glorification is one reason that no peaceful settlement has been found." *Time,* Sept. 21, 1992, p. 51.

64. The "classical" period of bardic poetry is usually put between 1200 and 1601, when the earl of Tyrone was defeated at the battle of Kinsale, and the English conquest of Ireland achieved a new level of rigor. For the response of the bards to this calamity, see Nicholas Canny, "The Formation of the Irish Mind," T. J. Dunne, "The Gaelic Response to Conquest and Colonisation," and Allan Macinnes, "Gaelic Culture in the Seventeenth Century." For the Gaelic poetry of the classical period, see Oscar Bergin, *Irish Bardic Poetry.* For the Gaelic poetry of the post-classical period, see *An Duanaire 1600–1900,* ed. and trans. Thomas Kinsella. Still valuable on the tradition of bardic invective is Fred Norris Robinson's "Satirists and Enchanters in Early Irish Literature." On this, see also Vivian Mercier, *The Irish Comic Tradition.* On the evidentiary uses of bardic poetry of the classical period, see Katherine Simms, "Bardic Poetry as a Historical Source."

65. Patterson, *Reading Between the Lines,* p. 102.

66. Hore, "Irish Bardism in 1561," pp. 165–66.

67. Patterson, *Reading Between the Lines,* p. 103.

68. Spenser, we should note, is not alone in his provisional relation to truth in Ireland. Although, when it comes to policing the bards, certainty is demanded and expected, in other contexts English policy makers can show this same curiously double sense of truth. It may be that Spenser's ambivalence is a feature of the official discourse itself; he merely exploits it. Sir John Davies, always confident of his grip on veracity, would ironically inform the earl of Salisbury that the writers of other dispatches "knowing all things *a priori,* in that they see the causes and grounds of all accidents, can give your Lordship more full and perfect intelligence than such an inferior Minister as I am, which come to understand things *a posteriori* only by the effect and by the success" ("A Letter from Sir John Davies, Knight, Attorney General of Ireland to Robert Earl of Salisbury Touching the State of Monaghan, Fermanagh, and Cavan Wherein is a Discourse Concerning the Corbes and Irenahs of Ireland," p. 345). And since in his day the English had great success at suppressing all competing belief in Ireland, his assured pragmatism probably suffered little contradiction. But earlier, before James I's conquest, we see a wariness in some official statements. In a dispatch on Irish policy, Henry VIII advised "sober waies, politique driftes, and amiable persuasions founded in lawe and reason" (Bradshaw, *Irish Constitutional Revolution,* p. 63). This king knows very well the need for obliquity, perhaps misstatement or evasion, in placating a barbaric people who do not always need to tolerate English truth, though he has no doubt that official disinformation

is entirely "founded in law and reason." Occasionally, "truth" comes to mean something like benevolence. Paradoxically, it implies a willingness not to impose English certainties unnecessarily. In 1537, John Allen urged that the Irish should have "truth used to them that they might perceive that we desire more the weal and quiet, than their cattle or goods" (ibid., p. 176), as if in Ireland truth could be employed or discarded at will. He too assumes that truth is something to be used, however charitably. Of course, when the conciliatory policies of Henry's early reign gave way to outright conquest, the full rigor of English truth was made clear to those who stood outside it. In 1569, a document placing Munster under martial law empowered Humphrey Gilbert "to annoy in every way any such malefactor by fire and sword according to the quality of the offense, and to use any kind of punishment upon the suspected person for the furthering of her Majesty's service for the better understanding of the truth" (Canny, *Elizabethan Conquest*, p. 101). It is truth in this brutally ineluctable sense that Irenius at once employs and evades.

69. Spenser's tacit secularism was not unprecedented. Sir John Perrot said that, in matters of state, "a man should set aside God, who in government admitteth no policy that is besides, much less directly against, His will" (Canny, "Identity Formation in Ireland," p. 172).

70. See n. 33.

71. Keohane, *Philosophy and the State in France*, p. 57.

72. "Use"—that is, custom—"becomes another nature" was a phrase often quoted in the early modern period. See Manley, *Convention 1500–1750*, *passim* but especially pp. 90–106.

73. Quinn, *The Elizabethans and the Irish*, p. 36.

74. Canny, *Elizabethan Conquest*, p. 123.

75. Quinn, *The Elizabethans and the Irish*, p. 45.

76. Sir John Davies, "A Letter from Sir John Davies to Robert Earl of Salisbury Concerning the State of Ireland," p. 384.

77. Ibid., p. 385.

78. Ibid., p. 389.

79. Quinn, *The Elizabethans and the Irish*, pp. 68–69.

80. Pocock, *The Ancient Constitution and the Feudal Law*.

81. Pocock, "The Ancient Constitution Revisited," p. 262, published together with a "reissue" of *The Ancient Constitution* by Cambridge University Press in 1987.

82. Pocock, *The Machiavellian Moment*, pp. 340–41.

83. Pawlisch, "Sir John Davies, the Ancient Constitution, and the Civil Law," p. 689. See also Pawlisch, *Sir John Davies and the Conquest of Ireland*.

84. Bradshaw, *Irish Constitutional Revolution*, p. 75.

85. Myers, introduction to *Discovery of the True Causes*, by Sir John Davies, p. 55.

86. Pocock, *Ancient Constitution*, p. 62. Here Pocock refers to the Old English specifically.

87. Ibid., pp. 60–61.

88. Ibid., p. 62.

89. Ibid.

90. Pocock, "Retrospect," p. 297.

91. Pocock, "Limits and Divisions," p. 317.

92. Pocock extends these claims well back into the medieval period. On the gradual expansion of the "Anglo-Norman kingship" into the march, for instance, see "Limits and Divisions," pp. 321–23.

93. Ibid., p. 335.

94. For an essay in which Pocock does consider inter-British influences within legal history, see "Cambridge Paradigms and Scotch Philosophers."

95. By "insularity," again, I mean a self-confirming belief in the unrivaled validity of common law, not necessarily an adherence to the doctrine of immemorial custom.

96. See, for instance, Pawlisch, "Sir John Davies," *passim.*

97. Pocock, "Retrospect," p. 262.

98. Ibid., p. 282.

99. Pocock, "Limits and Divisions," p. 320.

100. Pocock, "British History," p. 614.

101. Ibid., p. 616.   102. Pocock, *Ancient Constitution*, p. 63.

103. Ibid.   104. Ibid., pp. 62–63.

105. Though the second assertion reads in full: "It [brehon law] presented no striking points of resemblance, no principles of its own which might be found embedded in the common law and suggest new ideas as to how the latter had been built." Here one sense of insularity modulates into another.

106. Personal correspondence.

107. Pocock, *Ancient Constitution*, p. 34.

108. In fact, Irenius is wrong about the brehon law's orality; it was extensively codified.

109. I owe this comparison to John Pocock, who points out that both the policy of surrender and regrant "and Davies' more wholehearted substitution of primogeniture were designed to overcome" the problem of the non-inheritability of Irish allegiance. "The rationale was that the custom of partibility was incompatible with monarchy and therefore with settled government" (personal correspondence).

110. Pocock, "Retrospect," p. 275.

111. John Pocock has asked if Spenser is saying "that under Irish conditions, even the statutes of an Anglo-Irish Parliament can't enforce common law in an Anglo-Irish court working under [these] conditions," or if, more radically, Spenser "rejects the interpretive capacity of an English judge, sitting in an English court, interpreting a statute passed by an English parliament," thus rejecting the common law as such (personal correspondence). I would argue that he does both. Spenser's complaints are usually specific to the Irish situation, and he certainly does not directly challenge the legitimacy of the common law in England itself. Nonetheless, his legal critique is far reaching; it goes fundamentally to the premises of the English common law. He doubts the efficacy of *any* existing legal safeguard against prevarication and misprison—oath taking, judicial review, written statutory law—and dismisses them all, finally, in favor of a standard maintained by an absolute royal prerogative.

Spenser's *View* could be taken as a threat to the common law establishment, then, because he insinuated an attack on the bases of the common law in one kingdom, Ireland, that had disturbing implications for that law in another, England.

112. Spenser's specific complaint against the "statutes of the realm" of Ireland is that they are anachronistic and inappropriately rigorous, or, as he puts it, "impertinent and unnecessary, the which perhaps though at the time of making of them, were very needful, yet now through change of time, are clean antiquated, and altogether idle, as that which forbiddeth any to wear their beards all on the upper lip and none on under the chin . . . and that which maketh that all Irishmen that shall converse among the English shall be taken for spies and so punished" (31).

113. Patterson, *Censorship and Interpretation*, p. 44.

114. Pocock, "Retrospect," p. 283.

115. As Pocock points out, Spenser does "leave room here for Norman law's subsequent domestication as English custom" (personal correspondence).

116. Spenser, "Briefe Note," *The Works of Edmund Spenser*, vol. 9, pp. 241–42.

117. Spenser, "Briefe Note," *The Works of Edmund Spenser*, vol. 9, p. 236.

118. Maley, "How Milton and Some Contemporaries Read Spenser's *View*," p. 191.

119. Ibid.

120. See Falls, *Mountjoy*, and F. M. Jones, *Mountjoy 1563–1606*.

121. Harris, "The State of the Realm," p. 58.

122. On this settlement, see Moody, *The Londonderry Plantation 1609–41*.

123. Sir John Davies, "State of Monaghan," p. 359.

124. Canny, "Identity Formation," p. 178.

125. *Two Histories of Ireland*, ed. James Ware. I will cite the text as reprinted in *Ancient Irish Histories*.

126. Maley, "Milton and Contemporaries," p. 192.

127. Brady, "Spenser's Irish Crisis," p. 25.

128. Maley, "Milton and Contemporaries," p. 192.

129. *Ancient Irish Histories*, p. 237 (emphasis mine).

130. Canny, "Identity Formation," p. 191. Canny also speculates that the *View* saw print because its arguments "supported Wentworth's ambition to proceed with the Connacht plantation, an enterprise that had long been advocated by the New English in Ireland."

131. Ibid., p. 169.

132. Ibid., p. 177.

133. Ibid., p. 191.

134. *Ancient Irish Histories*, pp. 237–38.

135. Canny, "Identity Formation," p. 179.

136. *Andrew Marvell*, ed. Frank Kermode and Keith Walker.

137. Later commentators have often agreed that Spenser's *View* was fulfilled, if not vindicated, by Cromwell's invasion. Richard McCabe remarks that in the *View* Spenser dreamed a "Cromwellian dream a century [?] before Cromwell" ("The Fate of Irena," p. 119). W. B. Yeats saw a more direct connection. "He had studied Spenser's book," he said of Cromwell, "and approved of it . . . finding, doubtless, his

own head there, for Spenser, a king of the old race, carried a mirror which showed kings yet to come though but kings of the mob" (*Essays and Introductions*, p. 376).

138. Patterson, "The Egalitarian Giant," p. 114.

139. "Is it not ironic," asks Willy Maley, "that the utter extirpation of the Irish desired by Spenser under his beloved Gloriana could only be attained when the English throne was vacant, and unqualified executive power was placed in the hands of the viceroy?" ("Milton and Contemporaries," p. 201).

140. Canny, "Identity Formation," p. 200. Canny quotes *The Perfect Diurnall*, June 7, 1652, no. 130, p. 1928.

Chapter 3

1. Wallace, *Destiny His Choice*, p. 145. Further references will be given parenthetically in the text.

2. Legouis, *Andrew Marvell*, p. 10. "Cowardice" is Legouis's term for the allegation made against Marvell.

3. Kelliher, *Andrew Marvell: Poet and Politician, 1621–78*, p. 111.

4. Legouis, *Andrew Marvell*, p. 108.

5. The claim that Marvell was "opportunistic" is often attributed first of all to Legouis's biography (see n. 3). See Wallace, *Destiny His Choice*, p. 145, and Patterson, *Marvell and the Civic Crown*, p. 15. See also the unpublished dissertation by Robbins, "A Critical Study of the Political Activities of Andrew Marvell," cited by both of these critics.

6. Kermode and Walker, introduction to *Andrew Marvell*, ed. Frank Kermode and Keith Walker, p. xii. All citations of Marvell's verse will be from this volume.

7. Typically, Wallace hedges: "The opening stanzas, however, with what the rhetoricians might have called an insinuation, tacitly concede that his homecoming raises grave questions about the dangers of his supreme power which Englishmen ought to consider" (*Destiny His Choice*, p. 72).

8. Patterson, *Marvell and the Civic Crown*, p. 15. In line with Wallace, Patterson invokes "loyalism," along with "opportunism . . . or conservatism," whatever "one calls it," to stabilize Marvell's "political convictions" around the "tenacity of his belief in a mixed state and peaceful, constitutional government." This, she says, "remains believable as a motivating principle behind all the strategic shifts and occasional compromises which political action required."

9. For a detailed listing of the manuscripts of "The Loyal Scot," see *The Poems and Letters of Andrew Marvell*, ed. H. M. Margoliouth, vol. 1, pp. 384–87.

10. The phrase is Foucault's and entitles the introduction to Jonathan Goldberg's *Sodometries*.

11. Sedgwick, *Between Men*. There is also an echo of Sedgwick's title, of course, in my own.

12. Stevenson, "Cromwell, Scotland, and Ireland," p. 180.

13. Kermode and Walker, introduction to *Andrew Marvell*, p. viii.

14. Norbrook, "Marvell's 'Horatian Ode' and the Politics of Genre," p. 147.

15. Greene, "The Balance of Power in Marvell's 'Horatian Ode,'" p. 379.

16. Hirst, "The English Republic and the Meaning of Britain," p. 453. Hirst also notes that the appeal of a united Britain was far stronger in Scotland than in England (p. 457), and he is joined in this by Arthur H. Williamson, who argues that "Britain" not only held "far more serious meanings" for seventeenth-century Scotsmen than Englishmen, but it "is in many senses a Scottish idea" ("From the Invention of Great Britain to the Creation of British History," p. 275). In the 1650's, union between England and Scotland had a religious appeal on both sides of the border, although disproportionately. Despite "an exceedingly aggressive and hostile intellectual environment" (p. 272) in England, some few there saw such a coming together as divinely ordained (see also Hirst, "English Republic," pp. 464–66). But Scottish tradition, says Williamson, was more concerned with maintaining a sense of equilibrium with its powerful, dismissive neighbor to the south, and "could readily imagine a massive religiolegislative enactment that revaluated institutions and established new systems of authority" in the name of a British confederation. Consequently, the middle of the century in Scotland precipitated "an altogether unique moment in postmedieval British history." The covenanters, including those against whom Cromwell marched in 1650, "came far closer to achieving a Britain" (p. 275) than James I ever had. For a full-scale treatment of this argument, see Williamson, *Scottish National Consciousness in the Age of James VI.*

17. Hirst, "English Republic," p. 453.

18. P. B. Ellis, *Hell or Connaught!* p. 177.

19. B. Anderson, *Imagined Communities,* p. 36.

20. The "Civil War" was first renominated by Beckett in *The Making of Modern Ireland, 1603–1923.* On the implications of this nomenclature shift for a British historiography, see Pocock, "Limits and Divisions," pp. 325–27.

21. Hirst, "English Republic," p. 452.

22. Stevenson, "Cromwell, Scotland, and Ireland," p. 180.

23. Hirst, "English Republic," p. 453.

24. Pocock, "Two Kingdoms and Three Histories?" p. 305. Pocock does not apply this last phrase to Cromwell himself; it describes the eventual reaction to "a long series of steps" by which the Stuarts came to be seen as a "menace" to the tradition of English legal autonomy. The first of these steps, says Pocock, was "James VI and I's proclamation of union" in 1603, "which we may ascribe to the exigencies of 'multiple monarchy' and the 'British problem', and which ended in the imposition of English upon 'British' history" (p. 306).

25. See Hirst, "English Republic," pp. 459–63.

26. Ibid., p. 469.

27. Pocock, "Contingency, Identity, Sovereignty," p. 294.

28. Spivak, "Acting Bits/Identity Talk," p. 781.

29. For a comprehensive account of these events in terms of the interactions among three kingdoms, see Russell, *The Fall of the British Monarchies 1637–1642.*

30. Temple, *The Irish Rebellion; or, An History of the Attempts of the Irish Papists to Extirpate the Protestants in the Kingdom of Ireland; Together with the Barbarous Cruelties and Bloody Massacres which Ensued Thereupon*, p. 75. Further references will be included parenthetically in the text.

31. See Corish, "The Rising of 1641 and the Catholic Confederacy, 1641–5," pp. 291–92. To indicate the exaggerations that have attended this revolt: Temple claimed the toll was 300,000 over the two years, "cruelly murdered in cold blood, or destroyed in some other way, or expelled out of their habitations" (*Irish Rebellion*, p. 15). For a comprehensive account of the uprising and its causes, see Perceval-Maxwell, *The Outbreak of the Irish Rebellion of 1641*.

32. Pocock, "Limits and Divisions," p. 326.

33. Barnard, "Crises of Identity Among Irish Protestants 1641–1685," p. 50.

34. Ibid., p. 52.

35. The rebels at first tried not to " 'meddle with' the Ulster Scots, in the hope that this powerful group would not become involved, but within a few weeks they had, with a certain inevitability, been drawn into the conflict" (Corish, "Rising of 1641," p. 291). For a fine-grained account of the contacts between these two British peoples this period, see Stevenson, *Scottish Covenanters and Irish Confederates*.

36. Spenser, *A View of the Present State of Ireland*, p. 23.

37. I quote here the marginal note in the 1812 edition of Temple, *The Irish Rebellion*; the plantation itself was put in place during the reign of James I.

38. Stevenson, "Cromwell, Scotland, and Ireland," p. 150. On the fate of Ireland under Cromwell, see Barnard, *Cromwellian Ireland*.

39. Cromwell, *The Writings and Speeches of Oliver Cromwell*, vol. 2, p. 107.

40. Ibid., p. 124.

41. Hirst, "English Republic," p. 454.

42. Cromwell, *Writings and Speeches*, vol. 2, p. 197.

43. Hirst, "English Republic," p. 454.

44. Cromwell, *Writings and Speeches*, vol. 2, p. 198.

45. Stevenson, "Cromwell, Scotland, and Ireland," p. 158.

46. Worden, "Andrew Marvell, Oliver Cromwell, and the Horatian Ode," p. 174.

47. Greene, "Balance of Power," p. 390. Emphasis Greene's. Greene goes on to say of his own suggestion that this "harsh verdict doesn't really account for a text which has after all appeared as a formidable member of the small collection of major public poems our language affords" (pp. 390–91). I would add that the "Ode" may be so formidable a member of the body of political poems that "our language affords" because, as Greene himself implies, it problematizes the very notion of "our language" in seventeenth-century Britain, and thus calls up the constitutive questions of this polity. His verdict, then, may not be "harsh" and might help to account for the "Ode" quite well.

48. Worden, "Andrew Marvell," p. 174.

49. Ibid.

50. Norbrook, "Marvell's 'Horatian Ode,' " p. 159.

51. Worden, "Andrew Marvell," p. 174.

52. Ibid.

53. Walker, *Anarchia Anglicana; or, The History of Independency. The Second Part,* p. 203.

54. Greene, "Balance of Power," p. 386.

55. Barnard, "Crises of Identity," p. 43.

56. See the editors' note on line 35 of the "Ode" in Marvell, *Andrew Marvell,* p. 311.

57. On the "republican Britannia" that emerged with the "Cromwellian moment," see Armitage, "The Cromwellian Protectorate and the Languages of Empire," *passim.*

58. Wallace, *Destiny His Choice,* p. 111.

59. Armitage, "Cromwellian Protectorate," p. 535.

60. Ibid., p. 532.

61. Hirst, "English Republic," p. 466.

62. Ibid., p. 469.

63. Legouis, *Andrew Marvell,* p. 103. On the far-reaching imperial grandeur that Cromwell's ascendancy seemed to promise, see Armitage, "Cromwellian Protectorate," p. 534.

64. Legouis, *Andrew Marvell,* p. 103.

65. Levack, *The Formation of the British State,* p. 11. See also Omond, *The Early History of the Scottish Union Question,* pp. 122–46, and Mark Goldie, "Divergence and Union."

66. See Levack, *British State,* pp. 11, 45–46.

67. Omond, *Scottish Union Question,* p. 141.

68. "A Modern Account of *Scotland:* Being an exact Description of the Country, and a true Character of the People and their Manners, Written from thence by an *English* Gentleman," p. 123.

69. Ibid., p. 126.

70. Kelliher, *Andrew Marvell,* p. 103.

71. Benet, "'The Loyall Scot' and the Hidden Narcissus," p. 195.

72. Ibid., p. 205.

73. Ibid., p. 196. On the long-standing association of narcissism and homosexuality, and a critique of that association, see Warner, "Homo-Narcissism; or, Heterosexuality," *passim.*

74. See Rambuss, "Pleasure and Devotion," p. 277. See also Rambuss's "Engendering the Faith of Nations."

75. Note that Douglas's beauty is not itself sexually androgynous; instead, his "beauty" is distinct from his "sex" and "veils" it, however it is gendered.

76. Empson, *Using Biography,* p. 79.

77. Ibid., p. 16. Legouis called the "charges [of sodomy] made by [Marvell's enemies Samuel] Parker and his acolytes . . . ignominious" (Legouis, *Andrew Marvell,* p. 122).

78. See, for example, Rambuss, "Pleasure and Devotion," pp. 260–69. Tracing the argument for the "anachronism" of the term "sexuality" in a footnote (p. 277), Rambuss cites Foucault's *The History of Sexuality*; Alan Bray, *Homosexuality in Renaissance England*; and David Halperin, *One Hundred Years of Homosexuality*. Among these, Bray's scrupulously period-specific work has been crucial for early modern studies. See also his "Homosexuality and the Signs of Male Friendship in Elizabethan England," and Jonathan Goldberg's development of Bray's arguments in *Sodometries*, pp. 18–25.

79. Rambuss, "Pleasure and Devotion," p. 263.

80. Especially influential has been Butler's *Gender Trouble*.

81. Sedgwick, *Between Men*, p. 35. Sedgwick makes this point in the midst of an exemplary reading of Shakespeare's sonnets.

82. Bray, *Homosexuality*, p. 80.　　83. Ibid., p. 86.

84. Ibid., p. 103.　　85. Ibid., p. 104.

86. Ibid., p. 64.　　87. Legouis, *Andrew Marvell*, p. 121.

88. Ibid., p. 109.　　89. Ibid., p. 114.

90. Empson, *Using Biography*, pp. 14–15.

91. Ibid., p. 15. The specific relevance Empson has in mind is its bearing on the question of his marriage. In general, readers have been unconvinced by Empson's claims on this matter. "However that may be," Frank Kermode and Keith Walker respond firmly to his speculations, the "standard account" holds that the poet remained a single man throughout his life (introduction to *Andrew Marvell*, p. xiii).

92. Empson, *Using Biography*, pp. 86–87.

93. These phrases are found in "The First Anniversary of the Government under His Highness the Lord Protector," ll.159, 126, 395.

94. Empson, *Using Biography*, p. 44.

95. Ibid., p. 87.

96. Ibid., p. 86.

97. Bray, "Homosexuality and the Signs of Male Friendship," p. 41.

98. Goldberg, *Sodometries*, p. 17.

99. Ibid., p. 18.

100. Ibid., p. 20.

101. This might well be what Marvell was trying to do. If he was determined to prove that he "never had any, not the remotest relation to publick matters" (see n. 4) during the reign of the Lord Protector, he may have wanted to separate himself from the Cromwellian Britannia he had heralded in the "Ode."

102. See n. 59.

103. R. F. Jones, "Science and Language in England of the Mid-Seventeenth Century," p. 96.

104. See 1.1.187–206 of William Shakespeare's *Henry V*, ed. Gary Taylor. It is quite possible, of course, that Shakespeare is Marvell's source.

105. The reference here is of course to Benedict Anderson's well-known account of nation formation, *Imagined Communities*, in which he holds that such entities

come into being as they are linked by vernacular "print languages." From the early sixteenth century on, says Anderson, these languages were disseminated in Europe by the agency of cheap popular editions, news sheets, and later the novel; this created a shared readership that was newly "capable of comprehending one another via print and paper. In the process, they gradually became aware of the hundreds of thousands, even millions, of people in their particular language-field, and at the same time that *only those* hundreds of thousands, or millions, so belonged" (*Imagined Communities*, p. 44; emphasis Anderson's). The "nation" is thus fashioned as a common reading public. However, the example of "The Loyal Scot" suggests that reading and nation formation may work together in ways that are more complex than Anderson allows. As I have shown, the reader who is implied by the poem is not one who is necessarily assured of his or her alliances with "hundreds of thousands, even millions" of fellow Britons simply by virtue of his or her reading of a common text. On the contrary, this reader is reminded constantly of what separates him or her from these other readers; simultaneously, he or she is enlisted in the project of imagining a "national" community—"Britain"—that exists only to the extent he or she is willing to acknowledge it as such. Achieving national belonging, it seems, often requires more than the sense of shared literacy with others. Readers must also be willing to acquiesce in the strategies of nation formation that are inscribed in the disseminated texts. (Simply put, what they read and that they accept what they read matters at least as much as that they read.) Otherwise, it seems clear, reading within the "imagined community" can do as much to disrupt as to promote a shared "nationalism." National relations *among* readers are negotiated in the relation *between* the reader and the text.

106. Goldberg, *Sodometries*, p. 22.   107. Ibid., p. 20.
108. Colley, *Britons*, p. 1.   109. Bray, *Homosexuality*, p. 92.

Coda

1. All citations from *Spenser: Poetical Works*, ed. J. C. Smith and E. de Selincourt. Parenthetical references are to canto, stanza, and line numbers.

2. Roche, *The Kindly Flame*, p. 45.

3. David Lee Miller, *The Poem's Two Bodies*, p. 201.

4. Berger, *The Allegorical Temper*, pp. 103–4.

5. See Spenser's use of this term in his *View of the Present State of Ireland*, p. 30.

6. Berger, *Allegorical Temper*, p. 93.

7. Cf. David Lee Miller, *Poem's Two Bodies*, p. 207.

8. Ibid., p. 205. Emphasis Miller's.

Bibliography

Akrigg, G. P. V. *Jacobean Pageant, or the Court of King James I.* 1962. Reprint, New York: Atheneum, 1967.

Altman, Joel. "'Vile Participation': The Amplification of Violence in the Theater of *Henry V.*" *Shakespeare Quarterly* 42 (1991): 1–32.

Ancient Irish Histories. 2 vols. Dublin: Hibernia Press, 1809.

Anderson, Benedict. *Imagined Communities: Reflections on the Origin and Spread of Nationalism.* Rev. Ed. London: Verso, 1991.

Anderson, Perry. *English Questions.* London: Verso, 1992.

Armitage, David. "The Cromwellian Protectorate and the Languages of Empire." *Historical Journal* 35 (1992): 531–55.

Asch, Ronald G., ed. *Three Nations—A Common History? England, Scotland, Ireland, and British History c. 1600–1920.* Bochum: Universitätsverlag Dr. N. Brockmeyer, 1993.

Ashcroft, Bill, Gareth Griffiths, and Helen Tiffin. *The Empire Writes Back: Theory and Practice in Post-Colonial Literatures.* London: Routledge, 1989.

Avery, Bruce. "Mapping the Irish Other: Spenser's *A View of the Present State of Ireland.*" *English Literary History* 57 (1990): 263–79.

Bailyn, Bernard, and Philip D. Morgan, eds. *Strangers Within the Realm: Cultural Margins of the First British Empire.* Chapel Hill: University of North Carolina Press, 1991.

Baker, David J. "Off the Map: Charting Uncertainty in Renaissance Ireland." In Brendan Bradshaw, Andrew Hadfield, and Willy Maley, eds., *Representing Ireland: Literature and the Origins of Conflict, 1534–1660,* pp. 76–92. Cambridge, Eng.: Cambridge University Press, 1993.

———. "Some Quirk, Some Subtle Evasion: Legal Subversion in Spenser's *A View of the Present State of Ireland.*" *Spenser Studies* 6 (1986): 147–63.

———. " 'Wildehirissheman': Colonialist Representation in Shakespeare's *Henry V.*" *English Literary Renaissance* 22 (1992): 37–61.

Barnard, T. C. "Crises of Identity Among Irish Protestants 1641–1685." *Past and Present* 127 (1990): 39–83.

———. *Cromwellian Ireland: English Government and Reform in Ireland 1649–1660.* Oxford: Oxford University Press, 1975.

Bartley, J. O. *Teague, Shenkin, and Sawney.* Cork: Cork University Press, 1954.

Barton, Anne. "The King Disguised: Shakespeare's *Henry V* and the Comical History." In Joseph G. Price, ed., *The Triple Bond: Plays, Mainly Shakespearean, in Performance*, pp. 92–117. University Park: Pennsylvania State University Press, 1975.

Beckett, J. C. *The Making of Modern Ireland, 1603–1923.* London: Faber and Faber, 1966.

Benet, Diana Trevino. " 'The Loyall Scot' and the Hidden Narcissus." In Claude J. Summers and Ted-Larry Pebworth, eds., *On the Celebrated and Neglected Poems of Andrew Marvell*, pp. 192–206. Columbia: University of Missouri Press, 1992.

Berger, Harry, Jr. *The Allegorical Temper: Vision and Reality in Book II of Spenser's* Faerie Queene. New Haven: Yale University Press, 1957.

Bergin, Oscar. *Irish Bardic Poetry.* David Greene and Fergus Kelly, eds. Dublin: Dublin Institute for Advanced Studies, 1970.

Bhabha, Homi K. "Introduction: Narrating the Nation." In Homi K. Bhabha, ed., *Nation and Narration*, pp. 1–7. London: Routledge, 1990.

Bloom, Harold. Introduction to William Shakespeare's *Henry V.* Harold Bloom, ed. New York: Chelsea House, 1988.

Bottigheimer, Karl S. "Kingdom and Colony: Ireland in the Westward Enterprise 1536–1660." In K. R. Andrews, N. P. Canny, and P. E. H. Hair, eds., *The Westward Enterprise: English Activities in Ireland, the Atlantic, and America 1480–1650*, pp. 45–64. Detroit: Wayne State University Press, 1979.

Bradshaw, Brendan. *The Irish Constitutional Revolution of the Sixteenth Century.* Cambridge, Eng.: Cambridge University Press, 1979.

———. "The Tudor Reformation and Revolution in Wales and Ireland: The Origins of the British Problem." In Brendan Bradshaw and John Morrill, eds., *The British Problem, c. 1534–1707: State Formation in the Atlantic Archipelago*, pp. 39–65. London: Macmillan, 1996.

Bradshaw, Brendan, Andrew Hadfield, and Willy Maley, eds., *Representing Ireland: Literature and the Origins of Conflict, 1534–1660.* Cambridge, Eng.: Cambridge University Press, 1993.

Bradshaw, Brendan, and John Morrill, eds. *The British Problem, c. 1534–1707: State Formation in the Atlantic Archipelago.* London: Macmillan, 1996.

Brady, Ciaran. *The Chief Governors: The Rise and Fall of Reform Government in Tudor Ireland 1536–1588.* Cambridge, Eng.: Cambridge University Press, 1994.

———. "Comparable Histories? Tudor Reform in Wales and Ireland." In Steven G.

Ellis and Sarah Barber, eds., *Conquest and Union: Fashioning a British State, 1485–1725*, pp. 64–86. London: Longman, 1995.

———. "Reply." *Past and Present* no. 120 (1988): 210–15.

———. "The Road to the *View*: On the Decline of Reform Thought in Tudor Ireland." In Patricia Coughlan, ed., *Spenser and Ireland: An Interdisciplinary Perspective*, pp. 25–45. Cork: Cork University Press, 1989.

———. "Spenser's Irish Crisis: Humanism and Experience in the 1590's." *Past and Present* no. 111 (1986): 17–49.

Bray, Alan. "Homosexuality and the Signs of Male Friendship in Elizabethan England." In Jonathan Goldberg, ed., *Queering the Renaissance*, pp. 40–61. Durham: Duke University Press, 1994.

———. *Homosexuality in Renaissance England*. London: Gay Men's Press, 1982.

Breuilly, John. *Nationalism and the State*. 2d ed. Chicago: University of Chicago Press, 1994.

Brink, Jean R. "Constructing the *View of the Present State of Ireland*." *Spenser Studies* 11 (1990): 203–28.

Brown, Keith M. "British History: A Sceptical Comment." In Ronald G. Asch, ed., *Three Nations—A Common History? England, Scotland, Ireland, and British History c. 1600–1920*, pp. 117–27. Bochum: Universitätsverlag Dr. N. Brockmeyer, 1993.

———. *Kingdom or Province? Scotland and the Regal Union, 1603–1715*. New York: St. Martin's Press, 1992.

Bullough, Geoffrey. *Narrative and Dramatic Sources of Shakespeare*. 8 vols. New York: Columbia University Press, 1962.

Burgess, Glenn. *Absolute Monarchy and the Stuart Constitution*. New Haven: Yale University Press, 1996.

Butler, Judith. *Gender Trouble: Feminism and the Subversion of Identity*. London: Routledge, 1990.

Cairns, David, and Shaun Richards. *Writing Ireland: Colonialism, Nationalism, and Culture*. Manchester: Manchester University Press, 1988.

Campbell, Lily B. *Shakespeare's 'Histories': Mirrors of Elizabethan Policy*. San Marino, Calif.: Huntington Library, 1947.

Canny, Nicholas. "The Attempted Anglicization of Ireland in the Seventeenth Century: An Exemplar of 'British History.'" In Ronald G. Asch, ed., *Three Nations—A Common History? England, Scotland, Ireland, and British History c. 1600–1920*, pp. 49–82. Bochum: Universitätsverlag Dr. N. Brockmeyer, 1993.

———. "Edmund Spenser and the Development of an Anglo-Irish Identity." *Yearbook of English Studies* 13 (1983): 1–19.

———. *The Elizabethan Conquest of Ireland: A Pattern Established 1565–76*. Hassocks, Sussex: Harvester Press, 1976.

———. "The Formation of the Irish Mind: Religion, Politics, and Gaelic Irish Literature 1580–1750." *Past and Present* no. 95 (1982): 91–116.

———. *The Formation of the Old English Elite in Ireland*. Dublin: National University of Ireland, 1975.

————. "Identity Formation in Ireland: The Emergence of the Anglo-Irish." In Nicholas Canny and Anthony Pagden, eds., *Colonial Identity in the Atlantic World, 1500–1800*, pp. 159–212. Princeton, N.J.: Princeton University Press, 1987.

————. "The Ideology of English Colonization: From Ireland to America." *William and Mary Quarterly*, 3d ser., 30 (1973): 575–98.

————. "Introduction: Spenser and the Reform of Ireland." In Patricia Coughlan, ed., *Spenser and Ireland: An Interdisciplinary Perspective*, pp. 9–24. Cork: Cork University Press, 1989.

————. "Irish, Scottish, and Welsh Responses to Centralization, c. 1530–c. 1640: A Comparative Perspective." In Alexander Grant and Keith J. Stringer, eds., *Uniting the Kingdom? The Making of British History*, pp. 147–69. London: Routledge, 1995.

————. "The Permissive Frontier: The Problem of Social Control in English Settlements in Ireland and Virginia 1550–1650." In K. R. Andrews, N. P. Canny, and P. E. H. Hair, eds., *The Westward Enterprise: English Activities in Ireland, the Atlantic, and America 1480–1650*, pp. 17–44. Detroit: Wayne State University Press, 1979.

————. "Spenser's Irish Crisis: Humanism and Experience in the 1590's." *Past and Present* no. 120 (1988): 201–9.

Clarke, Aidan. *The Old English in Ireland 1625–42*. Ithaca, N.Y.: Cornell University Press, 1966.

Coleman, Christopher, and David Starkey, eds. *Revolution Reassessed: Revisions in the History of Tudor Government and Administration*. Oxford: Clarendon Press, 1986.

Colley, Linda. "Britishness and Otherness: An Argument." *Journal of British Studies* 31 (1992): 309–29.

————. *Britons: Forging the Nation 1701–1837*. New Haven: Yale University Press, 1992.

Collins, Arthur, ed. *Letters and Memorials of State*. 2 vols. London, 1746.

Corish, Patrick J. "The Rising of 1641 and the Catholic Confederacy, 1641–5." In T. W. Moody, F. X. Martin, and F. J. Byrne, eds., *A New History of Ireland: Early Modern Ireland 1534–1691*, pp. 298–316. Vol. 3. Oxford: Clarendon Press, 1976.

Cosgrove, Art. "Hiberniores Ipsis Hibernis." In Art Cosgrove and Donal McCartney, eds., *Studies in Irish History Presented to R. Dudley Edwards*, pp. 1–14. Dublin: University College, 1979.

Cromwell, Oliver. *The Writings and Speeches of Oliver Cromwell*. Wilbur C. Abbott, ed. Vol. 2. Cambridge, Mass.: Harvard University Press, 1939.

Davies, Sir John. *A Discovery of the True Causes Why Ireland Was Never Entirely Subdued [And] Brought Under Obedience of the Crown of England Until the Beginning of His Majesty's Happy Reign*. James P. Myers Jr., ed. 1612. Reprint, Washington, D.C.: Catholic University of America Press, 1988.

————. "A Letter from Sir John Davies, Knight, Attorney General of Ireland to Robert Earl of Salisbury Touching the State of Monaghan, Fermanagh, and Cavan Wherein is a Discourse Concerning the Corbes and Irenahs of Ireland." In Henry Morley, ed., *Ireland Under Elizabeth and James I*, pp. 343–80. London: George Routledge, 1890.

————. "A Letter from Sir John Davies to Robert Earl of Salisbury Concerning the State of Ireland." In Henry Morley, ed., *Ireland Under Elizabeth and James I*, pp. 382–90. London: George Routledge, 1890.

Davies, R. R. *The British Isles 1100–1500: Comparisons, Contrasts, and Connections.* Edinburgh: John Donald, 1988.

————. *Domination and Conquest: The Experience of Ireland, Scotland, and Wales 1100–1300.* Cambridge, Eng.: Cambridge University Press, 1990.

Dollimore, Jonathan, and Alan Sinfield. "History and Ideology: the Instance of *Henry V.*" In John Drakakis, ed., *Alternative Shakespeares*, pp. 206–27. London: Methuen, 1985.

Donaldson, Gordon. "Foundations of Anglo-Scottish Union." In S. T. Bindoff, J. Hurstfield, and C. H. Williams, eds., *Elizabethan Government and Society: Essays Presented to Sir John Neale*, pp. 282–314. London: Athlone Press, 1961.

Donne, John. *John Donne: The Complete English Poems.* A. J. Smith, ed. New York: Penguin, 1971.

Dunne, T. J. "The Gaelic Response to Conquest and Colonisation: The Evidence of the Poetry." *Studia Hibernia* 20 (1980): 7–30.

Edwards, Philip. *Threshold of a Nation: A Study in English and Irish Drama.* Cambridge, Eng.: Cambridge University Press, 1979.

Ellis, Peter Berresford. *Hell or Connaught! The Cromwellian Colonisation of Ireland 1652–1660.* New York: St. Martin's Press, 1975.

Ellis, Steven. "'Not Mere English': The British Perspective 1400–1650," *History Today* 38 (1988): 41–48.

————. *Tudor Frontiers and Noble Power: The Making of the British State.* Oxford: Clarendon Press, 1995.

Ellis, Steven G., and Sarah Barber, eds. *Conquest and Union: Fashioning a British State, 1485–1725.* London: Longman, 1995.

Elton, G. R. *The English.* Oxford: Blackwell, 1992.

————. *The Tudor Revolution in Government: Administrative Changes in the Reign of Henry VIII.* Cambridge, Eng.: Cambridge University Press, 1953.

Empson, William. *Using Biography.* London: Chatto & Windus, 1984.

Falls, Cyril. *Elizabeth's Irish Wars.* London: Methuen, 1950.

————. *Mountjoy: Elizabethan General.* London: Odhams Press, 1955.

Ferguson, Arthur B. *Utter Antiquity: Perceptions of Prehistory in Renaissance England.* Durham, N.C.: Duke University Press, 1993.

Foucault, Michel. *The History of Sexuality.* Vol. 1, *An Introduction.* Trans. Robert Hurley. New York: Random House, 1978.

Frame, Robin. *The Political Development of the British Isles 1100–1400.* Oxford: Oxford University Press, 1990.

Galloway, Bruce. *The Union of England and Scotland 1603–1608.* Edinburgh: John Donald, 1986.

Gellner, Ernest. *Nations and Nationalism.* Ithaca: Cornell University Press, 1983.

Goldberg, Jonathan. *James I and the Politics of Literature: Jonson, Shakespeare, Donne, and Their Contemporaries*. Baltimore: Johns Hopkins University Press, 1983.

———. "Shakespearean Inscriptions: The Voicing of Power." In Patricia Parker and Geoffrey Hartman, eds., *Shakespeare and the Question of Theory*, pp. 116–37. London: Methuen, 1985.

———. *Sodometries: Renaissance Texts, Modern Sexualities*. Stanford: Stanford University Press, 1992.

Goldie, Mark. "Divergence and Union: Scotland and England, 1660–1707." In Brendan Bradshaw and John Morrill, eds., *The British Problem, c. 1534–1707: State Formation in the Atlantic Archipelago*, pp. 220–45. London: Macmillan, 1996.

Gottfried, Rudolf. "Irish Geography in Spenser's *View.*" *English Literary History* 6 (1939): 114–37.

Grant, Alexander, and Keith J. Stringer, eds. *Uniting the Kingdom? The Making of British History*. London: Routledge, 1995.

Greenblatt, Stephen. *Shakespearean Negotiations: The Circulation of Social Energy in Renaissance England*. Berkeley: University of California Press, 1988.

Greene, Thomas. "The Balance of Power in Marvell's 'Horatian Ode.'" *English Literary History* 60 (1993): 379–96.

Greenfeld, Liah. *Nationalism: Five Roads to Modernity*. Cambridge, Mass.: Harvard University Press, 1992.

Gross, Kenneth. *Spenserian Poetics: Idolatry, Iconoclasm, and Magic*. Ithaca, N.Y.: Cornell University Press, 1985.

Gurr, Andrew. Introduction to William Shakespeare's *King Henry V*. Cambridge, Eng.: Cambridge University Press, 1992.

Hadfield, Andrew. "Certainties and Uncertainties: By Way of Response to Jean Brink." *Spenser Studies* 12 (forthcoming).

———. *Literature, Politics, and National Identity*. Cambridge, Eng.: Cambridge University Press, 1994.

Hadfield, Andrew, and Willy Maley. "Introduction: Irish Representations and English Alternatives." In Brendan Bradshaw, Andrew Hadfield, and Willy Maley, eds., *Representing Ireland: Literature and the Origins of Conflict, 1534–1660*, pp. 1–23. Cambridge, Eng.: Cambridge University Press, 1993.

Halperin, David. *One Hundred Years of Homosexuality*. New York: Routledge, 1990.

Harris, F. W. "The State of the Realm: English Military, Political, and Diplomatic Responses to the Flight of the Earls, Autumn 1607 to Spring 1608." *Irish Sword* 14 (1980): 58.

Hayes-McCoy, G. A. "The Completion of the Tudor Conquest, and the Advance of the Counter-Reformation, 1571–1603." In T. W. Moody, F. X. Martin, and F. J. Byrne, eds., *A New History of Ireland: Early Modern Ireland 1534–1691*, pp. 94–141. Vol. 3. Oxford: Clarendon Press, 1976.

Helgerson, Richard. *Forms of Nationhood: The Elizabethan Writing of England*. Chicago: University of Chicago Press, 1992.

Hesse, Carla, and Thomas Laqueur. "Introduction." *Representations* 47 (1994): 1–12.

Highley, Christopher. "Wales, Ireland, and *1 Henry IV.*" *Renaissance Drama*, n.s., 21 (1990): 91–114.

Hirst, Derek. "The English Republic and the Meaning of Britain." *Journal of Modern History* 66 (1994): 451–86. Reprinted in Brendan Bradshaw and John Morrill, eds., *The British Problem, c. 1534–1707: State Formation in the Atlantic Archipelago*, pp. 192–219. London: Macmillan, 1996.

Hobsbawm, E. J. *Nations and Nationalism Since 1780: Programme, Myth, Reality.* 2d ed. Cambridge, Eng.: Cambridge University Press, 1990.

Hore, Herbert F. "Irish Bardism in 1561." *Ulster Journal of Archaeology* 6 (1858): 165–67, 202–12.

James I. *The Political Works of James I.* Charles H. McIlwain, ed. Cambridge, Mass.: Harvard University Press, 1918.

Jones, Frederick M. *Mountjoy 1563–1606: The Last Elizabethan Deputy.* Dublin: Clonmore and Reynolds, 1958.

Jones, Gwynfor. "The Gentry." In Trevor Herbert and Gareth Elwyn Jones, eds., *Tudor Wales*, pp. 10–40. Cardiff: University of Wales Press, 1988.

Jones, R. Brinley. *The Old British Tongue: The Vernacular in Wales 1540–1640.* Cardiff: Avalon, 1970.

Jones, R. F. "Science and Language in England of the Mid-Seventeenth Century." In Stanley Fish, ed., *Seventeenth-Century Prose: Modern Essays in Criticism*, pp. 94–111. Oxford: Oxford University Press, 1971.

Jorgensen, Paul A. *Shakespeare's Military World.* Berkeley: University of California Press, 1956.

Kearney, Hugh. *The British Isles: A History of Four Nations.* Cambridge, Eng.: Cambridge University Press, 1989.

———. "Four Nations or One?" In Bernard Crick, ed., *National Identities: The Constitution of the United Kingdom*, pp. 1–6. Oxford: Blackwell, 1991.

Kelliher, Hilton. *Andrew Marvell: Poet and Politician, 1621–78.* London: British Museum Publications, 1978.

Kendrick, T. D. *British Antiquity.* London: Methuen, 1950.

Keohane, Nannerl O. *Philosophy and the State in France: The Renaissance to the Enlightenment.* Princeton, N.J.: Princeton University Press, 1980.

Kermode, Frank, and Keith Walker. Introduction to *Andrew Marvell.* Frank Kermode and Keith Walker, eds. Oxford: Oxford University Press, 1990.

———, eds. *Andrew Marvell.* Oxford: Oxford University Press, 1990.

Kinsella, Thomas, ed. and trans. *An Duanaire 1600–1900: Poems of the Dispossessed.* 1981. Reprint, Saint Paul: Irish Books and Media, 1985.

Kohn, Hans, *The Idea of Nationalism: A Study of Its Origins and Background.* New York: Collier Books, 1944.

Lacey, Robert. *Robert Earl of Essex.* New York: Atheneum, 1971.

Larkin, James F., and Paul L. Hughes, eds. *Stuart Royal Proclamations.* 2 vols. Oxford: Oxford University Press, 1973.

Leerssen, Joseph Th. *Mere Irish & Fíor-Ghael: Studies in the Idea of Irish Nationality,*

Its Development and Literary Expression Prior to the Nineteenth Century. Amsterdam: John Benjamins, 1986.

Legouis, Pierre. *Andrew Marvell: Poet, Puritan, Patriot.* Oxford: Clarendon Press, 1965.

Levack, Brian P. *The Formation of the British State: England, Scotland, and the Union 1603–1707.* Oxford: Clarendon Press, 1987.

———. "The Proposed Union of English Law and Scots Law in the Seventeenth Century." *Judicial Review,* n.s., 20 (1975): 97–115.

———. "Toward a More Perfect Union: England, Scotland, and the Constitution." In Barbara C. Malament, ed., *After the Reformation: Essays in Honor of J. H. Hexter,* pp. 57–74. Philadelphia: University of Pennsylvania Press, 1980.

Lloyd, J. E. *Owen Glendower.* Oxford: Clarendon Press, 1931.

Llwyd, Humphrey. *Breuiary of Britayne.* Trans. T. Twyne. London, 1573.

Lupton, Julia Reinhard. "Mapping Mutability; or, Spenser's Irish Plot." In Brendan Bradshaw, Andrew Hadfield, and Willy Maley, eds., *Representing Ireland: Literature and the Origins of Conflict, 1534–1660,* pp. 93–115. Cambridge, Eng.: Cambridge University Press, 1993.

McCabe, Richard. "The Fate of Irena: Spenser and Political Violence." In Patricia Coughlan, ed., *Spenser and Ireland: An Interdisciplinary Perspective,* pp. 109–25. Cork: Cork University Press, 1989.

McEachern, Claire. "*Henry V* and the Paradox of the Body Politic." *Shakespeare Quarterly* 45 (1994): 33–56.

McIlwain, Charles H., ed. *The Political Works of James I.* Cambridge, Mass.: Harvard University Press, 1918.

Macinnes, Allan. "Gaelic Culture in the Seventeenth Century: Polarization and Assimilation." In Steven G. Ellis and Sarah Barber, eds., *Conquest and Union: Fashioning a British State, 1485–1725,* pp. 162–94. London: Longman, 1995.

Maley, Willy. " 'Another Britain'? Bacon's *Certain Considerations Touching the Plantation in Ireland.*" *Prose Studies* 18 (1995): 1–18.

———. "How Milton and Some Contemporaries Read Spenser's *View.*" In Brendan Bradshaw, Andrew Hadfield, and Willy Maley, eds., *Representing Ireland: Literature and the Origins of Conflict, 1534–1660,* pp. 191–208. Cambridge, Eng.: Cambridge University Press, 1993.

———. "Rebels and Redshanks: Milton and the British Problem." *Irish Studies Review* no. 6 (1994): 7–11.

———. "Spenser and Scotland: The *View* and the Limits of Anglo-Irish Identity." *Prose Studies* 19 (1996): 1–18.

Manley, Lawrence. *Convention 1500–1750.* Cambridge, Mass.: Harvard University Press, 1980.

Marcu, E. D. *Sixteenth Century Nationalism.* New York: Abaris Books, 1976.

Marcus, Leah S. *Puzzling Shakespeare: Local Reading and Its Discontents.* Berkeley: University of California Press, 1988.

Marvell, Andrew. *Andrew Marvell.* Frank Kermode and Keith Walker, eds. Oxford: Oxford University Press, 1990.

————. *The Poems and Letters of Andrew Marvell.* 3d ed. H. M. Margoliouth, ed. Vol. 1. Oxford: Clarendon Press, 1971.

Mason, Roger A., ed. *Scots and Britons: Scottish Political Thought and the Union of 1603.* Cambridge, Eng.: Cambridge University Press, 1994.

Mathew, David. *The Celtic Peoples and Renaissance Europe: A Study of the Celtic and Spanish Influences on Elizabethan History.* London: Sheed & Ward, 1933.

Maxwell, Constantia, ed. *Irish History from Contemporary Sources (1509–1610).* London: George Allen & Unwin, 1923.

Mercier, Vivian. *The Irish Comic Tradition.* Oxford: Clarendon Press, 1962.

Miller, Christopher. *Blank Darkness: Africanist Discourse in French.* Chicago: University of Chicago Press, 1985.

Miller, D. A. *The Novel and the Police.* Berkeley: University of California Press, 1988.

Miller, David Lee. *The Poem's Two Bodies: The Poetics of the 1590 Faerie Queene.* Princeton, N.J.: Princeton University Press, 1988.

"A Modern Account of *Scotland*: Being an exact Description of the Country, and a true Character of the People and their Manners, Written from thence by an *English* Gentleman." *Harleian Miscellany* 6. London, 1745.

Montrose, Louis. "New Historicisms." In Stephen Greenblatt and Giles Gunn, eds., *Redrawing the Boundaries: The Transformation of English and American Literary Studies,* pp. 392–418. New York: Modern Language Association, 1992.

Moody, T. W. *The Londonderry Plantation 1609–41.* Belfast: William Mullan, 1939.

Morgan, Prys. "From a Death to a View: The Hunt for the Welsh Past in the Romantic Period." In Eric Hobsbawm and Terence Ranger, eds., *The Invention of Tradition,* pp. 43–100. Cambridge, Eng.: Cambridge University Press, 1983.

Mulcaster, Richard. *Positions.* Robert Herbert Quick, ed. London: Longman, Green, 1888.

Mullaney, Steven. *The Place of the Stage: License, Play, and Power in Renaissance England.* Chicago: University of Chicago Press, 1988.

Munden, R. C. "James I and the 'Growth of Mutual Mistrust': King, Commons, and Reform, 1603–1604." In Kevin Sharpe, ed., *Faction and Parliament: Essays on Early Stuart History,* pp. 43–72. Oxford: Clarendon Press, 1978.

Myers, James P., Jr. Introduction to Sir John Davies' *A Discovery of the True Causes Why Ireland Was Never Entirely Subdued [And] Brought Under Obedience of the Crown of England Until the Beginning of His Majesty's Happy Reign.* James P. Myers Jr., ed. 1612. Reprint, Washington, D.C.: Catholic University of America Press, 1988.

————, ed. *A History of Ireland in Elizabethan England: A Selection of Writings by Elizabethan Writers on Ireland.* Hamden, Conn.: Shoe String Press, 1983.

Nashe, Thomas. *The Works of Thomas Nashe.* Ronald B. McKerrow, ed. Vol. 1. Oxford: Basil Blackwell, 1958.

Neill, Michael. "Broken English and Broken Irish: Nation, Language, and the Optic of Power in Shakespeare's Histories." *Shakespeare Quarterly* 45 (1994): 18–22.

Norbrook, David. "Marvell's 'Horatian Ode' and the Politics of Genre." In Thomas

Healy and Jonathan Sawday, eds., *Literature and the English Civil War*, pp. 147–69. Cambridge, Eng.: Cambridge University Press, 1990.

Notestein, Wallace. *The House of Commons 1604–1610*. New Haven, Conn.: Yale University Press, 1971.

Omond, G. W. T. *The Early History of the Scottish Union Question*. Edinburgh: Oliphant, Anderson, & Ferrier, 1906.

Owen, G. Dyfnallt. *Elizabethan Wales: The Social Scene*. Cardiff: University of Wales Press, 1964.

———. *Wales in the Reign of James I.* Woodbridge, Suffolk: Boydell, 1988.

Patterson, Annabel. "Back by Popular Demand: The Two Versions of *Henry V.*" *Renaissance Drama*, n.s., 19 (1988): 29–62.

———. *Censorship and Interpretation: The Conditions of Writing and Reading in Early Modern England*. Madison: University of Wisconsin Press, 1984.

———. "The Egalitarian Giant: Representations of Justice in History/Literature." *Journal of British Studies* 31 (1992): 91–132.

———. *Marvell and the Civic Crown*. Princeton, N.J.: Princeton University Press, 1978.

———. *Reading Between the Lines*. Madison: University of Wisconsin Press, 1993.

———. *Shakespeare and the Popular Voice*. Cambridge, Eng.: Basil Blackwell, 1989.

Pawlisch, Hans S. *Sir John Davies and the Conquest of Ireland: A Study in Legal Imperialism*. Cambridge, Eng.: Cambridge University Press, 1985.

———. "Sir John Davies, the Ancient Constitution, and the Civil Law." *Historical Journal* 23 (1980): 684–702.

Penry, John. *A Treatise Containing the Aeqvity of an Humble Svpplication which is to be Exhibited vnto Hir Graciovs Maiesty and this high Court of Parliament in the behalfe of the Countrey of Wales, that some order may be taken for the preaching of the Gospell among those people*. Oxford, 1587.

Perceval-Maxwell, M. *The Outbreak of the Irish Rebellion of 1641*. Montreal: McGill-Queen's University Press, 1994.

Pocock, J. G. A. *The Ancient Constitution and the Feudal Law: A Study of English Historical Thought in the Seventeenth Century*. Cambridge, Eng.: Cambridge University Press, 1957.

———. "The Ancient Constitution Revisited," published together with a "reissue" of *The Ancient Constitution*. Cambridge, Eng.: Cambridge University Press, 1987.

———. "British History: A Plea for a New Subject." *Journal of Modern History* 47 (1974): 601–28.

———. "Cambridge Paradigms and Scotch Philosophers: A Study of the Relations Between the Civic Humanist and the Civil Jurisprudential Interpretation of Eighteenth-Century Social Thought." In Istvan Hont and Michael Ignatieff, eds., *Wealth and Virtue: The Shaping of Political Economy in the Scottish Enlightenment*, pp. 235–52. Cambridge, Eng.: Cambridge University Press, 1983.

———. "Contingency, Identity, Sovereignty." In Alexander Grant and Keith J.

Stringer, eds., *Uniting the Kingdom? The Making of British History*, pp. 292–302. London: Routledge, 1995.

———. "Deconstructing Europe." *History of European Ideas* 18 (1994): 329–45.

———. "History and Sovereignty: The Historiographical Response to European-ization in Two British Cultures." *Journal of British Studies* 31 (1992): 358–89.

———. "The Limits and Divisions of British History: In Search of the Unknown Subject." *American Historical Review* 87 (1982): 311–36.

———. *The Machiavellian Moment: Florentine Political Thought and the Atlantic Repub-lican Tradition*. Princeton, N.J.: Princeton University Press, 1975.

———. "Two Kingdoms and Three Histories? Political Thought in British Con-texts." In Roger A. Mason, ed., *Scots and Britons: Scottish Political Thought and the Union of 1603*, pp. 293–313. Cambridge, Eng.: Cambridge University Press, 1994.

———, ed. *The Varieties of British Political Thought 1500–1800*. Cambridge, Eng.: Cambridge University Press, 1993.

Pratt, Mary Louise. *Imperial Eyes: Travel Writing and Transculturation*. London: Rout-ledge, 1992.

Quinn, D. B. *The Elizabethans and the Irish*. Ithaca, N.Y.: Cornell University Press, 1966.

Quint, David. " 'Alexander the Pig': Shakespeare on History and Poetry." *boundary 2* 10 (1982): 63.

Rabkin, Norman. *Shakespeare and the Problem of Meaning*. Chicago: University of Chicago Press, 1981.

Rackin, Phyllis. *Stages of History: Shakespeare's English Chronicles*. Ithaca, N.Y.: Cor-nell University Press, 1990.

Rambuss, Richard. "Engendering the Faith of Nations: Richard Crashaw, the Ef-feminate Metaphysical." Forthcoming.

———. "Pleasure and Devotion: The Body of Jesus and Seventeenth-Century Religious Lyric." In Jonathan Goldberg, ed. *Queering the Renaissance*, pp. 253–79. Durham, N.C.: Duke University Press, 1994.

———. *Spenser's Secret Career*. Cambridge, Eng.: Cambridge University Press, 1993.

Renwick, W. L., ed. *A View of the Present State of Ireland*, by Edmund Spenser. Oxford: Clarendon Press, 1970.

Rich, Barnaby. *A New Description of Ireland*. London, 1610.

Robbins, Caroline. "A Critical Study of the Political Activities of Andrew Marvell." Ph.D. diss., University of London, 1926.

Robertson, John, ed. *A Union for Empire: Political Thought and the Union of 1707*. Cam-bridge, Eng.: Cambridge University Press, 1995.

Robinson, Fred Norris. "Satirists and Enchanters in Early Irish Literature." In David Gordon Lyon and George Foot Moore, eds., *Studies in the History of Religions Pre-sented to Crawford Howell Toy*, pp. 95–130. New York: Macmillian, 1912.

Roche, Thomas P., Jr. *The Kindly Flame: A Study of the Third and Fourth Books of Spenser's* Faerie Queene. Princeton, N.J.: Princeton University Press, 1964.

Russell, Conrad. "The British Background to the Irish Rebellion of 1641." *Historical Research* 61 (1988): 166–82.

———. "The British Problem and the English Civil War," *History* 72 (1987): 395–415.

———. *The Causes of the English Civil War.* Oxford: Clarendon Press, 1990.

———. *The Fall of the British Monarchies 1637–1642.* Oxford: Clarendon Press, 1991.

Sedgwick, Eve Kosofsky. *Between Men: English Literature and Male Homosocial Desire.* New York: Columbia University Press, 1985.

———. *Epistemology of the Closet.* Berkeley: University of California Press, 1990.

———. *Tendencies.* Durham, N.C.: Duke University Press, 1993.

Shakespeare, William. *Henry IV, Part I.* David Bevington, ed. Oxford: Clarendon Press, 1987.

———. *Henry V.* Gary Taylor, ed. Oxford: Clarendon Press, 1982.

———. *Henry the Fifth.* 1600. Reprint, Oxford: Clarendon Press, 1957.

Shuger, Debora. *Habits of Thought in the English Renaissance.* Berkeley: University of California Press, 1990.

Simms, Katherine. "Bardic Poetry as a Historical Source." In Tom Dunne, ed., *The Writer as Witness: Literature As Historical Evidence,* pp. 58–75. Cork: Cork University Press, 1987.

Sinfield, Alan. *Faultlines: Cultural Materialism and the Politics of Dissident Reading.* Berkeley: University of California Press, 1992.

Smith, Anthony D. *Theories of Nationalism.* London: Duckworth, 1971.

Spenser, Edmund. *Spenser: Poetical Works.* J. C. Smith and E. de Selincourt, eds. Oxford: Oxford University Press, 1912.

———. *A View of the Present State of Ireland.* W. L. Renwick, ed. Oxford: Clarendon Press, 1970.

———. *The Works of Edmund Spenser.* 10 vols. Edwin Greenlaw, Charles Grosvenor Osgood, and Frederick Morgan Padelford, eds. Baltimore: Johns Hopkins University Press, 1932.

Spivak, Gayatri Chakravorty. "Acting Bits/Identity Talk." *Critical Inquiry* 18 (1992): 770–803.

Stevenson, David. "Cromwell, Scotland, and Ireland." In John Morrill, ed., *Oliver Cromwell and the English Revolution,* pp. 149–80. London: Longman, 1990.

———. *Scottish Covenanters and Irish Confederates: Scottish-Irish Relations in the Mid-Seventeenth Century.* Belfast: Ulster Historical Foundation, 1981.

Taylor, Gary. *Three Studies in the Text of Henry V,* and Stanley Wells, *Modernizing Shakespeare's Spelling.* Oxford: Clarendon Press, 1979.

———, ed. *Henry V,* by William Shakespeare. Oxford: Clarendon Press, 1982.

Temple, John. *The Irish Rebellion; or, An History of the Attempts of the Irish Papists to Extirpate the Protestants in the Kingdom of Ireland; Together with the Barbarous Cruelties and Bloody Massacres which Ensued Thereupon.* 1646. Reprint, London, 1812.

Thompson, R. S. *The Atlantic Archipelago: A Political History of the British Isles.* Lewiston, N.Y.: E. Mellen Press, 1986.

Tillyard, E. W. *Shakespeare's History Plays*. London: Chatto, 1944.

Trouillot, Michel-Rolph. *Silencing the Past: Power and the Production of History*. Boston: Beacon Press, 1995.

Walker, Clement. *Anarchia Anglicana; or, The History of Independency. The Second Part.* 1649.

Wallace, John M. *Destiny His Choice: The Loyalism of Andrew Marvell*. Cambridge, Eng.: Cambridge University Press, 1968.

Ware, James, ed. *Two Histories of Ireland*. Dublin, 1633.

Warner, Michael. "Homo-Narcissism; or, Heterosexuality." In Joseph A. Boone and Michael Cadden, eds., *Engendering Men: The Question of Male Feminist Criticism*, pp. 190–206. New York: Routledge, 1990.

Wells, Stanley. *Modernizing Shakespeare's Spelling*, and Gary Taylor, *Three Studies in the Text of* Henry V. Oxford: Clarendon Press, 1979.

Williams, Glanmor. *Renewal and Reformation: Wales c. 1415–1642*. Oxford: Clarendon Press, 1987.

Williams, Gwyn. *Madoc: The Making of a Myth*. London: Eyre Methuen, 1979.

————. *The Welsh in Their History*. London: Croom Helm, 1982.

Williams, Penry. "Government and Politics." In Trevor Herbert and Gareth Elwyn Jones, eds., *Tudor Wales*, pp. 134–61. Cardiff: University of Wales Press, 1988.

————. "The Welsh Borderland Under Queen Elizabeth." *Welsh History Review* 1 (1960): 19–36.

Williamson, Arthur H. "From the Invention of Great Britain to the Creation of British History: A New Historiography." *Journal of British Studies* 29 (1990): 267–76.

————. *Scottish National Consciousness in the Age of James VI: The Apocalypse, the Union, and the Shaping of Scotland's Public Culture*. Edinburgh: John Donald, 1979.

Willson, D. H. "King James I and Anglo-Scottish Unity." In William A. Aiken and Basil D. Henning, eds., *Conflict in Stuart England: Essays in Honour of Wallace Notestein*, pp. 41–55. New York: New York University Press, 1960.

Worden, Blair. "Andrew Marvell, Oliver Cromwell, and the Horatian Ode." In Kevin Sharpe and Steven N. Zwicker, eds., *Politics of Discourse: The Literature and History of Seventeenth-Century England*, pp. 147–80. Berkeley: University of California Press, 1987.

Wormald, Jenny. "The Creation of Britain: Multiple Kingdoms or Core and Colonies?" *Transactions of the Royal Historical Society* 2, 6th ser. (1992): 175–94.

————. "James VI, James I, and the Identity of Britain." In Brendan Bradshaw and John Morrill, eds., *The British Problem, c. 1534–1707: State Formation in the Atlantic Archipelago*, pp. 148–71. London: Macmillan, 1996.

————. "One King, Two Kingdoms." In Alexander Grant and Keith J. Stringer, eds., *Uniting the Kingdom? The Making of British History*, pp. 123–32. London: Routledge, 1995.

Yeats, W. B. *Essays and Introductions*. New York: Collier Books, 1968.

Index

In this index an "f" after a number indicates a separate reference on the next page, and an "ff" indicates separate references on the next two pages. A continuous discussion over two or more pages is indicated by a span of page numbers, e.g., "57–59." *Passim* is used for a cluster of references in close but not consecutive sequence.

Library of Congress Cataloging-in-Publication Data

Baker, David J.
Between nations : Shakespeare, Spenser, Marvell, and the question
of Britain / David J. Baker.
p.   cm.
Includes bibliographical references (p.   ) and index.
ISBN 0-8047-2997-2 (cl.) : ISBN 0-8047-4184-0 (pbk.)
1. English literature—Early modern, 1500–1700—History and
criticism.   2. Politics and literature—Great Britain—History—16th
century.   3. Politics and literature—Great Britain—History—17th
century.   4. Shakespeare, William, 1564–1616—Knowledge—Great
Britain.   5. Spenser, Edmund, 1552?–1599—Knowledge—Great Britain.
6. Marvell, Andrew, 1621 — 1678—Knowledge—Great Britain.
7. National characteristics, British, in literature.   8. Literature
and history—Great Britain.   9. Great Britain—In literature.
10. Nationalism in literature.   11. England—In literature.
12. Renaissance—England.   I. Title.
PR428.P6B46   1997   97-8205
820.9′358—dc21   CIP
                                                              Rev.

Original printing 1997

Last figure below indicates year of this printing:

06   05   04   03   02   01   00

Milton Keynes UK
Ingram Content Group UK Ltd.
UKHW012219310823
427851UK00001B/113

9 780804 741842